THE GREATEST HEIST
STORIES EVER TOLD

THE GREATEST HEIST
STORIES EVER TOLD

EDITED BY TOM MCCARTHY

LYONS
PRESS

Guilford, Connecticut

An imprint of The Rowman & Littlefield Publishing Group, Inc.
4501 Forbes Blvd., Ste. 200
Lanham, MD 20706
www.rowman.com

Distributed by NATIONAL BOOK NETWORK

British Library Cataloguing in Publication Information available

Library of Congress Cataloging-in-Publication Data available

ISBN 978-1-4930-3998-2 (paperback)
ISBN 978-1-4930-3999-9 (e-book)

♾™ The paper used in this publication meets the minimum requirements of American National Standard for Information Sciences—Permanence of Paper for Printed Library Materials, ANSI/ NISO Z39.48-1992.

CONTENTS

INTRODUCTION

CRIME DOES PAY. AT LEAST FOR A WHILE.

You will see that quickly as you are drawn into the nine compelling and true stories of brilliant plans, guile, and nerves of steel in this arresting collection. The thieves awaiting you on the following pages seemed to have it all. They were clever and cool, and approached their goals with icy resolve. It took a lot of guts to do what they did and not fold under the pressure. After all, if those hard-wrought plans had failed, they would have had plenty of time in prison to think about what went wrong.

Hijack an airplane, demand a ransom and two parachutes, then disappear out the rear door in the middle of a storm? Invent a device that allows you to record the combination of any bank vault, then break into bank vaults twice? Rob a stage in broad daylight? Steal from a secret mob depository run by a boss known for his brutality? Why not? The rewards are much greater. Much like infamous robber Willie Sutton so presciently noted, the thieves in this collection did what they did because that's where the money was.

You'll soon see that, yes, planning is everything, and carrying out those plans is no easy task. And you'll also see that the benefits for these clever thieves were abundant—loads of money and the freedom to do whatever they wanted with it.

If only for a short time.

The problem with pulling off heists is that on the other side of the equation are police and detectives who are equally as clever and energetic and resourceful. While the thieves in these stories all make off with the goods and take advantage of their cleverness, the law always—or almost always—gets their man.

But still, the stories here do in a way celebrate the misdirected intelligence of thieves who, had they used their talents in more accepted fashions, would be pillars of the community—business executives or successful investors or highly regarded leaders. But that path did not seem to appeal to the criminals herein. Too mundane an existence, one might suppose. Too boring. So instead they set their sights on easy riches quickly gained with just a few hours of labor, albeit nerve-racking labor.

Easy money works that way. It appeals to a certain sort of mind. Over the years thoughts of piles of quick cash have lured some of the best minds of the criminal world. The heists in this collection were not simple—and the money involved was not the sort of trifling amounts that run-of-the-mill thieves covet. To acquire such bounty and get away with it calls for a certain intelligence. Ham-handed amateurs might try to knock off a convenience store, but a master thief has bigger ideas. The stories here are a tribute to the darkly misplaced use of some of the best minds in the world today—PhDs of the underworld.

There is much to admire in these crooks. *The Greatest Heist Stories Ever Told* will allow readers to appreciate the efforts that go into a truly magnificent heist. It is a celebration of stunning, well-planned, and audacious capers that left police and armies of investigators looking for answers and scratching their heads. Heists are smooth and often go undetected for days. They are often pulled off without physical violence—the only weapon on hand being brainpower. A well-executed heist leaves nothing but yellowing wanted posters pleading for information.

Almost always, anyway. The audaciousness of these crimes, one has to admit, is admirable.

Henry Hill, made famous later in the movie *Goodfellas*, and his friends stole millions from Lufthansa; the sophisticated George Leslie would steal more money than anyone ever had—but his plan required breaking into a bank twice to do so. One desperado, so clever in his plans, managed to rob a stage of tens of thousands and bury the money. But he met an untimely if not unexpected demise, and his map for a cohort leading to the treasure proved inaccurate. Perhaps the loot is still out there. The notorious Younger brothers, cocky and bold, thought the quiet citizens of Northfield, Minnesota, would cower while they robbed the town bank. They were wrong. A man who seemed to be a hardworking cabbie organized the perfect alibi for a big job and nearly got away with it.

There is much to admire on the other side as well. Police put in thousands of hours of painstaking investigation and sleepless nights, and doggedly persevere and pursue. And in the end, they always win. They get their man.

Almost always, anyway.

Maybe that's what assures us that there will always be more heists. There is always that golden chance of getting away with it.

ONE

The Lufthansa Heist

Henry Hill and Daniel Simone

THE STAGE WAS SET, THE CURTAIN ROSE, AND THE PERFORMERS READIED for Act One.

In this predawn hour of Monday, December 11, 1978, a black Ford van with six passengers is entering Kennedy Airport from the northeast end, a zone with a chain of cargo hangars. A silver Pontiac Grand Prix, the chase car, is trailing the van. The two-vehicle motorcade continues to travel southbound on the JFK Expressway, and at the Federal Circle intersection it veers off the ramp and heads east on Nassau Expressway. Within a half mile, the driver of the Ford van, Angelo Sepe, has in his sights the Lufthansa yellow fluorescent sign atop Cargo Building 261.

"It's a quarter-to-three. We're five minutes early," Sepe says.

DeSimone glances at his wristwatch. "You better slow it down, Angelo. We shouldn't get there before ten to three."

Sepe steers into a maze of parking lots until he reaches the targeted hangar, the German airline freight complex. The chase car passes the van, idles to the rear of the three-story Lufthansa building, and parks in front of a loading dock. The Ford van then stops near the main entrance, and everyone inside hardly breathes as they peruse the environment. White lighting splashes out of the third-floor office windows; at this restful hour, though, Kennedy Airport is dormant, and even a watchdog can find peace. The six armed robbers can hear the sound of a truck and the swishing tires of a courier panel-van somewhere in the distance. The takeoff and landing of aircrafts is nonexistent, an eerie contrast to the frenetic daytime traffic at the world's busiest airfield. The quietness and stillness is strange to the marauders; they've never roamed the inner roadways of the airport at three in the morning. It spooks and confuses them.

"Shit, I hope we don't run into ghosts," Sepe says. But in the perimeter of the Lufthansa compound no phantoms are in sight, and the burglars' breathing restarts, their hearts throttling back to a slower beat. Sepe then shifts the van into drive and eases on a hundred yards to the east of the hangar, where the chase car has been waiting. He brakes to a halt twenty feet from a chain-link fence. A padlocked gate encloses the loading ramp.

A square, man-size gaping hole opens widely on the side of the van as the door slides open. Four of the six men, Frenchy McMahon, Joe Manri, Tommy DeSimone, and Louis Cafora, have been in a squatting position on the metal floor. Sepe throws the selector lever into park. "OK, it looks clear. Get out now." He and the gunman seated to his right stay put in the vehicle, and their four compatriots, in a disguise of black ski masks and dark clothing, disembark. Two of them hop out with agility; overweight Manri and Cafora roll out as if they are two giant pillows bouncing off a bed.

In case someone spots them, Sepe waits three or four seconds— poised to scamper away—but the seas are at peace, and he climbs out of the van. The man in the front passenger seat, Paolo Licastri, also bails out. A short Sicilian immigrant without a visa, Licastri is on hand as John Gotti's envoy. Licastri and his bunch clump in front of the van.

McMahon peers at his watch. "OK, guys. Mr. Hychko should be coming soon."

Mike Hychko, a shipping clerk, is due back from collecting air bills from various airlines that, through Lufthansa, forward shipments to Europe. He regularly finishes these errands in time for the 3:00 a.m. meal break.

And here he pulls up with punctuality. Hychko, medium built with a square jaw and refined facial features, parks his pickup truck next to the Ford van, and the half dozen people grouped near it unnerve him. Five of the shadowy figures, he notices, are wearing wool caps. Hychko's eyes blink with alarm. "What're you guys doing here? And . . . and you can't park this van here by the gate."

The sixth interloper, Sepe, head and face uncovered, tackles Hychko. With the butt of his Colt .45 Gold Cup semiautomatic, a marksman competition firearm, Sepe thwacks the Lufthansa clerk on the skull and restrains him in a headlock. Hychko's wound gushes blood, tinting his light, wavy hair, and he roars out a piercing scream. "Rolf, Rolf, c'mon out here. Call Port Authority. I'm getting kidnapped. Call 9 . . ."

Manri rams his shotgun into Hychko's stomach. "Shut the fuck up, or I'll put a couple ounces of lead in your temple." Hychko's hollering is echoing, and he's writhing to break free from Sepe's forearm hold. The gash on his scalp is deep, and his face is sodden with blood. DeSimone pitches in and grapples Hychko from Sepe, who's fumbling to slip on his mask.

Too late. Hychko's memory bank has photographed a snapshot of Sepe.

Sepe puts on his ski cap. He plucks Hychko's wallet and waves it in front of the man's eyes. "OK, Mr. Hychko, I got your wallet, and now we know where you live. Somebody's gonna be parked on your block. If you rat on me, you can kiss your family good-bye. Got it?"

Anguishing over his fate, and more immediately, the life-threatening loss of blood, Hychko doesn't answer but nods in full understanding. DeSimone then handcuffs Hychko and bullies him. "Where's the three-sided key?" He raps the wounded man on his head. "Gimme the key. In which pocket do you have it?" DeSimone grabs the lapels of Hychko's coat and shakes him. "I said, gimme the fuckin' three-sided key."

The three-sided key? They have inside information, Hychko perceives. Panting, he mumbles, "It's . . . it's in my left side pocket."

DeSimone gropes in the pockets of Hychko's trousers and finds the specially shaped key that deactivates the loading ramp motion detectors, a system wired to the Port Authority headquarters at the airport. "Mr. Hychko, where's the switch for this key on the gates?"

Hychko's wincing contorts his face. "It's on the right post of the gate. Right there, you see it?"

DeSimone slides the key into the cylinder and switches the tumbler to the "off" position. "You better not have lied, Hychko. 'Cause if the alarm is still on, you're gonna be a bag of broken bones."

Hurriedly, with a bolt cutter Cafora swiftly shears the thick chain that's padlocked to the gates. He pushes them inward. DeSimone prods the wounded Hychko inside the fenced grounds, manhandling him to the top of the loading platform, the rest of the gunners following with soft steps. Sepe quickens his pace, trots ahead of DeSimone and Hychko, and reaches the small service door to the hangar. He presses the handle downward and steps indoors, everyone else at his heels. Werner had informed Manri that this door, the one used for foot traffic, will be unsecured. So far, Werner's input has been accurate, and the pirates are hoping the upcoming sequences will be faultless.

They storm inside, and a Lufthansa shipping agent, Rolf Rebmann, hears the shuffle of feet and a commotion of energetic movement. Rows of steel shelving stacked to the ceiling grid the ground level of the warehouse, and Rebmann's workstation is at the end of those lanes. He cranes his neck into the open space, and on seeing the charging gunmen, tenses. Rebmann's lips freeze, and he can barely speak. "Hey . . . hey, what's going on? Who are you?"

With the snap of a lisping snake, Licastri leaps at Rebmann's throat, and Sepe binds the man's wrists behind his back.

Rebmann struggles futilely and succumbs, his knees shaking. "Don't hurt me. I'll do whatever you want. I got two kids and a sick wife."

"Join the club," DeSimone replies. "I got a wife who plays sick, too. I've never known a married woman who isn't sick. The minute you marry them, they get sick and stop fucking."

Sepe says, "Take it easy, take it easy, Mr. Rebmann. Keep your mouth shut and nothin's gonna happen. And if any of you steps out of line, you'll all get it." To stress the threat, Sepe, in mock, raises the barrel of his semiautomatic to his temple. "See? Get my drift?"

The gunmen were clued in that at the end of the shelf rows, somewhere near the high-value vault, a security guard may be loafing out of sight. Up to now, the lone watchman has not yet detected the intrusion. Manri, whom Burke appointed in charge, directs the assailants, and in a whispery voice says, "Frenchy, you and Cafora go find the guard. He's an old dog, so go easy on him." Manri indicates the direction where the watchman may be stationed. "He's probably goofing off back there next to that pile of pallets. Go get him; we'll wait here."

McMahon and Cafora, crouching, walk stealthily down the aisles. They turn a corner and see the guard slurping hot soup from a Styrofoam cup and listening to a radio broadcasting the weather. His face is gaunt and gray. His frame, tall and fleshless, is curved forward, and from a side-view it forms a "C." He's a dozen years past his golden days and doesn't belong on the night shift protecting Lufthansa's cargo hangar.

The two commandos rush the watchman. He glimpses at them, and in a delayed reaction his body flexes, and the soup spills onto the floor. Cafora, his gun aimed at the wrinkled geriatric, says, "It's OK, Granpa. It's OK. Nothin's gonna happen. Come on with us." McMahon and Cafora each gently clasp one of his arms and walk him through the maze of shelving to reunite with their compatriots.

Petrified out of his wits and vibrating faster than a tuning fork, the brittle guard doesn't know how to react. His job calls for him to arrest trespassers and detain them until the police respond. How can this senior, who's in pain from a slipped disc and rheumatism, enforce security? He can scarcely stand upright, never mind wrangling 250-pound armed robbers.

For his will, though, he deserves an "A." "What'r you think you're doing? We got cops all over the airport. You don't know it, but the loading dock outside has an alarm, and you probably tripped it. And . . . and Port Authority will be here any minute."

McMahon chuckles. "We know about it, Pop. As we said, it's all gonna be all right. And because you're the oldest here, when we get upstairs tell everybody there to behave and not to do anything stupid. OK? And nobody will get hurt."

"Or killed," adds Cafora, and the watchman gasps, his freckled hands trembling.

Manri sees that McMahon and Cafora have the guard in their custody. "Good. You found the old man." Under his breath, out of earshot of the captives, he calls out, "Frenchy, Tommy, Roast Beef, and me will take these three with us and go upstairs to round up the rest of the night workers. Angelo, Paolo, you two stay down here. If anybody shows up, tie the fuckers and take them to the lunchroom."

Werner had instructed Manri to locate and account for the night supervisor, seven employees, and one guard. Nine in total. And Werner specified that at 3:00 a.m., the night shift groups in the lunchroom for the meal break. This was the significance of initiating the raid at 2:50 a.m.

Paolo Licastri questions Manri's directive, and in his thick Italian accent suggests, "Why I no go with you? If you gotta kill somebody, I can do easy."

"The Gent don't want nobody killed here tonight. And if you do, you'll be the next one to go. Got it?" Manri promised.

"Whatsa matta? Burke no have big *collioni*, eh? Ah, ah, ah."

Manri exhales heavily, bellies up to Licastri's chest, and hovers over him. "You just do what I say, you little prick." Inches from the Sicilian's eyes, Manri rams the air with his finger. "Because if you don't, we'll send you back to your boss, Mr. Gotti, in tomato sauce jars." This silences Licastri—for the moment.

Manri motions with his sawed-off shotgun for McMahon, DeSimone, and Cafora to follow him up the stairway. DeSimone and Cafora are dragging along the two Lufthansa cargo expeditors and the old gent, jabbing the younger two in their spines.

Manri flips off the light switch in the stairwell; he and his co-holdup men, flashlights in hand, nudge along the three captives, and they all file up to the third floor.

They're climbing two flights of stairs. Leading, Cafora stops on the landing and signals with his hand for everyone to halt. "Hold up." He can smell microwaved food, and murmurs are rumbling from one end of this floor.

"They're supposed to be in the lunchroom," McMahon says under his breath.

The melody of a song is seeping from the cafeteria. Faintly audible, the lyrics are escaping into the hallway: "Monday, Monday, can't trust that day . . ."

Handcuffed and standing between the watchman and Hychko, Rebmann informs them, "They're all in the cafeteria. The supervisor, Rudi

Eirich, is the only one who doesn't come up here." This submissiveness is Rebmann's way of ingratiating himself in the hope the brutes will spare him harm.

Suddenly, a chirping of rubber soles, then the jolly whistling of a man nearing the stairwell.

"I guess they're not *all* in the lunchroom. Are they, Mr. Rebmann?" DeSimone chides. "Listen, Rebmann. Don't try to be cute, because you're gonna get your ears cut off. You're already a donkey, and you'll look even stupider without ears. So who the fuck could be walkin' around in the hallway?"

Rebmann's intent to cooperate is misconstrued and reeks of deception. He explains, "No . . . no. That . . . that could be the supervisor, Eirich. I . . . I told you he's the . . . the only one who doesn't come to the lunchroom on his meal break."

"Shut the fuck up and don't say another word," Cafora shushes, tightening his jaws.

Manri prods DeSimone to step out into the corridor with him and grab hold of whoever is wandering outside the cafeteria. Guns up high, the two robbers spring into the brightly lit hallway and plant their feet two yards from Cargo Agent John Murray. Not to draw the attention of those in the cafeteria, DeSimone says quietly but harshly, "Put your hands up. What's your name?" His .38 Magnum pearl-handle Smith & Wesson is aimed at Murray's midsection.

The abrupt images of the masked gunmen terrify Murray. Only because adrenaline is anesthetizing him, he dares to ask, "Who are *you?*"

Manri and DeSimone move in, flanking Murray, the shotgun and the Smith & Wesson scraping his temples.

"We're asking the questions, not *you.*" Manri's eyes are spearing Murray's through the eyeholes of the ski mask. He jams the barrels of the shotgun into Murray's forehead. The cargo agent twitches, the veins in his temples now blue and swelling. "If you wanna be a wiseass, a blast from this thing will make a tunnel through your head."

DeSimone has ten pairs of handcuffs in a satchel strapped to his shoulder. He pulls out one set and fetters Murray's hands, while Manri holds the shotgun inches from him. "Where's everybody else?"

Murray points with his chin at the doors of the lunchroom. "Some of them are in there."

"Where's everybody else?"

"The supervisor is downstairs in his office. Rolf Rebmann, Mike Hychko, and the security guard are somewhere in the warehouse," John Murray answers genuinely, unaware three of his coworkers have already been corralled.

Werner had said the night supervisor, Rudi Eirich, often stays in his office on the warehouse level. Manri does some math in his head. "Mr. Murray, how many people should be in the cafeteria?"

"Probably seven." Murray assumes he is the only one captured; otherwise, he would've confirmed only four workers in the lunchroom.

Werner had also spoken about a cleaning service. "Where are the porters, Mr. Murray?"

Murray is shaking as loosely as a leaf in the wind. "They're . . . they're gone. They leave early." Judging by the scent of fresh wax and the high luster of the blue vinyl-tiled floor, Manri and DeSimone believe him.

Manri knows of the independent contracted porters, the number of personnel in the building, and their identity. It's clear, Murray thinks, a Lufthansa employee must've spelled out the indispensable facts to the robbers. And though the sight of Manri's shotgun is short-circuiting Murray's brain, he's convinced the ringleader of this holdup is Louis Werner.

Everyone in the building now accounted for, Manri and DeSimone walk Murray to the stairwell, and Manri nods at his companions to take the captives into the cafeteria. He touches his nose as a reminder to maintain silence. "We got everybody who's supposed to be in the building. There should be four more in the lunchroom down the hall."

Single file, the four thugs herd the hostages down the tunnel-like corridor. They stride up to the swinging doors of the lunchroom; DeSimone kicks them open and hurls Murray inside. McMahon gives Hychko and Rebmann each a hard push, and Cafora and Manri lurch in with the watchman.

In this moment, the four in the cafeteria are unflustered by the incursion. "Oh, c'mon, what kind of a joke is this. You guys got nothin' better to do?"

"It's . . . it's no joke," warns Rebmann, his mouth quavering.

"Oh, please. Get the fuck outta here. Who do you think you're fooling?" says one of the workers.

Manri flaunts his weapon. "This ain't no joke, and if you don't believe this shotgun is real, lemme put a shot in your fuckin' head."

The harrowing invasion nearly ceases the heartbeat of the Lufthansa night shift, and the leisurely meal break erupts into bedlam.

His shotgun sweeping side to side, Manri shouts, "Get on the floor face down, and don't look up."

Two of the Lufthansa staffers had been dozing. Having been jarred from sleep, but not quite fully awake, their grogginess sees this head-whirling moment as the absurdity of a dream.

The seven hostages do as they're told and scramble to the floor.

Manri yells out, "Like I said, everybody keep your fuckin' eyes down and don't look around the room."

One of the detainees, Wolfgang Ruppert, can't seem to concentrate on keeping his gaze on the pavement; his eyes rove from Cafora, to McMahon, to Manri.

Cafora goes up to Ruppert and presses his booted foot on the man's neck. "We told you not to look around. If you lift your head again, you better say your last prayer."

Ruppert complies and starts weeping. "I have a family of five. Two of my sons are three and four years old. They need me."

Cafora grins. "Yeah, well, everybody needs their fathers."

One by one, the captors rifle through the pockets of the prisoners, take their wallets, and hurl them at DeSimone for him to keep in his satchel. The robbers then take turns addressing the Lufthansa staff. This tactic is to lessen the chance for the gunmen to leave traits or clues of their identities. McMahon is in rotation to speak. Mimicking a professional master of ceremonies, he clears his throat. "You all must've heard the story of the unsung hero. The message I'm trying to drive home is this; we're as concerned for your safety as you are yourselves."

Burke had chosen McMahon to give this speech because his manner was the exception within the Robert's Lounge gang; his pronunciation was indistinct, unlike the rest of them, whose New York Brooklynese accent could be singled out even by a foreigner. "We got your wallets, and we know who you are and where you live. So please do what we say. If any of you doesn't obey, *remember*, we can find you. You should also understand that the damage we're going to do tonight to Lufthansa, a corporation with millions and millions of dollars, will be as minute as a mosquito bite on a horse. But if you try to be a hero, well . . . it may cost you your life. Now that's a big loss. So no heroes, please!"

Manri and DeSimone lift Murray to his feet and shove him into the corridor. "Mr. Murray, pay attention," Manri says. "I want you to call your supervisor and have him come up here."

"You mean Rudi Eirich?" Murray asks.

"Yeah, him."

Supervisor Rudi Eirich is responsible for the high-value vault and the alarm keys.

"You want me to get him up here? What do you want me to say to him?"

Cafora is up at bat to do the talking. "How about telling him he's got a call from headquarters in Germany. When Germany phones, he's gotta take the call. Right? So don't play stupid. If you don't get Eirich here, I'm gonna mix your brains in your dinner." Cafora glances at his watch. "Germany is six hours ahead of us. Let's see, it's 3:15 here. There, it's 9:15 in the morning. So it's likely they could be calling. Right?"

Holding Murray by the arms, Manri and Cafora take him to his workstation. Cafora unshackles him so he can dial. The cargo agent picks up the phone on his desk and punches in Eirich's extension.

Manri grasps Murray's wrist and interrupts his dialing. "Before you call Eirich, lemme warn you. Don't get the idea to use tricky words to give your boss a heads-up. Remember what we said in the lunchroom: no heroes, please."

Murray bobs his head and redials. "Rudi, it's John Murray. Listen, I . . . I got a call on hold from Germany. They wanna talk to you. Said it's important."

Manri and Cafora assume Eirich to be saying, "Switch the call to my extension."

"No . . . no, Rudi," Murray stammers. "The call . . . the call came in on the open line." The open line is a dedicated telephone toll cable for overseas communications.

There's a lapse in the phone conversation. Seconds pass, and Murray hangs up the receiver. "Mr. Eirich's coming." He's perspiring but is relieved.

Cafora removes his gun from Murray's temple. "Good, good."

Manri, too, bows with appreciation. "Good job, John." By now, they're on a first-name basis.

Towing Murray along, Cafora and Manri go to the far end of the hallway where the steel door to the stairs is. They keep Murray standing against the wall, and the two holdup men position themselves out of sight on the sides of the stairwell.

Manri says to Murray, "Don't make a move." Forty seconds click, and Eirich hasn't arrived. Manri frowns at Murray. "I hope you weren't foolish enough to have said something to give Eirich a hint."

Murray's forehead douses to a drench. "Hell, no! He . . . he'll be here. It's a long walk from his office. He'll be here . . . soon."

He isn't lying. In ten seconds, Eirich pushes open the fireproof door and urgently emerges from the stairway. To his dismay, a mouth-fluttering dread, Eirich runs into the deadly end of a high-caliber pistol and a stubby, double-barreled shotgun. And so sinister are the sizes and shapes of the felons toting the artillery.

"What the hell . . . ," Eirich utters, and his body braces.

Cafora wiggles the tip of his gun on Eirich's cheek. "Relax, relax. You missed the speech in the cafeteria. The bottom line is we don't want you to be a hero. Everything's gonna work out, and nobody will get harmed. *Or killed.*" Cafora nods. "Let's have your wallet."

Hands trembling, Eirich promptly produces it.

"In the next half hour," Manri forewarns, "a couple of hot-headed guys, who have no respect for a human life, will be parking themselves in front of your house. Know what I mean?" He nods, and Manri says, "I know you do, Mr. Eirich. Now let's go to the cafeteria."

Envisioning a prelude to death, Eirich lowers his head, and the two robbers pull him by the arms for the hike to the lunchroom.

On seeing his staff sprawled on the cafeteria floor with an armed, hooded burglar standing over them—a heart-skipping picture—Eirich wets his underwear. More wrenching, he sees blood dripping from Hychko's scalp, leaching onto the pavement as though it were a red, slow-moving river.

Manri bumps Eirich's back with the shotgun barrels. "These are eight of your people. Is everyone here, or is someone missing? And don't bullshit me."

Eirich counts eight pathetic men, one's hair bloody and tangled. "Yes, they're all here." His fingers unsteady, he indicates Hychko. "Eh, he's losing a lot of blood. He needs an ambulance." The supervisor feels his urine warming the left thigh and frets that the expanding stain on his pants might be noticeable.

"Yeah, yeah. The sooner you get the money room opened and closed, the sooner we get out of here, and the sooner you'll be able to get help for Hychko. OK?" Manri waves the shotgun in the direction of the stairs. "Let's go downstairs."

Manri, Cafora, and McMahon take Eirich two floors below to his glass-enclosed office, where the alarm control panels are mounted on a wall. Cafora tugs roughly at Eirich's sweater. "You got the key for the alarm?"

Shivering from fright, Eirich straightens his collar and points to a safe anchored under the control panels. "When I'm in the building, I keep it in there."

With his forehead, Manri nods at the safe. "Get it."

Burke's orders to his field marshal, Joe "Buddha" Manri, are not to injure anybody. And unaware of such considerateness, these hell-bent raiders portend a fatal ending. Hand trembling, Eirich works the combination dial, opens the safe door, and reaches in for the key.

All the while, Licastri and Sepe have been standing by on the loading platform. Earlier, Licastri removed a key from Rebmann's pocket, and with it, he turns on the switch next to the overhead door. It opens, and Sepe backs the Ford van into the cargo bay. The van now indoors, Licastri switches the door shut.

Manri instructs Eirich to disarm the alarm, a delicate procedure. The position of the switch must be precise, a deliberate exactness intended to trip unauthorized tempters. Eirich steadies his thin fingers, huffing and wiping his brow. He sets the knob to the supposedly correct setting. "The alarm is off."

"Hear me out, Eirich, before we go and unlock the door to the vault, let's get one thing straight. If you're doin' some kind of trick and an alarm goes off at the Port Authority, we'll . . ."

Eirich loses his composure and bangs on the alarm panel. "Oh, stop this shit. I don't want to be no hero, and I don't want any trouble. I got a family to go to. All I want is for you people, whoever you are, to take what you want and get the hell out of here. And leave my workers unhurt. God damn it!"

Eirich's outburst surprises the robbers, and Manri doesn't want to test Eirich's sincerity. "Here's what I'm gonna do. If you got nothin' to worry about, then when we leave here, you won't mind coming with us until we're out of the airport. All right?" Manri squares his shoulders and speculates, "If you did what you weren't supposed to do, and we get a tail of cops on our asses, well, then we can kill you right then and there. How's that?"

Cafora breaks out into a laugh. "That's a good one, Joe."

Eirich doesn't see the humor, his knees are as rubbery as overcooked linguini, and he feels he's about to faint.

McMahon and Joe Manri leave Eirich's office, and Cafora stays to guard him. McMahon and Manri huddle in a corner to mull over the supervisor's fate.

"Joe," McMahon says, "I don't think it's a good idea to take Eirich with us."

Manri crimps his lips. "Why not?"

McMahon shakes his head negatively. "Let's say we make it out of the parking lot, and somewhere down the highway we get into a chase with the cops. You know how DeSimone and that nut-job Licastri are. They got balls but no brains, and the common sense of a two-day-old spic."

The common sense of a two-day-old spic! McMahon's disparagement incenses Manri, a South American himself, though he can't defend against the slur. It must remain secret that he isn't of Italian descent. Inwardly, he's boiling with rage and would love to strangle McMahon.

"If things get hairy," McMahon reasons, "with Eirich *and* those two empty-headed nitwits in the van, anything can go wrong. Then we'd have a murder rap on our hands." Affecting a psychological dominance, he palms his gloved hand on the wall above Manri's left shoulder. McMahon's uniqueness to the Robert's Lounge gang is one of value; though he's a schizophrenic, his cleverness and keenness are talents Burke needs to restrain the rest of the louts in check.

Seething, Manri glares fiercely at McMahon and doesn't answer.

McMahon pauses and lets four to five seconds linger. "Me, I'd rather take my chances with the cops. I mean, Sepe is a hell of a driver." McMahon senses he's mollifying Manri.

Manri studies the cement floor, and McMahon recaps, "I believe Eirich is playing it straight. He doesn't seem the type to risk it all. And for what? So when he retires, Lufthansa will give him a twenty-dollar watch?"

Manri isn't the sharpest knife in the drawer, though his smarts are a notch above the rest of Burke's flock. He mulls for a moment or two. "All right, Frenchy, I'll go along with you on this, but if something goes wrong, it's on you. Let's get Eirich to open the vault."

⌁

The high-value chamber is built as two separate vaults, an outer and an inner. The cartons of money are stored in the inner room. To access the second vault, after deactivating the alarm, one must unlock the door (Door 1) to the outer chamber. Once inside there, Door 1 must be closed before opening the one to the second vault (Door 2), a critical step. If Door 1 and Door 2 are simultaneously left open, a warning sounds off at the Port Authority.

Settled on trusting Eirich, Manri and McMahon trot back to his office.

"Are we taking him with us?" Cafora asks.

"No, we ain't," Manri answers with an air of finality.

"Why not?"

"Let's just get this done," Manri says.

McMahon looks severely at Eirich. "OK, the moment of reckoning is here."

Manri presses the barrels of his weapon against Eirich's spine, and they fast-step to where the vault is, McMahon following them.

Again, Manri prods Eirich with the shotgun. "Open it. So far you've done good. Don't blow it now, Eirich." The four-inch-thick cast-iron door can only be unlocked by turning three handles to the left and to the right in a preset sequence, and Eirich does so. No alarms or sirens, so far.

"Thank God!" Eirich mutters, his inhalations slowing.

The faces of Manri, McMahon, and Cafora are glistening with perspiration, and their pulses have suddenly quickened. They seem to be wondering if a silent alarm is alerting the police. A battalion of cops could be here in two to three minutes and surround the Lufthansa complex.

"Get inside." Manri jostles Eirich through the doorway of the vault. "There's supposed to be an alarm button somewhere on a wall. Where is it?"

Eirich points to a red knob next to the light switch. "It's right there."

"OK, Eirich, sit down in the middle of the floor."

Listening for sirens, a torrent of misgivings rushes through Cafora's mind. He's been keeping watch on Eirich; McMahon snaps him out of his anxieties. "Pay attention and make sure Eirich don't go near that red button over there."

"How many times do I have to say it? I don't want trouble," Eirich appeals.

"Yeah, yeah, we believe you, but we can't take chances," Manri says. "Now you're the man of the hour, Mr. Eirich. Stand up and shut the outer door airtight before you open the second one."

Only a handful of Lufthansa managers know that coded succession, and a name booms in Eirich's mind, *Louis Werner*. The robbery isn't yet over, and two employees of the German airliner have already pegged blame on Werner.

Eirich gives the gunmen access to the inner vault. Hundreds of packages in a variety of dimensions and sizes are piled on steel shelving. A clipboard hangs on a shelf post, and a sheaf of invoices and bills of lading are clipped to it. Manri leafs through the paperwork to pinpoint the parcels with the cash. Werner's data has been on point; one night's work, at last, is about to make everyone flush.

But what if there isn't any money? Well, then, Mr. Werner should buy a ticket to the far end of the world because Jimmy Burke will hunt him until the end of time.

In the outer vault, from where he's standing Eirich can spy Manri sifting through the tissue-thin freight manifests rubber-banded to the clipboard. The tale-tell signs of an insider's role are plain, and Eirich can't contain his curiosity. "One thing I'd like to know."

"Yeah, what's that?" Cafora says, his gun pointed at Eirich.

"I'd love to know who's your inside man."

"Maybe we'll send you a postcard with his picture," Cafora jokes. "We *do* have your address, you know."

McMahon snaps the clipboard from Manri and quickly isolates the money packets. "Here, Joe! I think these are what we're looking for."

Teeth gritting, Manri reproves, "Watch yourself! Don't call me by my fuckin' name in front of Eirich."

McMahon covers his mouth, glances slyly around him. "Shit, I'm sorry." Unfazed by the blunder, McMahon speedily unravels one of the bundles, and the content is green. "Yeah! These are the ones," he gloats, his broad grin flashing through the mouth opening of his ski mask.

Sepe has been in the driver's seat of the Ford van, waiting for Manri's cue to back it close to the vault. His heart is racing; he's imagining a SWAT team staking out the loading dock outside, waiting to ambush the robbers. In the interim, Licastri joins Cafora in guarding Eirich. Manri motions for Sepe to start the engine; Sepe glances at him through the side-view mirror and rolls the van so the rear bumper is four to five feet from the vault. He jumps out of the cab and helps his confederates transfer the one-cubic-foot boxes from the inner room, across the outer vault, and into the van. The engine is running, and the exhaust fumes are fouling the cargo bay with carbon monoxide.

"Shut off the motor before we all get gassed," McMahon squawks.

The stickup men need six minutes to load the loot.

Manri and McMahon practically lift Eirich by the armpits. "This is your final act, Mr. Eirich," McMahon jibes. "Now look into my eyes. Without fuckin' around, close the doors of the vaults, *the right way*."

Eirich first closes Door 2 and then opens Door 1. Despite Eirich's assurances, McMahon and Cafora fear the unknown, an automatic signal going off at the Port Authority. McMahon prompts, "C'mon, Mr. Eirich, let's make this fast and finish locking Door 1. We wanna get out of here."

Eirich completes securing the outer vault door, and Licastri and Sepe board the Ford van, now laden with three hundred pounds of treasure. McMahon, Cafora, and Manri haul Eirich upstairs to the lunchroom. DeSimone has the cargo agents sitting quietly on the floor, and he's been hankering for one of them to provoke him.

Cafora and McMahon are prodding Eirich, Manri strutting ahead. They bound into the cafeteria, and DeSimone seems glad to see them. He slides the ski mask over his forehead and wipes his cheeks of perspiration. "Did you find what we came for?"

"Pull down your damn cap, man," shouts Manri. "What're you, a moron?"

McMahon glances at two of the Lufthansa shipping clerks, who are in a direct line of sight to where DeSimone is standing. He stews, realizing a second gunman has revealed himself to the Lufthansa workers.

Rebmann and Murray surely will not forget DeSimone's visage. Hychko also has locked Sepe's face in his mind from the glimpse he caught of it earlier.

McMahon points his gun to the floor and draws an imaginary ring with the left hand. "All right, everybody. Sit on the floor in a circle with your asses inside the circle."

The armed men string together the cargo agents, arms behind their backs, and DeSimone gags everybody's mouth with silver duct tape, a well-thought-out drill.

DeSimone is about to strap the tape on Eirich's mouth, and the supervisor recoils, his face red and filmy. "This is not necessary, goddamn it! Even if we wanted to scream for help, nobody can hear us. We're too far from the other buildings. We've been gentlemen all through this."

DeSimone hurls the tape at Cafora and pats Eirich on the shoulder. "You're right. You have been gentlemen. If you weren't, by now you'd be at the pearly gates talking to St. Peter."

Eirich gazes pitifully at Hychko, though he can't make out the seriousness of the man's lacerations, a sickening flesh of blood and pulp on his cranium. Eirich implores the robbers, "Hychko is in bad shape. He needs medical care. Immediately!"

"He'll get it soon enough. First we gotta finish our job," Cafora says with the callousness of a hangman.

Of the nine hostages, eight are handcuffed. The burglars do not cuff Murray and loosely rope his wrists, enabling him to free his hands and phone for assistance.

Manri scowls at Murray, his jaws clenched. "Wait twenty minutes before you call 911. Even if you get free, WAIT twenty minutes. GOT IT?"

The Port Authority can block the four airport exits within fifteen minutes. Three days ago, during the same early morning hours, Manri and McMahon drove from the Lufthansa cargo hangar and out of the airport in six minutes. Ample time to escape.

To ensure the victims are tied snugly, McMahon checks each one. "Remember, no heroes, please! When you're asked what we sounded like, be smart, say you were too shook up and don't remember a thing. We're going to remind you again. We know where you live."

McMahon and DeSimone are ready to follow Manri and Cafora to the stairway. They quick-step four or five paces, and then turn around to face the lunchroom. Unscripted, McMahon bids, "Good night, and have a nice day tomorrow. You're going to be on TV and in newspapers, so dress up in your Sunday clothes."

"Let's get out of here." DeSimone taps McMahon's forearm, and they scurry to the stairway.

They catch up with Manri and dash below to the ground level. Cafora remains on the landing, slams the door, and counts to sixty.

". . . fifty-eight, fifty-nine, sixty." He plows his 360 pounds into the door and forcefully reopens it, bursting into the corridor, an intimidating effect.

Burke's highwaymen regroup on the loading ramp and pile into the Ford van. McMahon presses the "Up" button on the wall, and the corrugated roll-up door of the warehouse starts to open. The van exits, and he walks out the side door of the cargo bay. McMahon jogs to where the chase car, the Pontiac Grand Prix, is parked, and folds his six-foot-one frame into the bucket seat on the passenger side. He tears off the woolen ski mask, and a gust of wind refreshes his cheeks. The engine is idling, and the heater fan is blowing warm air.

"Turn off the damn heater," McMahon complains. "I'm sweating like a pig."

"How did it go?"

"All right. We got it, Frank." McMahon vents his face with a hand and lays his head on the headrest. He lets out a sigh of relief and shuts his eyes.

Licastri engages the "Down" switch, and the twenty-four-foot-wide door begins to lower, its rollers screeching loudly, fracturing the complacency of the early dawn. With Sepe at the steering wheel, the van turns left out of the driveway of the Lufthansa compound and then onto the Nassau Expressway.

"Stay close behind the van and keep checking for cars that might be following us," McMahon says to his driver, Frank, Burke's oldest son.

Duly respecting the forty-five-miles-per-hour speed limit, Sepe decelerates and shifts his eyes from the solitary road to the rearview mirror. "Oh, shit!" he exclaims.

"What's wrong?" Manri asks.

"Some kind of car with flashing lights is creeping up behind the Pontiac. Could be cops."

Everybody becomes rigid and stares through the rear windows of the van.

"Fuck," Cafora curses, "an alarm must've gone off."

"Hit the gas, Angelo. Floor the goddamn pedal," DeSimone yells out, gritting his teeth.

Panic breaks out inside the van. Manri looks at the closely tailing Pontiac carrying McMahon and Frank Burke, and squints to focus three hundred feet farther back on the vehicle with the orange emergency beacons, flashes careening in the darkness.

They scramble for their weapons. "Cool it, cool it," Manri yells out. "They're not cops. Those lights are orange. It must be a tow truck or somethin'. Only ambulances, fire trucks, and police cruisers have red emergency lights. Everything else got orange lights."

"Whew!" The desperados exhale heartily, releasing a surge of breath they'd been holding in, and bellow in unruly laughter, palms slapping with one another.

"A close one," cries out Cafora, wheezing and winded.

"You ain't shittin'," Sepe remarks.

~~

A tune comes on the radio, and Paolo Licastri amplifies the volume to the maximum. It's a new hit, "Gonna Fly Now," from the soundtrack of the film *Rocky*. The music incites Burke's scholars to a rocking mood; they're richer than an hour ago and clap to the beat of the song. Manri quells the excitement. "Whoa, whoa! Cool it. Paolo, turn it down. You can hear it from outside. Let's not attract attention at the last minute."

"It's all under control, man. I got an eye on the rearview mirror. All is quiet, and the seas are calm," Sepe wisecracks. "Just Frank and Frenchy in the Pontiac. We're home free. WE'RE HOME FREE!!!!"

Sepe veers onto the entrance ramp of the northbound lanes of the Van Wyck Expressway and hums in sync with the radio.

DeSimone is sulking over the ultra-foolish move of removing his ski mask in the Lufthansa cafeteria, but rises above it, dreaming about tomorrow, the heftiest payday of his felonious career. And to forget the dark thought of that stupider-than-stupid move back there, he jokes, "How can you go through life with a name like that Lufthansa worker, Wolfgang Ruppert?" DeSimone was a bully from the moment he'd sloshed out of his mother's womb, and in his school days, had he come across a boy named Wolfgang, he might've slapped him just for laughs.

"If my old man named me Wolfgang, I'd kill the bastard," Sepe assures.

Rowdy guffaws crackle in the crowded van, and foul odors from perspiring bodies taint the air. And though the temperature is at the freezing mark, the passengers feel as if they're broiling in an oven—it's been a nerve-racking night.

Paolo Licastri, though, has been moping; he can't relate to the humor in DeSimone and Sepe's heckling. His English isn't much better than that of a retarded parrot. Moreover, he's stewing over Manri's orders back at the Lufthansa hangar not to harm anybody, offending him in the company of his equals, a discourtesy he will not ever bury.

In the dawning hours of December 11, 1978, the Lufthansa cargo complex underwent two cleaning services, one by the contracted porters, and the second a costly scrubbing by the Jimmy Burke company of convicts. Afterwards, as John Murray unshackled his wrists, he bolted to his workstation and sent a Mayday call to the Port Authority headquarters a mile to the west of Lufthansa.

Fingers fluttering, Murray dialed the Port Authority. "Eh, this . . . this is Cargo Building 261 re . . . reporting an armed robbery. I'm, eh . . . Shipping Agent John Murray. One of us is bleeding badly. Please send an ambulance."

"Emergency response units will be on the way, Mr. Murray."

In the next twenty minutes, as the magnitude of the theft flew over the wires to the regional and federal law enforcement agencies, a fleet of police autos, unmarked vehicles, ambulances, crime scene trucks, and Brinks patrol cars swooped into the Lufthansa parking field.

Nine miles from Lufthansa ground zero, traveling south on the Van Wyck Expressway, exhaustion was weighing on Sepe's eyelids, and the Ford van swerved slightly, riling McMahon, who was watching the zigzagging getaway vehicle from the chase car. "Damn, look at this jerk Sepe driving all over the road. He's gonna get stopped."

Indeed, if the gunmen attracted the interest of a cruising patrolman, a shootout could definitely ensue.

"Ouh!" Cafora yelped. "Angelo, what're you, sleeping at the wheel? Paolo, give'm a smack before he falls asleep."

Paolo Licastri refrained; nobody could slap Sepe and go on unscathed.

Sepe shook off his doziness. "I'm OK. We only got a few blocks to go."

"You sure?" Manri second-guessed. "'Cause I can drive the rest of the way."

"Nah, nah, I'm all right."

They were headed to Metropolitan Avenue in Maspeth, Queens, where an industrial park with factories and commercial buildings spanned blocks on end.

"Slow down, Angelo. It's the second building on the left," Cafora said.

"Are you sure?" Sepe questioned.

"You're a real mammalook. Wasn't I here just a couple of hours ago to drop off Jimmy?"

Sepe decelerated. "I see it." He nosed the van into the driveway of the warehouse, and Manri bounced out. He banged on the roll-up door, and in seconds it began rising. The warehouse was John Gotti's contribution.

The gangly black man, Stacks, was waiting inside, his finger on the button of the electric opener. "All right! All right! C'mon in. You got plenty o' room," he directed, waving on the Ford van. Sepe drove it in, the Pontiac chase car immediately behind.

Outdoors the street resumed its stillness. Inside the warehouse, the lighting was dusky at best, and everyone spilled out of the van. Draped in a black, full-length wool coat, its collar and a white cashmere scarf enveloping his neck, Burke came forth from the shadows, seemingly in a slow-motion, soundless stroll, hands deep in his pockets. He smiled at Manri. "How did it go?"

"Smooth, Jimmy. Smooth," Manri informed him, kissing his thumb and index fingers. To feel accepted, he overcompensated in mimicking the Burke gang of Italians.

A flush warmed the Gent's face, and he had the look of a child who couldn't wait to unwrap a gift. "What're you waitin' for? Unload the cash and lemme get it out of here."

This startled the robbers. "Jimmy," Licastri spoke out, "why we no count the money now?"

Everyone else gazed at the floor, and Burke stared at Licastri. "You think we're gonna stand here counting for the next three hours? I wanna be off the streets in case the cops put up roadblocks."

"How I know how much we steal?" Paolo Licastri clucked his tongue, his rotting teeth as pointy as a pitchfork.

"You're gonna have to trust me. And if you don't, tough shit. Now let's get this cash out of the van," Burke said.

In a minute, the warehouse changed into a setting reminiscent of Santa Claus's shop of elves. Everyone lined up, forming a human conveyor belt. They unloaded the cartons of money from the van, and reloaded them into a switch car, a second vehicle for ferrying the booty to where it'd be hidden—a precaution if perchance a witness had seen the black Ford van on the Lufthansa property. Burke and his stickup men packed the bundles into the trunk of the switch car, a white Toyota Corona. As a decoy, they added twelve pounds of foul-bagged bluefish over the packets of cash. This tactic, Burke's idea, served two objectives: it hid the money, and if an inquisitive cop started searching the trunk, the nostril-gassing odor would fend him off from digging further. Who'd conceive of cash camouflaged under rotting fish?

Sepe pinched the tip of his longish nose, the outline of a ski jump. "Whooh! Sure as shit, nobody's gonna wanna go near this car."

"Pheeew. Jimmy, after this run, you're gonna have to junk it," Manri said. "You'll never get the stink out of this car."

"OK, we're done," Burke said, wired energy in his speech. "Frenchy, let everybody squeeze into the Pontiac and drive them back to Robert's Lounge. Frank and me will go stash the loot." The Gent's son, Frank, a tall, skinny nineteen-year-old, would be inhaling the putrid fish fumes, and Senior . . . well, he'd be basking in the defeat of the Red Baron.

The Toyota loaded, Burke said to Stacks, "Listen carefully." He dropped his hands on the black man's shoulders. "This van's gotta disappear faster than immediately. Understand? You know where to take it. Change the plates and go there now."

"I got you, Jimmy," Stacks said.

The gunners changed their clothes. Manri threw the outfits and ski masks into the van. John Gotti had arranged for an auto-wrecking yard in the Flatlands section of Brooklyn to crush-compact the getaway vehicle and all the paraphernalia used in the robbery.

Burke's thieves huddled around him. "All right," he coached. "After we all leave here, I want you to do whatever you've been doin' and don't change your routine. I don't want none o' you to phone each other. If you got something to say, do it in person. NO PHONE CALLS. Got it?" The Gent peered at them one by one. "Five days from today, Joe Buddha's gonna come to see you all and square up with your cut." Burke leered at Licastri. "Paolo, tell John that I myself will be straightening out with him." The whole crew gave signs of understanding, and disbanded. Licastri, though, wore a glare of disdain for Burke.

$$\sim$$

Frank and his father drove to their house in Howard Beach and pulled into the driveway, the black, overcast sky losing its darkness and streaking to a violet hue, shades of the new aurora. The Gent got out of the Toyota, took a remote control out of his coat pocket, clicked it, and the garage door opened. He waved Frank on to roll the car in. In the middle of the garage floor was a four-foot by twelve-foot wooden hatch. Beneath it, the Gent had dug a pit two yards deep, originally for a mechanic to work on the undercarriage of an automobile.

Into that hole, an oily and grease-saturated trench, Burke ditched the Lufthansa haul.

Minutes after Burke and Frank had driven out of the warehouse, Stacks snuffed out the lights, backed the Ford van out onto the sidewalk, and the electric overhead door closed automatically. He was headed east on Metropolitan Avenue and tuned the radio to an FM jazz station. He hummed, floating into a reverie while listening to the fast-skipping blues notes of the sax musician, Sonny Stitt. Stacks glanced at the digital clock on the dashboard: 5:54 a.m. "I gotta get this van to the junkyard before it gets light out," he muttered to himself. A distraction titillated his thoughts, Shelly, a "fine sistah" with whom he curled up from time to time. She fashioned a claret-dyed Afro, a cushiony fluff in style with the one Angela Davis trended in the late sixties. Shelly had had four children with four different men, or possibly five. She herself had lost count.

Stacks was cruising at forty-five-miles-per-hour, careful not to speed; the license tags on the van, number 508HWM, were stolen. Sonny Stitt's saxophone was lulling Stacks into the mood, and he suddenly longed to stop by Shelly's; he'd stay with her for a couple of lines of cocaine, a romp in the sack, and then scram to the Flatlands quarters of Brooklyn to dump the van.

At the auto-wrecking yard, the operator had been waiting to crush the Ford van into a bale of scrap metal. Stacks, instead, boarded the west-bound lanes of the Belt Parkway at the Cross Bay Boulevard intersection. He traveled on the Belt for seven minutes and exited on Rockaway Parkway. He then swung north for two miles toward Canarsie until reaching East 95th Street. Shelly lived in a garden apartment, a drug exchange center, crack leading the neighborhood commodity. The tenants were five-dollar prostitutes, drugrunners, social assistance scammers, and addicts. A balanced blend of citizens. On the grounds outdoors, weeds were littered with trash and newspaper debris, empty bottles of Gypsy Rose wine strewn here and there.

Clunkers with rotted fenders lined both sides of the block. The late-model Ford van, clean and shiny, was bluntly out of place on this ghetto street. Stacks absentmindedly parked it near a fire hydrant; he locked the door, and traipsed to Shelly's doorway.

Nailed to the door was a piece of cardboard with a handwritten message, "Bell No Work." Stacks knocked. No answer. He knocked again, and after thirty seconds in the frosty climate he heard the jangling of a safety chain and the clanking of the doorknob.

"Who is it?"

"It's Stacks, baby. Open up."

The door opened, and Shelly appeared, yawning and sleepy, a brown infant crying in her arms. "Stacks, it's five o'clock in da mornin', honey. Whatchu doin' here so late?"

He hugged "his lady" and kissed her, the baby howling louder. "I wanted a snort o' coke, baby. And I know you got a little stash," he said, plugging his nostril with a thumb, a hint of his craving.

"C'mon in," Shelly mumbled with reluctance, her hand shielding the child's scalp. "Hurry up and close the door. The cold be comin' in." Rocking the tot in her arms, she went into the tiny kitchen. Sprinklings of cat litter on the tattered vinyl flooring crackled under her sandals, and a mountain of crud-plastered dishes covered the sink, a chipped and dented basin. In the den Stacks sat on a red velour couch, the edges of the armrest frayed and stained with a rainbow of spillages from chicken soup to urine. An acidy smell of sour milk fouled the air.

Awake for the past thirty hours, Stacks rubbed his eyelids. Shelly plopped a ceramic sugar bowl on the glass coffee table, and in it was a dusting of cocaine. Stacks coiled his arm around Shelly's caramel-toned thigh and giggled. "All right! All right, baby. I knew you'd come through for your Stacks." He kissed her upper leg, inching closer to the vagina. "I goin' come through for you."

Shelly pushed Stacks's head aside. "Whatchu mean?"

His pulpy lips widened and, teeth missing, his mouth opened to a gaping hole. "Baby, we just done a big, big score, and I'm gonna be comin' into a piece o' change."

"Oh, Stacks, nobody goin' give you nothin'. You been sayin' this since I know you. It never be happenin'."

"It be happenin', baby. You'll see."

"Don't be a fooh, Stacks. Stop believin' them white boys. They like to keep everythin' for themselves. And you gotta watch out for those Aitalians. They be bad people."

Stacks didn't care to dwell on this. "Baby, they won't be messing with this nigga." He enfolded his arms around Shelly's buttocks, a pair of basketballs, and lapped at her navel. She hugged his cheeks, and they began snorting the cocaine. At some point, Stacks, ever the lover, lifted Shelly off the couch and carried her to the bedroom, a darkish room with newspapers on the windows. They tumbled in the hay for an hour; Stacks fell asleep, the baby shrilling in the background, and the Ford van—stolen plates and all—illegally parked at the fire hydrant.

——⌣——

By daybreak, law enforcement agencies understood the enormity of the theft, and more and more representation from the NYPD, FBI, the Queens district attorney, Port Authority, New York State troopers, and Brinks detectives were teeming into the Lufthansa cargo hangar.

Dense pewter clouds were spitting out watery snowflakes, and within minutes into the inquiry the scene of the robbery underwent a transformation; a cargo shipping plant had turned to a boxing ring. Ranks of investigators from the many police forces were growing uncivilized, hostility mounting by the hour. The sparring for top command of the investigation was brewing antagonism, and blows were about to fly, literally.

Two

The Great Taxicab Robbery

James H. Collins

On Thursday, February 15, 1912, the New York evening papers had a startling news story.

Between ten and eleven o'clock that morning two messengers were sent in a taxicab from the East River National Bank, at Broadway and Third Street, to draw $25,000 in currency from the Produce Exchange National Bank, at Broadway and Beaver Street, in the downtown financial district, and bring it uptown. This transfer of money had been made several times a week for so long a period without danger or loss that the messengers were unarmed. One of them, Wilbur F. Smith, was an old man who had been in the service of the bank thirty-five years, and the other was a mere boy, named Wardle, seventeen years old. The taxicab man, an Italian named Geno Montani, seemed almost a trusted employee, too, for he operated two cabs from a stand near the bank, and was frequently called upon for such trips.

While the cab was returning uptown through Church Street with the money, five men suddenly closed in upon it. According to the chauffeur's story, a sixth man forced him to slacken speed by stumbling in front of the vehicle. Immediately two men on each side of the cab opened the doors. Two assailants were boosted in and quickly beat the messengers into insensibility, while their two helpers ran along on the sidewalk. The fifth man climbed onto the seat beside the chauffeur, held a revolver to his ribs, and ordered him to drive fast on peril of his life. This fellow seemed to be familiar with automobiles, and threatened the driver when he tried to slacken speed. That is a busy part of the city. Yet nobody on the sidewalks seemed to notice anything out of the ordinary. The cab dodged vehicles, going at high speed for several blocks. At Park Place and Church Street, after a trip of eleven blocks, at a busy corner, the chauffeur was ordered to stop the cab, and the three robbers got down, carrying the $25,000 in a leather bag, ran quickly to a black automobile without a license number, which was waiting for them, and in a few moments were gone.

Information came chiefly from the chauffeur, because the two bank employees had been attacked so suddenly and viciously that they lost consciousness in a moment. When the chauffeur looked inside his cab after the crime, he said, he saw them both lying senseless and bleeding. They could give no description of the assailants. Eye-witnesses were found who had seen men loitering in the neighborhood where the cab was boarded shortly before the crime, but their descriptions were not very useful.

That night the New York evening papers published accounts of the crime under great black headlines, and on the following morning every news item of a criminal nature was grouped in the same part of the papers to prove that the city had entered one of its sensational "waves of crime." And for more than a week the public read criticism and denunciation of the police force.

Now, let us follow the police story. We will begin at the very beginning, watch the incidents and characters unfold, and give quite a little attention to the technical methods by which results were arrived at. For the story is a study in clean, straightforward detective work, and that work ought to be better known by the public, so that intelligent public opinion may back up honest police effort.

The story starts with a burly, genial man, sitting in a big office at Police Headquarters. The office is that of the Second Deputy Police Commissioner, and the man is the Commissioner himself, George S. Dougherty.

Commissioner Dougherty dominates the story. The taxicab robbers were caught by his methods, plans, and supervision, backed by the splendid team work of the men under him. His own sources of information supplied the clues, and his personal skill in examining criminals brought out the confessions that saved the city the expense of trials with all but one offender. It is far from the writer's wish to indulge in hero-worship, however, so these details will appear in their proper place in the narrative.

George Dougherty has had nearly twenty-five years' experience in criminal work in New York, and over the whole country. Until his appointment by Mayor Gaynor in May, 1911, he was connected with the organization. Bank and financial crimes have long been his specialty, so the taxicab case fell right into his own province. He knows the ways of forgers, bank sneaks, swindlers, burglars, and "yeggmen," and is personally acquainted with most of the criminals in those lines in and out of prison. He has also had much to do with protecting the crowds at races, ball games, aeronautic meetings, and other big gatherings. As executive head of the detective bureau, five hundred plain-clothes policemen scattered over Greater New York cover all crimes of a local and routine nature, and are subject to his call when a special case like the taxicab robbery comes up for his personal attention.

On an ordinarily quiet morning at Police Headquarters, there will be a steady stream of people passing into Dougherty's office. Several assistants guard the doors leading from two ante-rooms, and marshal the visitors. Now a group of detectives enters and hears a talk on methods. Then two detectives come in, make a report and receive further instructions. Then there will be an interruption, perhaps, while an assistant soothes and sends away a crank who occasionally turns up with a purely imaginary affair of his own, and two more detectives pass in accompanied by a man and a woman who look just like the people one sees dining at a fashionable uptown restaurant. The woman's furs are magnificent, and her hat a costly Fifth Avenue creation.

"A couple of taxpayers?" speculates the group of reporters, waiting outside to get a statement about some important case.

"Two of the cleverest check swindlers in the country," corrects a detective, and presently the reporters are called in, and Dougherty recites names, dates, and facts connected with the gang to which these prosperous "taxpayers" belong, gazing reflectively out of the window as details come back in memory, and chuckling with the delighted journalists as the pithy slang and professional names of the underworld are jotted down on their pads. They fire a scattering volley of questions at him and depart, and then his secretary announces that the saloon-keeper who knows a good deal about the Blind Puppy Café case is outside, but refuses to talk to the police at all.

"Hullo!" is the Commissioner's off-hand greeting as the cautious saloon-keeper comes in, and in two minutes the latter is answering questions freely.

"Why, say!" he exclaims. "I'll tell *you* anything."

Then a humble little woman in a cheap hat and a long cloak is brought in. For more than an hour she has been waiting outside, with her eyes fixed patiently on the door leading to the inner office.

"Stand there," says the Commissioner, with gruff kindness, and he makes a formal statement about her husband, who has been arrested with a criminal gang, and is pretty certain to go to prison. He tells her what has been done in the case, and what will follow, and the little woman listens mutely. When he finishes, her eyes fill with tears. But she makes no reply, nor any sound. The Commissioner winks fast as he looks out of the window again, and then says, sympathetically, "That's the best that can be done. But don't you worry. Come in and see me again. Keep in touch with me, and don't worry yourself. Come in and talk with me—come in tomorrow." And she bravely wipes her eyes and goes out with her trouble.

The procession continues.

Police captains and detectives in squads, prisoners and witnesses in twos and threes, newspaper men in corps and singly, and occasionally a cautious gentleman who wants to see the Commissioner alone, and is anxious that nobody say anything about this visit to Police Headquarters—for he is an informant.

The taxicab robbery took place on a quiet morning like this.

Suddenly, around eleven o'clock on Thursday, February 15, a brief message comes from the second precinct, stating that a robbery has been committed in the financial district. A little later there is a fuller report over police wires. The details are few, as will be seen by the general alarm that presently goes out over the city:

Police Department, City of New York,
February 15, 1912.
To all Boroughs—notify the patrol platoon immediately.
Arrest for assault and robbery three men:
No. 1, about 35 years, five feet eight or nine inches in height, 160 or
170 pounds, small stubby dark mustache, dark complexion, medium
build, dark suit and cap, no overcoat.
No. 2, about 35 years, five feet ten inches in height, slender build, dark
hair, possibly smooth shaven, light brown suit, no overcoat, wore a cap.
No description of No. 3.
Stole $25,000 in five and ten dollar bills, contained in a brown
leather telescope bag, 24 inches long, 16 inches square, from two bank
messengers in a taxicab about 11 this a.m., at Park Place and Church
Street, and escaped in a five- or seven-seated black touring car, top up.
Look out for this car, bag, and occupants on streets, at ferry entrances,
bridge terminals, railroad stations. Inquire at all garages, automobile
stands, stables, etc.
If found, notify Detective Bureau.

Before noon, the Commissioner has postponed appointments, assigned routine business, and is engaged in an investigation that will keep him busy until that morning, twelve days later, when the first arrests are made, and the case is, in police parlance, "broken."

Where do the police begin in such a crime? What do they start with when there is apparently so little to work upon?

In spite of the wide popular interest in police and criminal matters, the average citizen has no very clear idea. Even the newspaper reporter, following police activities every day, is not well informed in technical details. Some information is necessarily withheld from him, and he is a busy young man, with his own technical viewpoint, working hard to get his own kind of information.

This lack of knowledge leads to a feeling of mystery, helplessness, and terror after a sensational crime, and to criticism of the police. They are at work, skillfully, honestly, diligently. But results take time. It would do little good to make arrests without evidence. The citizen's sympathies are aroused by brutal lawlessness, and he urges that somebody be caught and punished. If results are not at once apparent, he jumps to the conclusion that the police are "demoralized." He would be startled if he could see how quickly and persistently the underworld takes steps to strengthen him in that conclusion, and use him to discredit the police.

Sixty detectives are immediately called into the case. Five of them go down to the scene of the robbery, with orders to work there until further notice. They make a thorough search of the neighborhood, following the route taken by Montani's taxicab, and questioning merchants, newsdealers, porters, truckmen, and other persons likely to have information as eye-witnesses. They go through the streets that may have been taken by the escaping robbers, and work over the whole ground. This search through one of the busiest sections of New York in a busy hour, amid the excitement created by the crime, may appear like hopeless business. But, as will be seen presently, it yields important results. Other detectives search garages for the black automobile without a license number in which the robbers are reported to have got away. Four uniformed policemen on beats along the route taken by the taxicab are questioned. Other detailed inquiries of the same nature are started.

But the most important work of the first day centers at Police Headquarters, where a conference is held by Commissioner Dougherty and his assistants, and in the examination of Montani, the taxicab driver.

Strip all the labels off a suit of clothes and lay it before a committee of tailors. In a few moments certain points would be agreed upon. It may be a new suit, or an old one, a fine piece of tailoring, or a cheap hand-me-down. The committee could often identify the cheap suit and tell the name of its manufacturer, while with a seventy-five-dollar suit it might be possible to determine the maker's name. This holds true of many other lines of work, and it is particularly true of criminal investigation.

Who cut and made that suit of clothes?

The conference sat down to determine this, judging the robbery strictly as a piece of workmanship. Names of known bank criminals were brought up, one by one, and details gone over. It soon became clear that none of the men identified with bank crime were likely to have the brains, skill, or organization to plan and execute so complicated a robbery.

34

The criminals had known the habits of the bank in conveying cash uptown. They knew the route, and were aware that the guard was only an elderly man and a seventeen-year-old boy, both unarmed. They had boarded the cab at the best point, and evidently made arrangements for stopping it. There was teamwork in every detail. It showed marked insight, for instance, to provide additional men to boost each assailant in at the doors. For young Wardle, the bank employee, had made a plucky attempt to shove his robber out and shut the door, and might have succeeded had there not been an outside man. Robberies are committed under exciting conditions. They sometimes fail because criminals balk. That outside man was there not only to help his "slugger" into the cab, but to *force* him in if he shrank, and make certain he did his work. Whoever planned such details, it was agreed at the conference, possessed more cunning than the ordinary bank criminal.

Montani Is Examined

When Montani, the taxicab driver, arrived at Police Headquarters, he was willing to talk, and seemed anxious to help the police in every way. He knew suspicion might be directed toward himself, but did not resent that. He talked like a man confident of the truth of his story, and certain that he would be found blameless.

Montani is an Italian, from the northern part of Italy, about thirty years old, five feet six inches high, rather stout and thick-set, with very dark complexion. The striking feature of his countenance, his large, intelligent brown eyes. Commissioner Dougherty found himself thinking of Napoleon in connection with Montani.

The first examination lasted all afternoon, Montani going out to lunch with the Commissioner. Hundreds of questions were asked bearing on the robbery, the appearance of the criminals, and Montani's past and personal affairs. The story was gone over again and again, and different questioners relieved each other. Yet the taxicab man never lost his temper or patience, and did not contradict himself in any important particular.

Montani had been in this country since the age of twelve, it appeared, had a wife and two children, and was the owner of two taxicabs operated from a stand at a hotel near the bank, whose money he regularly carried.

He had owned three cabs, but lost one through business reverses. In fact, he had passed through money troubles, and his story excited sympathy. Starting originally as a truckman for a salvage company, his ambition and intelligence had won him such confidence that this company lent him money to set up trucking for himself. Still more ambitious, he had become a taxicab proprietor. Through the trickery of an ill-chosen partner, however, he had lost some of his savings. He seemed a little bitter about this, and it was a circumstance not likely to escape an expert police examiner, for the loss of money through fraud, coupled with temptation, is often the starting point in crime.

The Italian's former employers spoke highly of his character when questioned by detectives. He gave the names of chauffeurs who had worked for him lately, and of business people who knew him, and careful investigation failed to disclose any suspicious circumstances. Montani quite won the newspaper men—so much so that, when he was discharged in court a few days later for apparent lack of evidence, the newspapers criticised the police for having held him at all.

And yet, before that first night, Montani himself, largely through simple answers to questions, had become so involved that there was ground for holding him under arrest.

In the questions and cross-questions, the checks and counter-checks of a skillful examiner, there are possibilities little suspected by those not familiar with that kind of work.

Montani had slowed down his cab at the point where the robbers boarded it. He said that an old man had suddenly got in front, and he had slackened speed to avoid running over him. But detectives along the route found eye-witnesses who had seen the robbers board the cab, and who could testify that there had been nobody in front of the vehicle.

Both of his cabs had stood in line near the bank that morning, the one driven by himself being second, and the other, in charge of an employee, was first. When the call came from the bank, Montani answered it himself out of his turn, sending the other cab uptown, as he explained, to have some tires vulcanized. But it was not a good explanation.

He said that as soon as the robbers left his cab he had raised a cry for help. But eye-witnesses were found who denied this.

Instead of running north after the robbers' automobile when he had taken a policeman aboard his cab, he ran south, away from it. This action, he maintained, was taken under orders from the policeman. But the latter denied that.

He was not able to explain how the robbers had known where to post their automobile so it would be waiting at the spot where they finished their work.

Interest centered in this mysterious black automobile without a license number. For, though Montani was an experienced chauffeur, and his replies to other questions showed that he had seen both the rear and the side of that car, he was unable to tell its make.

Meanwhile, it was learned that three men had hurriedly boarded an elevated train near the scene of the robbery shortly after, not waiting for change from a quarter. The ticket-seller was unable to describe them, but connected them with the robbery when he heard about it.

Montani was held in the custody of the Commissioner that night, to be put through further examination in the morning. But long before morning the police were working on an entirely new development.

THE FIRST DIRECT CLUE

The law-abiding citizen goes around New York with little knowledge of the crowding underworld all about him. It is perhaps just as well that he knows nothing of the lives and morals of hundreds of people who elbow him on the streets, sit beside him in the cars, and scrutinize him with a strictly professional eye in many places.

Nor has he any clear conception of the relations that a good police officer maintains with members of this underworld. It is a world just as complete as that of business or society, however, and much of the time of a detective or police official is spent keeping track of people in it, forming acquaintances and connections in various ways, and establishing the organization of informants that will help in the detection and prevention of crime. A good detective is like a good salesman—he keeps track of his "trade."

Shortly after midnight of the first day, Commissioner Dougherty received a message over the telephone that sent him uptown to meet an informant. At two o'clock in the morning of Friday, February 16, he and this person had a talk at a fashionable uptown hotel. Indeed, most of the meetings with informants during this case were held at two well-known hotels, perhaps the last places in the city that anybody would connect with such conferences.

Informants are not always right, nor always possessed of useful information. But this one had the first real clue.

On the afternoon of the robbery, it was learned, a fellow known as "Eddie Collins" had come to his rooming house, on the lower West Side, told a woman with whom he lived, known as "Swede Annie," to pack up and be ready to leave the city in a hurry, and presently disappeared with her. He was also reported to have a large roll of money. With a rough estimate of the size of this roll, given by the informant, and a dummy roll of "stage money" made up for the purpose, the police were able to judge that Collins must have had between $3,000 and $5,000. That would have been his probable share in a division of the stolen currency among five men.

The house where Collins had lived was kept by a Mrs. Sullivan. Steps were at once taken to "surround" this woman, as the operation is known technically. For before a possible source of information like Mrs. Sullivan is followed up, it is necessary to know something about it. The person in question may be criminal, or in league with the underworld. On the other hand, he or she may be quite innocent, and willing to aid the police. The "surround" is an interesting operation. It is often made without the knowledge of the person investigated. In many cases it takes time.

Mrs. Sullivan came through the ordeal handsomely.

She proved to be a wholesome, hard-working landlady, keeping a house that sheltered occasional suspicious characters, but entirely honest herself. She was not only able to furnish information about her late lodgers, but willing.

"Sure, it's a good deal I know about that Collins, as he calls himself," she said, "and mighty little that's good."

It seems that about two weeks previously Collins had offered to pay the landlady if she would appear in a Brooklyn court and testify to the good character of a criminal named Molloy, who was being held for trial on a charge of robbery.

"They're paying fifteen to twenty dollars for 'character' witnesses," said her lodger.

"And do you think I'd take the stand and perjure myself swearing for a man I never heard of?" asked the indignant landlady.

"Oh, that's nothing to some of the things we do," was the reply.

Several days later, while she was putting some laundry into Collins' bureau drawer the landlady caught sight of two new blackjacks. She asked Collins what he was doing with such weapons.

"Aw, we use them in our business," he said. Then, with the confidence often bred in criminals by success, he told her he knew a gang that was planning to rob a taxicab that carried money uptown to a bank every week. Mrs. Sullivan questioned him as to details, and he assured her it would be an easy job.

"For we've got it all fixed with the chauffeur," he said.

At that point, however, like many an honest person who might aid the police with information, Mrs. Sullivan let the matter drop out of her mind. It is a simple thing to mail a letter or telephone to Police Head-quarters, giving such information, and the experience of the Detective Bureau is such that the information can be investigated without involving innocent persons. But perhaps Mrs. Sullivan concluded that, in a big city like New York, it is well for people to keep their mouths shut. Or maybe she decided that Collins was merely boasting.

On Friday, less than twenty-four hours after the robbery, a "network investigation" was begun.

Sixty detectives searched that part of the city where Collins and Annie had lived, seeking further information. Photograph galleries and other places were investigated on the chance of finding pictures. Den-izens of the underworld were talked with casually. Professional crimi-nals, prostitutes, dive-keepers, receivers of stolen goods, and other shady characters were brought before Commissioner Dougherty in couples and half-dozens for quick cross-examination. By Saturday evening the police had some highly important information.

It was learned that Annie had been seen going away on the after-noon of the robbery in a taxicab, accompanied by two men, one of whom was Collins, and the other unknown. Good descriptions were secured of

Annie and her sweetheart, especially of her hat, which was a cheap affair, but conspicuous by reason of a row of little red roses. It was also discovered that Collins had been a boxer, that he hailed from Boston, and that his real name was Eddie Kinsman. Finally, the police secured two photographs, one an indifferent picture of Kinsman, and the other an excellent portrait of Annie. These were quickly put through the department's photograph gallery, where there are facilities for making duplicates in a hurry, and more than a hundred copies were soon ready for work, which will be described in its proper place.

The trail now seemed to lead to Boston. At all events, further information was to be secured there. And here came in a little refinement imparted by Commissioner Dougherty's experience with the Pinkerton forces. For where this private detective organization works unhampered over the whole country, the official police forces in most cities confine their searches to their own territory. When it is believed that criminals have left town, as in this case, a general description is telegraphed to other cities. Dougherty's method, however, is always to send a man from his own staff, with detailed instructions. There are no local boundaries for him.

Late on Saturday night Inspector Hughes, of the Detective Bureau, slipped out of headquarters with Detective O'Connell, and took a train for Boston. Their departure was kept strictly secret. They bid good night to associates, saying that they expected to be up and at work again early next morning, and until their return on Monday everybody who asked for the Inspector was told that "he is usually around the building somewhere."

MONTANI POINTS OUT "KING DODO"

All through Friday and Saturday, while the network investigation was going on, Commissioner Dougherty continued his examination of Montani.

Some important information against him now came from outside.

It developed that Montani had been involved several months before in an insurance case, claiming indemnity for a burned automobile under a policy. He had presented, as part of its value, a bill for repairs amounting to $1,348. The insurance company, however, had found that this bill was fraudulent, that the repairs had never been made, and had obtained a statement to that effect from the Italian chauffeur. Out of pity for his wife and two children the case was not pressed against him. Now that he was involved in another crime, however, the insurance people came forward and laid the facts before the police.

Of course, Montani knew nothing about this new development.

For two days the chauffeur was questioned at intervals, and the inquiry centered chiefly on the knotty points in his story of the crime. He was particularly pressed for better explanations of the slackening of his cab when the robbers boarded it, but stuck to his original statement about a man getting in front of the vehicle. He described this person as an old man, and said he must have been in league with the criminals. As the police had good evidence that there had been nobody in front of the taxicab, however, this point was returned to again and again, and toward night on Saturday, February 17, the little chauffeur began to feel the strain.

On his way to supper that evening with men from the Detective Bureau, Montani was taken through the Bowery. Suddenly he stopped, dramatically, and exclaimed: "There! That is the old man who got in front of my cab!"

His finger indicated a Bowery character as typical as anything ever seen in melodrama—a ragged little old figure with an amazing set of whiskers, engaged in picking up cigar butts along the gutters. He was immediately taken to headquarters.

No detail of his work interests Commissioner Dougherty more keenly than his study of the many picturesque characters who turn up as an important case unfolds. He has a ready appreciation of everybody who appears, from the society lady who lost her jewels to the typical Bowery loafer. He is as ready to look at facts from a criminal's point of view as that of an honest man. He has often gone half across the country to get acquainted with a good burglar, and in this warm human interest lies the basis of his skill as an examiner of suspects. These details are set down, not in glorification of Dougherty, but for the guidance of every police officer interested in his methods.

The moment Dougherty laid eyes on this new character, with his magnificent whiskers, he gave him a nickname.

"King Dodo!" said the Commissioner, and by that name he was known insofar as he figured in the case at all. "King Dodo" proved to be entirely innocent, and nothing more than the victim of a chance move of Montani's, who evidently thought that he ought to produce something tangible to back up his assertion that the cab had been intercepted by an old man. "King Dodo" established a perfect alibi, proving that he had been elsewhere at the time of the robbery, and after being questioned and the truth of his story established, he was released, there being no reason for holding him.

"I feel safe," said the Commissioner solemnly, "in paroling you on your own responsibility, to appear again if wanted."

That may have been a heavier responsibility than had been put on his shoulders in years. But he rose to it. Two days later a decently dressed, clean shaven, elderly gentleman came in and asked for the Commissioner. He was "all dolled up," in police parlance, and looked like a retired small shopkeeper. The staff did not recognize him for a moment. But it was "King Dodo," doing his best to fill the part of a minor figure in the great taxicab mystery. There being nothing for him to do, he dropped back into private life.

On his Sunday visit to Boston Inspector Hughes talked with Chief Inspector Watts of that city, learned where Kinsman lived, and that his family was a respectable one; found a bright patrolman named Dorsey who knew Kinsman, and gave more information about his personal appearance, habits, and career as a boxer, desertion from the Navy, and so forth; and made arrangements to have the Kinsman home watched so that news of his return would be secured immediately. It was clear that Kinsman had not returned to Boston.

Discovery of Kinsman's Trail

As soon as Inspector Hughes returned from Boston, on Monday morning, the Commissioner took steps to question the crews of every train that had left New York since one p.m. on the day of the robbery.

Just the other afternoon the writer sat with a squad of young detectives at Police Headquarters and heard a talk on methods given by Dougherty, and one point clearly brought out was the usefulness to the thief-catcher of routine information.

He began by relating an amusing incident. Some days before a detective had turned up at headquarters for instruction, and naïvely asked the Commissioner to lend him a pencil and a slip of paper, so he could make some notes. Another detective was found who had only a hazy idea of the location of New York's telephone exchanges. Taking these as his text, the Commissioner explained the value to every police officer of what might be called "time-table" information—knowing the depots and ferries, what roads run out of them, the cities reached, the number and character of trains, the general methods of dispatching trains, and so forth. The Commissioner himself is as well informed on such matters as any railroad man, and thoroughly familiar with routine methods in many other lines of work and business. How such knowledge can be employed was shown by the next move in the taxicab case.

Detectives were sent to every railroad terminal to secure lists of trains, learn the names of the crews, and make out schedules of the time when each crew would be back in the city. Then each man was found and carefully questioned. His memory could be helped by pictures of Kinsman and Annie, and by intimate details of personal appearance and manner.

The search bore fruit, though it took time.

On Wednesday Detective Watson, who was a railroad engineer before he joined the police, found that Train No. 13 on the New York Central had taken on three passengers answering the descriptions on the afternoon of the robbery. They had boarded the train at Peekskill, the town to which, as it was subsequently learned, they had ridden in a taxicab. The conductor's attention had been drawn to Annie by her smoking a cigarette on the sly in the toilet of the day coach. He remembered her high cheek bones, and the black velvet hat with its little roses, and the athletic build of her men companions, who both appeared to be boxers. It was also established that the trio had gone to Albany, for one of the trainmen distinctly remembered helping Annie down at that station.

"PLANT 21" IS ESTABLISHED

Monday, February 19, was an important day in more ways than one.

While the train investigation was going on, it was learned that a woman known as "Myrtle Horn," an intimate of Annie's, had moved to a lower West Side rooming house, taking Annie's trunk with her, as though Annie expected to return to the city. After a preliminary survey, this house was visited by Commissioner Dougherty in person. He explained that he was a contractor, about to build a section of the new subway, and that he was looking for a quiet room at a reasonable price where he might have some of the comforts of home. After a little talk with the landlady it became clear that she was honest and trustworthy, with no information of the new lodger who had taken her front room in the basement. Arrangements were quickly made to put this house, inside and outside, under constant surveillance.

Along in the evening Mrs. Isabella Goodwin, a police matron, was installed there. The Commissioner brought her, and carried her bundle. The landlady and the matron had never seen each other in their lives, but kissed ostentatiously, and made considerable fuss on the chance of being overheard. Mrs. Goodwin was "planted" as the landlady's "sister," who had come from Montreal to live with her and help in the housework until she could find a position in New York. The Commissioner grumbled a little about her stinginess in refusing to pay an expressman to bring her bundle, and then took his departure, explaining that the train had been late, and the baby was not well, and his wife, Aggie, would be worried about him, and so forth. Mrs. Goodwin established herself in a room at the rear of the basement, handy to that occupied by Myrtle Horn, and kept her eyes and ears open as she went about the housework, slipping out to report when she had any information, and receiving instructions.

Outside surveillance on this house was conducted from an empty store across the street. Arrangements for the use of such property are usually made by the police without difficulty, though occasionally a close-fisted owner expects rent. Blinds were put up over the windows, peep-holes made, and a few hammers provided, with some nails and boards. Then six of the best "shadow men" in the Detective Bureau were stationed there. They made a little noise occasionally, in "getting the store ready for a big firm moving up from downtown," and watched the house day and night. Whenever Myrtle went out she was followed. If she had visitors, they were investigated. This store was known by the code term of "Plant 21," so that reports could be sent without disclosing police information.

Montani Goes Free

On Monday, too, Montani was arraigned in court, and discharged for what appeared to be lack of any evidence against him.

At this point the Commissioner took the liberty of fooling the newspaper men for the good of his case.

Newspaper criticism for three days had been particularly severe. Editors made many charges, and were fertile in suggestions as what ought to be done to reorganize the presumably "demoralized" police department. The present writer feels confident, however, that a careful search of the files for those days will disclose hardly any suggestions likely to be at all helpful to public servants in the discharge of duty. Many questions with no real bearing on the case had been brought up by the journalists, and the Commissioner, who was patient in answering the newspaper men, began to be a little tired.

On Sunday night his big office was filled with reporters. They sat about everywhere. He had admitted them because he wanted them to see that he was working. From time to time they quizzed him in this fashion:

"Is it true that you and Commissioner Waldo have quarreled?"

"Is Waldo going to resign?"

"Do you favor the Sullivan law against pistols?"

"Will the 'dead line' be maintained now?"

"Hadn't the daily 'line up' of criminals ought to be restored so that detectives will know crooks when they see them?"

"Hasn't Mayor Gaynor tied the hands of the police?"

And so forth, and so forth, and so forth.

Suddenly, on Sunday night, Dougherty turned and read the newspaper men a lecture. He said that he wanted them to understand that he was no spring chicken at his business, that he was working eighteen hours a day, and that he knew he would show results if the people would only be patient and give him time. His only recommendation in the way of new laws or reforms was for a statute that would enable the police to put known criminals, without occupation or visible means of support, at work mending roads. He outlined a plan which, rather strangely, did not get any attention in the newspapers at all. His idea of dealing with idle criminals, he said, was to have a cart, with commissary and sleeping quarters for twelve men. As soon as twelve idle criminals with records had been sentenced, they would pull this cart out of town themselves, under guard, and go to work repairing roads. If that plan were adopted, New York would not only be as free from criminals as the District of Columbia, where a similar measure is enforced, but the roads all around the city would be so well cared for that they could be used as roller-skating rinks.

The newspapers next morning were quite certain that Commissioners Waldo and Dougherty had quarreled, and when the journalists went down to report Montani's examination in court they were decidedly partial to the taxicab man.

Dougherty had told the newspaper men beforehand that he had evidence enough to have Montani held for trial. He had made very positive statements about this. Montani would be arraigned, he predicted, and if discharged on one count, would be immediately arrested on something else. If he was discharged on that, he would still be arraigned on further charges.

It needs no very brilliant imagination, therefore, to picture the effect upon the newspapers when Montani, after being arraigned on the doubtful points in his own account of the crime, and those not too vigorously pressed, was discharged, with comment by the court upon the flimsiness of the police case. There was one striking discrepancy in the evidence presented at that examination which, if pressed, should have resulted in the holding of Montani for trial. He still insisted that he had stopped his cab because an old man had got in front of it, but this was denied by a witness. That point was permitted to pass by Lieutenant Riley, who appeared for the police. Montani could have been re-arrested on charges based upon his attempt to defraud the insurance company. But he was permitted to go free. That course had been decided on at Police Headquarters after some difference of opinion.

The newspapers were now more pessimistic than ever in their comments. They contrasted this outcome with Dougherty's promises that the chauffeur would be re-arrested. It was taken as a confession of police incompetency and bewilderment—which, as will be seen in its proper place, was very useful in its way. Montani went free, and was jubilant, calling on the Commissioner next morning to thank him. But from the moment he left court until he was arrested again, the Italian chauffeur never got out of sight of the Police Department.

What Developed on a Busy Tuesday

It was on the day after Montani's release that Commissioner Dougherty began to uncover more interesting characters in the taxicab drama.

Bit by bit, through points supplied by informants and persons who had come in contact with him in various ways, a very good working knowledge of the fugitive Kinsman was pieced together. It appeared that he had come to New York the previous summer, from Boston, and after a brief career as a boxer, had gone to work in a Sixth Avenue resort known as the "Nutshell Café," where he was a waiter. Among his associates there had been two characters who invited further inquiry.

The first of these was a fellow called "Gene," described as having a "parrot nose," and a criminal record. He had been a close pal of Kinsman, and had also introduced another intimate, a wily little Italian called "Jess," who had formerly owned a thieves' resort that he called the "Arch Café." A good description of Jess was secured.

There was some delay while the Commissioner "surrounded" this last-mentioned resort to find out if it was a place where any information might be obtained openly. The question was decided in the negative. So a plain-clothes man was quietly "planted" there to pick up information.

When a criminal is arrested (or "falls") it is customary in the underworld to raise a fund for his defense. The Arch Café was a center for the deposit of such "fall money." It was learned that a hundred dollars had been raised for the defense of a man named Clarke, alias "Molloy," under arrest in Brooklyn for robbery. This was the same Molloy to whose fine character Kinsman had asked his landlady to swear in court. The Italian named Jess had taken charge of Molloy's defense fund, but squandered it in a spree. Later, making it good, he had sent it over to Molloy's relief by Kinsman's pal, "Dutch," and an Italian known as "Matteo."

District inspectors of police were then called upon to find a detective who knew Jess, and an Italian plain-clothes man, Antony Grieco, who had grown up in that part of New York where Jess had kept a café, and who knew the latter well, was detailed with another detective to look him up and keep him under surveillance. They found that Jess, whose last name was Albrazzo, had headquarters in a tough resort in Thompson Street, kept by an Italian named James Pasqualle, better known as "Jimmie the Push." From that time Jess was kept "on tap," to await further developments.

Then the Commissioner undertook to find out more about the character called "Gene." Working in New York, as waiters and bartenders, were many members of a criminal band known as the "Forty Thieves of Boston." The Commissioner called in all of them that he could find, and sounded each for information about this "Gene." After the time of day had been passed, the talk would turn on members of the band and criminals in general, and after curiosity had been excited, "Gene" would be referred to casually. If the party interviewed said he knew "Gene," the Commissioner would probably be sceptical, ask his last name, press for details of appearance and habits, and then pass to some other subject.

It was found that "Gene's" last name was Splaine, that he had served a term in prison in Boston as a boy, and that, by his general description, he must be the third fugitive accompanying Kinsman and Annie. When Detective Watson got better descriptions of the third man at Albany, and comparisons were made with sources of information in New York, it became practically certain that Gene Splaine was with Kinsman.

Annie Shows at "Plant 21"
It was on this day, too (Tuesday, February 20), that "Swede Annie" suddenly stepped into police view, *wearing a new hat*. She turned up quietly at the house where Myrtle Horn had moved with her trunk, and began living in the front basement room. Matron Goodwin and "Plant 21" immediately reported her presence, and from that time the shadow men across the street had something to do besides driving nails. For whenever Annie or Myrtle went out of the house they were followed.

Shadowing is a highly interesting kind of police work, at which some men have exceptional ability.

The general conception is that of a detective following closely behind the suspected person, with his eyes glued to him, and cautiously crouching behind lamp-posts and trees when the victim turns suddenly. But that is far from the real thing. The work is done in ways altogether different. Shadow men operate in pairs, as a rule, and keep track of their party from vantage points not likely to be suspected. They dress according to the character of the case, always in quiet clothes, changed daily, and with absolutely no colors that will attract attention or lead to recognition through the memory. They know how to follow when the person under surveillance rides in cabs, cars, or trains, to cover the different exits from a building into which he or she may have gone, and to loiter several hours around a given neighborhood, if need be, without attracting the attention of honest citizens.

This work is done by shifts. The operators relieve each other almost as regularly as office employees, no matter how far the trail may have taken them. They are in constant touch with headquarters for the purpose of making reports and receiving instructions.

In this branch of detective work, as in many others, the chief requisite is resourcefulness. The detective of fact wears little disguise apart from clothes that fit the surroundings he moves in. But he has an instant knack at accounting for himself as a normal character who has happened quite naturally into the scene. Ready wits do the trick—not false whiskers. Thus it came about that whenever Annie and Myrtle were hungry, and sat down in a restaurant, what they said was noted by a couple of fellows at another table, who quickly made a party of the chance patrons they found there, discussing wages or the suffragettes. Or if Annie used the telephone in a drug store, a polite young man turning over the directory said to her, "Go ahead, lady—I'm in no hurry," and listened.

At the same time, Matron Goodwin was reporting conversation from inside the house. It appeared that Kinsman had sent Annie back to the city after buying her a new hat and giving her $125. He promised to write soon, but did not tell her where he was going. Toward the end of the week, as no letter arrived, Annie began worrying, and was talkative. She feared that Eddie no longer loved her. She reproached herself for letting him go without taking her along, and spoke of setting out to find him.

THE TRAIL IS TAKEN UP

It was now Wednesday, February 21, and all the careful detail work began to come together.

It was this day that Detective Watson found the crew of Train No. 13, on the New York Central, which had taken Kinsman, Annie, and Splaine aboard at Peekskill the afternoon of the robbery after they had ridden out of New York in a taxicab to avoid possible police surveillance at the railroad stations. Commissioner Dougherty dispatched Watson to Peekskill and Albany with thorough instructions. His motto in working out a case is, "Supervision is half the battle."

"When you get to Albany," he said, "go to that big hat store on Broadway near the station. I'll bet that's where Annie's new hat was bought—they sell the best millinery in the country outside of New York."

Nothing important was learned at Peekskill, but at Albany, sure enough, Detective Watson found the saleswoman right in "that big hat store" who had sold the new hat, and secured Annie's discarded headgear. The new hat had cost twenty-five dollars. The old one looked as though it might have cost ninety-five cents—a "Division Street Special." Its black velvet was of the cheapest grade, the famous little red roses proved to be, on close inspection, nothing more than little loops of pink cotton cloth, and the general state of the hat indicated that it was about time Annie had a new one. This interesting "bonnet," however, seemed just then more handsome than any costly article of millinery ever smuggled over from Paris. It was immediately sent to New York by express, with a copy of the sales slip covering the purchase. The saleswoman was able to add one or two details of description, and remembered how, after the woman had selected a hat, the two men had joked about who was to pay for it.

"She's your girl," said Splaine, and so Kinsman had paid the bill with five five-dollar bills.

Nothing could be learned as to the direction in which the two men meant to travel. Detective Watson now began a search among train crews running out of Albany, and Commissioner Dougherty, in New

York, got the Albany ticket-sellers by long-distance telephone. His knowledge of how railroad tickets are sold, accounted for, taken up, cancelled, and checked by the auditing department made it possible to sift matters down to the strongest kind of probability. After considerable telephoning, aided by Detective Watson on the spot, it was determined that Kinsman and Splaine had been the purchasers of two consecutively numbered tickets for Chicago sold together on Friday morning, twenty-four hours after the robbery, and that they had gone west on Train No. 3, leaving Albany at 12:10 p.m. Their tickets were available for that train, and the conclusion was strengthened by calculating Annie's movements. For it was found that she had come back to New York the same day, between four and five in the afternoon. She had kept out of sight until she appeared at Myrtle Horn's lodging and was reported by Matron Goodwin and "Plant 21" on Tuesday. But she must have taken a train from Albany about the time that the men were starting for Chicago, reaching New York at 3:45 p.m.

Commissioner Dougherty felt that the chances of finding his men in Chicago were so good that, without wasting time in an investigation of the crew of Train No. 3, he put Detectives Daly and Clare aboard a Chicago train that same night. Kinsman and Splaine would both find congenial company among the pugilists in Chicago.

These detectives were given names to conceal their identity, and ordered to report under the code term of "Orange Growers" to eliminate all flavor of police business. They received detailed instructions about where to go and what to do. Again the Commissioner covered the trail when it led out of New York by sending capable assistants, instead of merely wiring the police in other cities. Before the "Orange Growers" departed, the "boss" gave them a little talk about expenses.

The detective attached to a municipal police force is very often hampered by fear of making unusual expenditures. Accounting routine is strict. Telegrams are often limited to the minimum of ten words where a hundred are needed to send a working description or report. The long-distance telephone is used as a luxury, and in many instances where the plain-clothes man can get valuable information through an informant he pays the shot out of his own pocket because there is no other way of paying it, and trusts to the chance that this private investment out of his salary will help him "break" a knotty case.

Commissioner Dougherty told the "Orange Growers" that they would be kept on this trail if it led all around the world. They must not consider expenditure when there was vital information to put on the wire. He expected them to turn to the long-distance telephone whenever they needed new instructions in a hurry. Briefly, he took the blinders and shackles off them, and sent them out to do good work, and the outcome justified this far-sightedness.

At that period of the winter trains were delayed everywhere by storms, so the "Orange Growers" had opportunities to make inquiries at stations and railroad restaurants all along the line to Buffalo. They were in search of their "brother," who was described in terms of Kinsman's personal appearance, and was supposed to be on his way somewhere with another man. At Syracuse an observant waitress remembered their "brother" distinctly, having served both the men when their train stopped for supper. Finally, the two "Orange Growers" got snowed up in Michigan for a time, and there we will leave them for the present.

Montani Quizzed Once More

By Thursday many loose ends of the case were being brought together so effectually that the outlook seemed exceedingly bright.

But only to the executive circle in Dougherty's office.

Outside, all was dark. Newspaper criticism had become more caustic than ever, and the public, after the ingrained habit of New York, was turning its attention to fresher news sensations.

At a big annual dinner of police officials held that evening, February 22, the atmosphere of gloom resting upon the department was most tangible. The fourteen hundred guests, who were chiefly police inspectors, captains, and lieutenants, felt that a stigma lay upon the service with which they were identified. They had no means of knowing, of course, that one week from that night the gloom would have lifted, criticism be turned to praise, and that policemen generally would be, as a witty lieutenant put it, "back to our official standing again—which never was so very high."

Montani had called at Police Headquarters repeatedly, accompanied by his unseen shadowers. He professed to be anxious to furnish further information, if it lay in his power, and the Commissioner chatted with him cordially, leading him to believe that he no longer rested under the slightest suspicion.

On Friday Dougherty made an interesting effort to "break" Montani.

He now had a minute physical description of Kinsman, as well as two photographs of him. The chauffeur was asked to describe once more the man who had sat upon the cab seat with him. The questions went over details from head to foot, and were prompted by details of Kinsman's real appearance.

Montani said the man had large brown eyes, which was true.

He remembered that he had talked with a good American accent, and used words not common to the criminal, which was also more or less true.

He suddenly recalled a gold-filled tooth in the robber's upper right-hand jaw, a point already furnished by informants.

In fact, as this new examination went on, it became clear to the Commissioner that Montani was actually describing Kinsman, changing only one detail. He said that the robber had had a dark mustache, while it was certain that Kinsman had been smooth-shaven.

Suddenly the Commissioner tried what is known as a "shot."

The examiner in such an inquiry is often in possession of incriminating evidence. Instead of producing it bluntly as evidence, however, he will perhaps let it slip out bit by bit, as though by awkwardness, meanwhile maintaining an appearance of absolute confidence in the suspect's integrity. A classic example of this device is found in the Russian writer Dostoevsky's *Crime and Punishment.* The skillful "shot" is usually far more disconcerting than evidence produced openly to overwhelm. For the suspect assumes that the examiner really knows nothing, and has merely blundered. So he is on his guard outwardly. But he also worries inwardly, and this trying conflict between inner doubt and the need for keeping up outer calm will often break him down completely.

Dougherty's "shot" was a photograph of Kinsman.

By pre-arrangement an assistant came into the office and began turning over some papers on the Commissioner's desk. The photo of Kinsman popped out where Montani could see it plainly, and then was hurriedly put out of sight again. The Commissioner scolded his assistant, and the latter stood shamefaced and silent.

But in this instance the device failed.

Montani not only betrayed no interest in Kinsman's picture, but took the awkward assistant's part, and asked the Commissioner not to scold him.

Montani had planned his crime, fitted the plan with men, laid out every detail in his mind, and arranged his story beforehand. He expected to be arrested, and said so. He admitted that there were inconsistencies in his story, but hoped to clear them up. He had discussed the crime with Jess and Dutch, and had not been seen in the company of the other criminals. So, having settled on his story, Montani stuck to it without variation under every form of pressure. Others forgot what they had arranged as their defense, or departed from it, or broke down and confessed. But not Montani. He alone went to trial, and stuck to his story until the end.

THE "ORANGE GROWERS" IN CHICAGO

When Daly and Clare, the two New York detectives working as the "Orange Growers," arrived in Chicago, they went to Police Headquarters in that city, made inquiries about Kinsman and Splaine, and secured the aid of Chicago detectives. Then they put up at a hotel where, by arrangements with the house detective, they occupied a room on the second floor handy to a little-used stairway leading to a side street, which would make it easy to slip in and out without going through the lobby. On the trip from New York both of them had neglected shaving, and Daly was an especially tough-looking citizen, for his beard grows out stiff and bristly, with black and red intermixed, and a little green to help the general effect. With suits of old clothes and sweaters they were so little like their official selves that for several days, though they went rather freely around resorts frequented by crooks who knew them in New York, they were not recognized.

The "Orange Growers" now became a pair of hardened "yeggmen," or bank robbers, and for three days were busy visiting thieves' haunts all over the city, from the Levee district to the Stockyards. It was found that

Kinsman and Splaine had put up at a high-class boarding house in a fashionable residence section. Kinsman seemed to be doubtful about the impression Splaine might make there, though in the opinion of the police Splaine was by far the more intelligent of the pair. So he took the landlady aside and asked her, privately, if she had objections to a prize-fighter in her house. The landlady replied, "Why, no! if he is a gentleman—many prize-fighters are just like other people!" Thereupon, Kinsman undertook that Splaine should behave himself. He also wanted to know if valuables were safe there, and the astonished landlady assured him that her house was like a home, that the guests were like one big family and seldom locked their doors, and that Mr. Smith, well known as an officer in one of the leading banks, had lived there for years.

The pair had spent considerable time in criminal haunts, but had now disappeared. Kinsman, as it was learned later, had returned to New York. Splaine was apparently in Chicago still, spending his money, but the two "Orange Growers" seemed never to catch up with him. Their man had always gone around the corner within the past hour.

Finally they planned a ruse with the aid of two Chicago detectives. Splaine had been intimate with a certain woman of the underworld, known as "Josie." Clare went to her, represented himself as a "stick-up man," said he and his partner were after that guy with all the money and diamonds, meaning Splaine, and that they meant to rob him. If Josie worked with them, like a good girl, she would come in for her third of the plunder.

Josie professed ignorance. She was sure, so help her Mike, cross her heart, that she knew nothing about no gent with any money or diamonds—no such a party had been near the house in months, worse luck. Clare argued awhile with no results, and then said he would come back a little later and bring his pal. Then Daly was introduced to Josie as the extremely undesirable citizen who would do the strong-arm work. But Josie still insisted that she had no idea what they were talking about.

They went out, and within a few minutes the two Chicago detectives, Dempsey and McFarland, known by Josie as officers, came in, described the disguised Clare and Daly as two of the most desperate "yeggmen" in the country, said that they had warrants for them, and asked if they had been seen. Josie crossed her heart again, and said that there had been nobody around there all evening—believe her, it was like living the simple life, and if things kept on bein' so quiet she'd blow the town and go back to Keokuk.

Then, enter the two "Orange Growers" once more, to be warned by the fair Josie.

"Say, the bulls are after you boys, an' you better pull your freight, 'cause if you stay around here they're goin' to *get* you."

"Aw, hell!" was the reply, "We'd just as easily kill a cop or anybody else. We stick in this house till you tell us where we can reach that guy with the money and the diamonds—understand?"

Then Josie broke down, and told them Splaine had been there early in the evening, but had gone away to take a train out of town. She did not know the railroad, and urged them to leave. This was evidently the truth, so they hurried to Police Headquarters, telegraphed descriptions to other cities with a request that arriving trains be watched, and went to bed to get a little sleep, so that they could be at work early the next morning.

But in the morning word came from the Memphis Police that Splaine had been arrested there on alighting from a train, and they thereupon notified New York, went to Memphis, secured Splaine on extradition papers, and brought him back to the metropolis.

The Traps Are Sprung

On Saturday afternoon, February 24, while most of the energy of the Detective Bureau was centered on the taxicab case, a brutal murder was committed in Brooklyn.

Word came that a Flatbush merchant had been found dead in his store, shot by unknown criminals whose motive was robbery. They had taken his watch and five safety razors.

Inspector Hughes was sent to the scene of the crime, and Commissioner Dougherty quickly followed. The murder occurred about one p.m. By six o'clock the same day the number of the watch had been learned through a canvas of jewelers in the neighborhood, it being on record by one of them who had repaired it, and the watch and two of the safety razors had been found in pawnshops. Descriptions of the murderers were obtained, and by three o'clock Sunday, the following day, their identity had been established. Within thirty hours after the crime these men had been arrested, positively identified as the pawners of the stolen articles, and completely tied up in their own statements.

At half-past nine Sunday night, while the Commissioner, Inspector Hughes, and Captain Coughlin, in charge of Brooklyn detectives, and Lieutenant Riley were winding up their work on this murder case, word suddenly came over the telephone to Commissioner Dougherty from an informant that Eddie Kinsman had been seen in New York with "Swede Annie," and that he was accompanied by an unknown man, wearing a red necktie, supposed to be Gene Splaine. At the same time Matron Goodwin, stationed inside Annie's lodgings, telephoned that she had information indicating that Kinsman had returned to the city.

When the Commissioner motored over to New York, he found his men covering a hotel on Third Avenue, not far from 42d Street. Kinsman and Annie were inside.

The Commissioner hurried to the 18th precinct police station and sent out a call for twenty-five detectives. Team work on the case had developed to such a degree by this time that, though the men came from many stations, they were all on hand in record time, a matter of twenty or thirty minutes. Then a squad of these plain-clothes men was sent to watch every railroad station and ferry house, each accompanied by one of the men from "Plant 21," familiar with Annie from having followed her movements for a week. Surveillance on the hotel was strengthened, and steps taken to ascertain whether the unknown man in the red tie was really Splaine.

While making these arrangements, a curious incident occurred, showing how small New York is, after all, with its five million people. As Dougherty sat in the 18th precinct station, Detective Rein brought in a prisoner arrested for shooting a citizen. He was drunk and extremely disagreeable, and gave his name as "Steigel," living at 98 Third Avenue. Something in this address echoed to something in Dougherty's memory—a keen one for names, dates, addresses, and facts generally. He investigated further, and found that this prisoner was no other than the criminal Molloy, whose urgent need of "character witnesses" had played so important a part in furnishing the first information in the taxicab case.

By some mischance, these operations came to the ears of the newspaper men. Word went about, beginning in Brooklyn, that important arrests were to be made. The reporters followed the Commissioner in a crowd when he refused to make a statement. They not only hampered the work, but greatly endangered the outcome. On the following day, Monday, the papers published information about the police activities of the night before. The hazard here may be appreciated when the reader is told that Kinsman had been a persistent reader of newspapers from the day of the robbery, and that it was largely the pessimistic newspaper comment upon Montani's release in court that led him to return to New York. Deceived by the newspaper chorus of "police demoralization," and the easy way in which Montani had got free, he concluded that the taxicab investigation had been given up as hopeless.

Kinsman was arrested in the Grand Central Station at half-past eleven Monday morning, with Swede Annie and the unknown in the red tie. They were about to set out for Boston.

There were some amusing circumstances in the arrest.

Kinsman's immunity overnight, and police precaution in deferring the arrest until the last moment, on the chance that other persons would join the party, gave him a false confidence. He afterward admitted that ideas of a "pinch" at that time were far from his mind.

When a criminal thought to be dangerous is to be arrested in a crowded place like the Grand Central Station, police officers operate by methods that prevent a struggle. As two detectives closed in on the party, Kinsman watched one of them out of the corner of his eye. While a waiter at the "Nutshell Café," he had often thrown objectionable guests out onto the sidewalk. He now fancied that one of the detectives resembled a man he had once "bounced," and was ready to fight if attacked.

"I was just folding it up," he said, referring to his fist, "and getting ready to land on him when one had me from behind and the other in front. Then I knew they were cops."

Annie was gorgeously dressed in a new blue suit and fine fur coat, bought out of the taxicab money. The unknown man proved to be

Kinsman's brother, who had come down from Boston with him. Kinsman had visited his native city before returning to New York, but had escaped the police net there by stopping at a hotel and sending for his brother. He sent a grip home by this brother, and it was afterward found to contain three packages of bills of $250 each in the original wrappers of the bank.

As soon as word of these arrests was telephoned to Police Headquarters, the other traps were sprung. Detectives brought in Montani, Jess Albrazzo, and Myrtle Horn, the latter, with Annie, being held as witnesses.

⌒

Now begins some of the most interesting work connected with the taxicab case—the examination of the first prisoners, which led to confessions, the implication of other guilty persons not yet under arrest, and the voluntary pleas of guilty in court, which saved costly trials in all but Montani's case.

This sort of work is familiar under the term of "third degree." It is popularly supposed to be accompanied by force and sometimes brutality—and in wrong hands often is. Commissioner Dougherty's experience with a commercial detective agency, however, has led him to develop intelligent methods. The commercial detective organization has none of the authority of an official police force, and at the same time, through its national operations and the general character of its work, deals chiefly with the most accomplished criminals. Therefore, tact and legal subtlety are depended upon in examining suspects, and the Commissioner long ago learned to get his results mainly by straight question and answer. He puts his own wits against those of the suspect, backed by experience in many other cases. He has a practical grasp of criminal psychology, as well as many ingenious ways of using evidence to the best purpose, overwhelming the suspect, and breaking down stolidity and deception. Dougherty is not only opposed to force in the "third degree," but knows that it is of absolutely no use.

The first prisoner examined was Eddie Kinsman.

When he was brought to Police Headquarters Kinsman appeared to be thoroughly satisfied with himself, and confident that no policeman would get anything out of *him*. He proved to be a good-looking young fellow, of athletic build, and by no means a fool.

Methods of examination are never twice alike, for they depend upon the case and the suspect. As a rule, however, when the criminal first sits down to answer Commissioner Dougherty he is astonished by that gentleman's apparent lack of guile, and ignorance of worldly knowledge. When Dougherty composes himself for an inquiry, he is rather a heavy-looking citizen, not unlike a country magistrate, and his first questions, put for the purpose of determining the suspect's character and previous surroundings, usually relate to bald routine matters, such as name, age, residence, education, family, and so on.

"Gee!" thinks the suspect. "This guy is the biggest lobster I ever got up against! I wonder how he ever got to be a police commissioner. He must have a strong political pull."

Kinsman was ushered into a large, quiet office, where this bureaucratic official began by asking his name, birthplace, and other details.

"Will you kindly stand up a minute while I get your height?" asked the questioner, and Kinsman did so in a patronizing way. Then the dull-looking gentleman turned back Kinsman's coat and looked at the little label sewed in the inside pocket.

"I see that you have been in Chicago recently," he observed. "This suit was made by a tailor there. You ordered it February 17th, two days after the robbery."

He looked into Kinsman's hat.

"That was bought in Chicago, too."

He examined the label on Kinsman's tie.

"This was also bought in Chicago."

He turned up the label at the back of the neck of the new silk underclothes worn by the prisoner.

"Those were bought in State Street, Chicago, and from a very good store, too—I know it well."

Kinsman now began to be pugnacious and defiant.

"See here!" he said. "You must take me for a boob."

"Yes, I think you are a boob," replied the Commissioner. "You might as well have made your getaway with a brass band as to take Swede Annie with you to Albany, attracting attention all the way, and then send her back to New York with a hundred dollars to tell the police where you had gone."

Suddenly Lieutenant Riley, personal aide, walked into the Commissioner's office carrying a cheap article of millinery—a shabby black velvet hat with a row of little red roses across the front. Commissioner Dougherty apparently grew very angry.

"What do you mean by bringing that thing in here now?" he exclaimed. "I am not ready for that—take it away."

This "shot" had been previously arranged, of course, but Riley pretended to be injured when called by his superior.

"Cripes!" exclaimed Kinsman. "Annie's old hat. How did you get that so quick?"

"Oh, that is only one thing we've got on you," replied the Commissioner. "We know that you went to Peekskill in a taxicab with Annie and Splaine on the afternoon of the robbery. We know that you took Train 13 to Albany, and where you stopped that night, and where you bought Annie's new hat, and how much you paid for it, and what train you took to Chicago Friday noon. Suppose you tell me something more about your movements?"

Kinsman became scornful.

"If you know all that," he said, "maybe you know more about where I went and what I did than I do myself. So what would be the use of me telling *you* anything?"

While certain people were being found outside, the Commissioner worked upon the prisoner along another line. Enough of Kinsman's personality was now disclosed to show that he was vain and egotistical. This side of his nature was therefore fed with flattery. He was assured that the taxicab robbery had been a wonderful "stick-up." Everybody in New York had been astonished. The whole country was talking about it, and about him. He must be an awfully bright, cunning fellow to have planned and carried out such a piece of crime.

Kinsman warmed up genially under this admiration, and seemed to be more confident than ever that so shrewd a young man as himself would have little difficulty in fooling the police.

But presently self-satisfaction was subjected to shock after shock.

Detectives were bringing in Montani, Myrtle Hoyt, Rose Levy, Mrs. Sullivan, the landlady with whom Kinsman had lived, and her housekeeper. Jess Albrazzo was under arrest. Kinsman's brother was there for examination, and Inspector Hughes and Lieutenant Riley were bringing in startling intelligence every few minutes.

The housekeeper was ushered in, and told how Kinsman had given her five dollars from a huge roll of bills before leaving for Peekskill.

Commissioner Waldo came in and sat while Mrs. Sullivan told what she knew about her late lodger.

Kinsman's brother gave information about the former's movements from the time he had arrived in Boston until he brought him to New York to have a good time, and Kinsman knew that at the home of his parents in Boston the police would surely find money in the original wrappers of the bank.

The prisoner was put under pressure to explain how a man like himself, known to be working as a waiter in a cheap resort, could suddenly have come into possession of such sums. Statements from the women in the case had been secured, and were produced, and finally Kinsman was brought to detailed admissions, one by one. He agreed that it was true he had gone to Peekskill in a taxicab with Annie and Splaine, that he had gone to Albany, had bought Annie a hat there, had gone to Chicago, and so forth. Opportunities were given him to see Montani and Jess, under arrest. Nothing but the truth was told him, yet by degrees he was led to see himself surrounded on all sides by evidence and confessing accomplices. At last he broke down completely, his vain self-confidence destroyed, and made a detailed confession.

Kinsman's story brought up fresh circumstances and new actors in the taxicab case.

He told how he had come to New York nine months before, to have a good time and make money, and how, after going penniless and hungry, and getting a few dollars for taking part in a boxing match, he had become a waiter at the "Nutshell Café." There he soon made the acquaintance of criminals, meeting Gene Splaine, "Dutch" Keller, "Joe the Kid," "Scotty the Lamb," and other characters who were afterward to assist in the taxi robbery. There he also met "Swede Annie" and became her sweetheart, and finally, Jess Albrazzo, a dark little Italian who seemed to exert marked influence over all the others. It was from Jess that Kinsman first heard about the plan to rob a taxicab carrying money to a bank. This "swell job" was discussed, and Jess told him he had a friend named Montani who carried the bank's cash, and would cooperate in stealing it. The job would be easy, because Montani would run the cab through a side street, and the only guard was an old man and a boy, neither of them armed.

One Sunday night, two weeks before the crime, Jess took Kinsman and other accomplices over the route, after all had drunk themselves into optimistic mood, and pointed out the bank from which the money was drawn, the streets through which Montani would run, the place where the gang could board the cab, and the point at which they could leave it and escape uptown. Details were discussed. There was a difference of opinion as to methods, and the plotters parted that night with the understanding that each would submit his own ideas of how the robbery could be most effectively and safely carried out. Eventually there was a definite agreement as to boarding the cab, preventing an outcry, making the getaway, and splitting up the money.

According to Montani's information, the bank messengers usually carried between $75,000 and $100,000. When the day for the robbery had been set, word suddenly came that there would not be so large a sum. This was disappointing, but the gang decided to put their project through, nevertheless. Kinsman was busy at the café, where he worked until four o'clock on the morning of February 15, and "Dutch" called for him several times, asking if he was going to "lay down on the job." Finally Kinsman got away, went to a room in a lodging house taken by "Dutch," and found the gang all there smoking and drinking. At five o'clock they all went to sleep. At eight everybody was awakened. "Dutch" and Splaine took blackjacks, and offered Kinsman a revolver, which he refused, saying he could take care of himself with his hands, being a boxer. There were six in the party—Kinsman, "Dutch," Splaine, "Joe the Kid," Jess, and "Scotty the Lamb," whose part was to stumble in front of Montani's cab at the place selected for the boarding, and thus give the chauffeur a colorable reason for slackening speed if eye-witnesses afterward called his honesty into question. The gang had breakfast in a cheap restaurant, stopped for a drink at the saloon of "Jimmie the Push" in Thompson Street, where the booty was to be divided, and proceeded downtown, after parting with Jess. The latter was the organizer, and took no part in the robbery; as he explained, he was known as a friend of Montani's, and wanted to arrange so that he could prove an alibi if suspected, proving that he had not been near the scene of the crime when it was committed.

At that saloon they had met a trio of Italian criminals known as the "Three Brigands," who said they were not to take part in the robbery, but would be on hand to see that it was vigorously put through.

Arrived upon the ground, at Church Street and Trinity Place, Splaine and Kinsman waited on the west side of the thoroughfare, while "Dutch" and "Joe the Kid" stood on the opposite side. "Scotty the Lamb" posted himself fifty feet off.

As Montani's cab came speeding along, "Dutch" raised his hat as a signal. "Scotty the Lamb" did not have time to step in front of the vehicle before it slackened, and the robbers were aboard. "Dutch" opened one door and struck the old bank teller, Wilbur Smith, and "Joe the Kid" boosted Splaine in on the other side, where he assaulted young Wardle. Kinsman mounted the seat beside Montani, and the latter put on full speed, telling Kinsman to point his finger at his side as though he had a revolver. The cab slipped past trucks and dodged pedestrians. Kinsman said he seemed to see policemen everywhere, and was dazed when the vehicle stopped at Park Place and Church Street. All the criminals got off there, "Dutch" lugging the brown bag containing the money. Splaine and "Dutch" were both covered with the bank guards' blood. Taking Kinsman, they jumped aboard a street car. It was crowded. Several passengers noticed the bloody men, but were told that there had been a fight, and the occurrence was not reported to the police. After riding two or three blocks they got off, boarded an elevated train, rode to Bleeker Street, and went to a back room in "Jimmie the Push's" saloon, where the money was to be divided. Here they found Jess and the "Three Brigands," and the latter now set up a claim for a share in the booty. Matteo, leader of the trio, pulled out a revolver, and there was a discussion. Finally the bag was opened, and found to contain $25,000. There were three packages of

$5,000 each and one of $10,000. Matteo grabbed the latter package, saying that his gang was to get $3,000 apiece, and that the odd $1,000 would go for "fall money" to get Molloy out of jail in Brooklyn. The robbers then divided the remainder, Jess taking $3,000 for himself and another $3,000 for Montani, Splaine getting $3,000, Kinsman $2,750, "Joe the Kid" $250, and "Scotty the Lamb" nothing. Kinsman then told how he had called for Swede Annie, and left town in a taxicab, going as far as Peekskill, to avoid the police at the Grand Central Station.

Jess Confesses and Assists

The next prisoner examined was Jess Albrazzo, a dark little Italian, who appeared to be somewhat ignorant.

In this examination the Commissioner had ample outside proof, and he also employed what he calls his "psychological study." Years ago, in dealing with negro suspects in Southern crimes, Dougherty devised a little instrument that he dubbed his "lie watch." This was a dial with a needle, hung round the suspect's neck. If the latter told the truth, the needle presumably pointed to "Truth," and if he didn't, it pointed to "Lie." Being out of the suspect's sight, it had a strong effect.

From that, Dougherty went into studies of the mental states of suspects under examination, and found rough physiological indications, which he uses as a guide to the integrity of the suspect. Investigations of European criminal experts like Professor Hans Gross amply demonstrate that there is a real scientific basis for such methods.

Dougherty took it a little easier with Jess. They sat down, and the Commissioner went over the Italian's movements for the past few months, showing him how thoroughly he was implicated. Jess had worked for Montani, and been intimate with the rest of the taxicab "mob." He and Montani were confronted with each other, and points brought out in Kinsman's confession were skillfully used.

At one point in this examination the Commissioner rose from his desk, took the lobe of Jess's ear between his thumb and finger, pinched it slightly, looked at the ear closely, and then walked out of the room.

Jess was all on edge with curiosity.

"Why did he pinch my ear?" he asked of Lieutenant Riley.

"To see if you are telling the truth," was the answer, and in a moment the Commissioner came back and examined that ear again.

"Yes, he's lying," he declared. "Look at his ear—can't you see it yourself?" Others were invited to look at Jess's ear, and the little Italian became so curious that he actually tried to look around the side of his skull and see his own ear!

This psychological study was backed up with abundant proof that Jess had not told the whole truth. Presently he weakened and confessed. He told how he had handed $2,000 in a collar box to "Jimmie the Push" on the day of the robbery, which was to be taken to a Bowery bank and put in a safe deposit vault for Montani. He agreed to accompany the police to Jimmie's place in Thompson Street, and late that evening a party made up of Commissioner Dougherty, Inspector Hughes, and Lieutenant Riley went there, taking Jess along.

"Jimmie the Push's" place is one of the most picturesque thieves' resorts in lower New York.

"Typical of the old village," as Dougherty puts it. "In fact, this whole case has a strong flavor of the little old village of New York."

Jimmie was out when they got there, but this saloon was in charge of the biggest, swarthiest Italian bartender in town, a tough Hercules weighing somewhere around three hundred pounds. The room was crowded with motley characters, drinking beverages known to the neighborhood as "shocks" and "high hats." For their edification, a tramp magician was taking coins out of his ears, his nose, and the air.

Jess was not known to be under arrest, and immediately sent a boy called "Reddy" to fetch the proprietor, who had known the three police officers for years. Presently Reddy came back and said that Jimmie would come in about half an hour, as he was playing cards and had a fine hand.

Reddy was sent back to impress upon Jimmie that Jess wanted to see him right away—it was very important. In about two minutes, just as the Commissioner had bought a "high hat" for everybody in his party, Jimmie appeared. He was told that Jess had got into trouble in connection with the taxicab robbery, and asked about the money in the safe deposit vault. "Jimmie the Push," with his partner, Bob Deilio, had by this time been implicated themselves, for it was clear that the money had been divided in their resort, and that probably they had taken part in the planning, and the decidedly one-sided division of the spoils. Jimmie was led to believe that he did not rest under suspicion, however, and that he was only asked to aid the police. He said Jess had handed him a collar box on the day of the robbery, asking him to put it in a vault in his own name, but that he had had no idea what the box contained, and had left it lying behind the bar for a couple of days before he got a chance to go to the bank with it. He readily promised to appear at Police Headquarters the following morning, bring the key to the safe deposit box, and help recover the money. Thereupon the police officials bade him good night and went away. But no chances were taken on "Jimmie the Push." From that moment he was shadowed.

That Monday was a busy day in many other ways.

Developments came thick and fast.

Kinsman's home in Boston was visited, and $750 of the bank money recovered in the original wrappers. It had laid in his grip, unknown to the honest Kinsman family.

Swede Annie, Myrtle Horn, and a girl named Rose Levy were examined, quickly broke down, and made tearful statements to be used in evidence. These women were held only as witnesses, and as the case cleared up after a few days' detention, were released.

The girl, Rose Levy, greatly attracted the Commissioner. She was only nineteen years old, a mild-mannered little Jewess with jet black hair and very remarkable eyes. The Commissioner went into details of her personal story. It seems that she had left her home in Brooklyn two months before, after a quarrel with her mother, and had come to New York looking for a position. But she quickly fell into the lower world, became known as Jess's girl, and was ambitious to be "one of the gang." After a fatherly talk she was persuaded to return to her home and live a decent life. But within a week she was back in New York again, in her old haunts, trying to raise money to help Jess, for whom, she told the Commissioner, she would willingly work for the rest of her days.

Before visiting Jimmie's saloon the Commissioner called up the "Orange Growers" in Chicago, had a long talk with them, told what progress was being made, and put new life into them.

More Money Recovered

True to his word, "Jimmie the Push" walked into Police Headquarters at nine o'clock Tuesday morning, February 27, closely followed by his unseen shadowers. He produced the key of the safe deposit vault, and went with officers to see the money recovered. There was $2,000, as Jess had stated, still in the wrappers of the bank. Jimmie was still permitted to go free, under the impression that he had come through the ordeal "clean," while fresh evidence was being obtained against him.

That morning the Commissioner also took Kinsman down over the route of the robbery, to have him explain it in his own way. This was done to strengthen the case against Montani, and upset his story in court.

Then "Scotty the Lamb" was located, arrested, brought to headquarters, and led to confess. "Scotty the Lamb" was in some respects a pathetic figure in the case, and also a humorous one. He had been in charge of the lunch kitchen at the Arch Café when Jess owned it, and later worked as a dishwasher in a Washington Square hotel. A Scotch youth, from Glasgow, he had been in this country about four years, and while no criminal record appeared against him, he was plainly in the company of thieves most of the time. According to his statement, he had been promised $25 for doing some work for Jess, and without inquiring into the nature of it at all, had shown up with the gang and gone along to do his minor part of a "stall," stumbling in front of the cab. But before he could get out into the street, the cab had been boarded. So poor "Scotty the Lamb," without a nickel for carfare, plodded all the way uptown again to the saloon where the money was to be divided, and got nothing whatever. He was a cheerful soul, however, and the life of the party when the gang was locked up, cracking jokes, and taking the view that, as sentences ought to be proportioned to the amount of money each member of the gang had got in the division, and he had got nothing, he might be let off with six months' imprisonment.

"Scotty, haven't you got any overcoat?" asked Inspector Hughes, sympathetically, as they were going to court one brisk morning. "Did you *ever* have an overcoat, Scotty?"

"No, sir, I never had an overcoat," replied Scotty, and then as he thought of his prospects for going to prison, added drolly, "And now I don't expect, sir, that I ever will!"

THE FINE ITALIAN HAND

The next step in the case was that of arresting "Jimmie the Push" and his partner, Bob Deilio.

Another phase of the robbery now began to come out plainly.

Up to the present time the main burden of proof pointed to the four "hold-up" men of American birth as the chief actors in the crime. Montani and Jess, the two Italians, appeared to be accessories.

But as the tangled threads were unravelled, one by one, it was found that the Italians involved outnumbered the American thugs, and that furthermore they had outwitted them.

When Bob Deilio was arrested he drew $215 in five-dollar bills out of his pocket and handed it to the police, admitting that it was part of $5,500 of the stolen money. The rest, he asserted, had just been paid for rent of the two resorts operated by "Jimmie the Push" and himself.

Jimmie and Bob were taken to Police Headquarters and examined, with Jess present. Commissioner Dougherty played one against the other so skillfully, with cross-questions and counter pressure, that in a little while each was excitedly telling tales on his two companions with the desperate hope of clearing himself, and denunciations flew back and forth among the trio as evidence came out that was likely to send them all to prison. Their confessions were obtained, and used in a new effort to break down Montani. But this was without results. The little Italian chauffeur still stuck doggedly to his original story.

From these new confessions it appeared that the Italians had planned the crime, enlisted the American hold-up men to carry out the dirty work, and laid a counter-plot for holding them up in turn when the money was divided. The "Three Brigands" were ostensibly offered a chance to take part in the actual robbery, but refused on the plea that it would be too risky, and that they did not believe Montani could carry it out successfully. On the morning of the crime they walked north over the route. When they met the taxicab coming south, with a policeman on the seat beside Montani and two unconscious bank messengers inside, they knew that the project had succeeded. So the "Three Brigands" hurried uptown to "Jimmie the Push's" saloon. They got there so quickly that they were ahead of the robbers. Jess made a rehearsed protest when they insisted in sharing in the plunder, but the "Three Brigands" drew revolvers, threatened to make a disturbance that would bring in the police, and finally helped themselves to $10,000. When the thugs who had done the actual work left the saloon, they had only $8,000 all told. The Italians, who had "played safe" at every point, had $17,000.

One of the Brigands Comes In

The actual whereabouts of the "Three Brigands" was not known to the police then. But there were certain channels through which news might reach at least one of them. Word was sent through those channels, therefore, that it might be best for them to appear and give an account of themselves, and on Friday, March 1, just at the time Splaine had been brought back from Memphis, the little leader of the brigands, Matteo Arbrano, an undersized Italian wearing spectacles, who had carried out the job of robbing the hold-up men, surrendered himself to the District Attorney.

Arbrano said that he had divided his $10,000 with his two companions, Gonzales and Cavaquero, and immediately left New York, taking a steamer for Mexico by way of Havana. At the latter city he stopped overnight, met a woman and accompanied her to a resort, was drugged and robbed of $2,700, and woke on the Prado with only $100 left, a single bill that had been concealed in his shoe. With that he returned to New York. The story is regarded by the police as more picturesque than convincing. It is probable that Matteo's share of the plunder, with that of other Italians involved, has been carefully "planted."

Pauli Gonzales, another of the brigands, was traced to Vera Cruz, Mexico. In the present state of that country, however, it was found impossible to arrest and extradite him upon the evidence at hand.

Three other persons concerned in the robbery are still at large at this writing—"Dutch" Keller, "Joe the Kid," and an "unknown" whose identity is concealed for police reasons.

Montani pleaded "Not guilty," and stood trial. After two days, exactly a month and a day subsequent to the robbery, he was convicted by a jury, and sentenced to not less than ten years and not more than eighteen years and two months in prison, with hard labor.

A word must be said about the prompt action of the District Attorney's office in the taxicab case. Where crime has had such publicity there is an opportunity to make a demonstration of great value by pressing the prosecutions. It was not lost. Under Assistant Charles C. Nott, Jr., evidence was succinctly laid before judges and juries, the trials finished in a matter of hours, and convictions and sentences secured within six weeks after the robbery. Furthermore, the various sentences were just, being carefully graded according to the part played by each offender, his character and previous record, and his individual effort in facilitating justice.

THREE

The Geneva Bank Job

Allan Pinkerton

(In the pages which follow I have narrated a story of actual occurrence. No touch of fiction obscures the truthful recital. The crime which is here detailed was actually committed, and under the circumstances which I have related.—AP)

It is a hot, sultry day in August, 18—, and the shrill whistles from the factories have just announced the arrival of six o'clock. Work is suspended for the day, and the army of workmen are preparing for their homes after the labors of the day.

At the little bank in Geneva the day has been an active one. Numerous herders have brought their stock into market, and after disposing of them have deposited their moneys with the steady little institution, in which they have implicit confidence, and through which the financial affairs of the merchants and farmers round about are transacted.

The last depositor has departed, and the door has just been closed. The assistant cashier and a lady clerk are engaged within in settling up the business of the day. At the Geneva bank the hours for business vary with the requirements of the occasion, and very frequently the hour of six arrives ere their customers have all received attention and their wants have been supplied. This had been the case upon this day in August, and breathing a sigh of relief as the last customer took his leave, the front door was locked and the work of balancing up the accounts was begun.

Suddenly, a knock is heard at the outer door, and Mr. Pearson, the assistant cashier, being busily engaged, requested the young lady with him to answer the summons. As she did so, two men, roughly dressed, and with unshaved faces, burst into the room. Closing the door quickly behind them, one of the men seized the young lady from behind and placed his hand upon her mouth. Uttering a piercing scream, the young lady attempted to escape from the grasp upon her, and with her teeth she inflicted several severe wounds upon the ruffianly hand that attempted to smother her cries. In a moment she was knocked down, a gag was placed in her mouth, and she was tied helplessly hand and foot. While this had been transpiring, the other intruder had advanced to the assistant cashier, and in a few moments he too was overpowered, bound, and gagged. In less time than is required to tell the story, both of them were lying helpless before their assailants, while the open doors of the bank vault revealed the treasures which had excited the passions of these depraved men, and led to the assault which had just been successfully committed.

No time was to be lost, the alarm might be sounded in a moment, and the thieves, picking up a valise which stood nearby, entered the vault, and securing all the available gold, silver, and bank-notes, placed them in the satchel and prepared to leave the place.

Before doing so, however, they dragged the helpless bodies of the young man and woman into the despoiled vault, and laying them upon the floor, they deliberately closed the doors and locked them in.

Not a word had been spoken during this entire proceeding, and now, in silence, the two men picked up the satchel, and with an appearance of unconcern upon their faces, passed out of the bank and stood upon the sidewalk.

The streets were filled with men and women hurrying from their work. The sun was shining brightly in the heavens, and into this throng of human beings, all intent upon their own affairs, these bold burglars recklessly plunged, and made their way safely out of the village.

How long the two persons remained in the bank it is impossible to tell; Miss Patton in a death-like swoon, and Mr. Pearson, in the vain endeavor to extricate himself from the bonds which held him. At length, however, the young man succeeded in freeing himself, and as he did so, the young lady also recovered her consciousness. Calling loudly for help, and beating upon the iron door of their prison, they indulged in the futile hope that someone would hear their cries and come to their rescue.

At last, however, Mr. Pearson succeeded in unscrewing the bolts from the lock upon the inside of the doors of the vault, and in a few minutes thereafter, he leaped out, and dashing through a window, gave the alarm upon the street. The news spread far and wide, and within an hour after the robbery had taken place, the town was alive with an excited populace, and numerous parties were scouring the country in all directions in eager search of the fugitives. All to no avail, however, the desperate burglars were not discovered, and the crest-fallen bank officers contemplated their ruin with sorrowful faces, and with throbbing hearts.

Meanwhile, Miss Patton had been carefully removed to her home, her injuries had been attended to, and surrounded by sympathetic friends, who ministered to her wants, she was slowly recovering from the effects of the severe trial of the afternoon.

An examination of the vault revealed the fact that the robbers had succeeded in obtaining about twenty thousand dollars in gold, silver, and currency—all the available funds of the bank, and the loss of which would seriously impair their standing, and which would be keenly felt by everyone interested in its management.

Though sorely crippled by their loss, the bank officials were undismayed, and resolved to take immediate steps for the capture of the criminals, and the recovery of the stolen property. To this end they decided to employ the services of my agency at once, in the full hope that our efforts would be crowned with success. Whether the trust of the directors was well founded, and the result so much desired was achieved, the sequel will show.

On the evening of the same day on which this daring robbery occurred, and as I was preparing to leave my agency for the day, a telegram was handed to me by the superintendent of my Chicago office, Mr. Frank Warner. The message read as follows:

GENEVA, *August* —, *18*—.
Bank robbed to-day. Twenty thousand dollars taken.
Please send or come at once.
(Signed,) HENRY SILBY, *President.*

This was all. There was no detail of particulars, no statement of the means employed, only a simple, concise, and urgent appeal for my services. As for myself, realizing the importance of promptness and despatch in affairs of this nature, and fully appreciating the anxiety of the bank officials, I resolved to answer their call as speedily as possible. But few words of consultation were required for the subject, and in a short time I had selected the man for the preliminary investigation, and requested his presence in my office. John Manning was the operative chosen for this task, an intelligent, shrewd, and trusty young man of about thirty years of age, who had been in my employ for a long time. Well educated, of good address, and with a quiet, gentlemanly air about him that induced a favorable opinion at a glance. Frequently, prior to this, occasions had presented themselves for testing his abilities, and I had always found him equal to any emergency. Sagacious and skillful as I knew him to be, I felt that I could implicitly rely upon him to glean all the information that was required in order to enable me to devise an intelligent plan of detection, and which would, as I hoped, lead to eventual success.

Giving John Manning full instructions as to his mode of proceeding, and cautioning him to be particular and thorough in all his inquiries, I directed him to proceed as soon as possible to the scene of the robbery, and enter at once upon the performance of his duties.

In a very short time Manning had made his preparations, and at eight o'clock that evening he was at the depot awaiting the departure of the train that was to bear him to his new field of operation. After a journey of several hours, in which the detective endeavored to snatch as much comfort as possible, the train drew up at the neat little station at Geneva, and Manning was upon the ground and walked to his room at the Geneva Hotel.

The next morning, as the hour was still too early for a conference with the bank officials, he resolved to stroll about the town and ascertain the locality of the Geneva bank, before entering upon the duties of the investigation.

His stroll, however, was not a very extended one, for as he started from the hotel he noticed upon the opposite side of the street the sign of the bank. The building in which it was located was a large, square brick structure, occupied in part by the bank, and in part as a store for the sale of hardware and agricultural implements. The upper floor was used as an amusement hall, and was called the "Geneva Opera House." Here the various entertainments of a musical and dramatic nature were given, to the intense delight of the people of the village.

There was no notice of the bank having suspended operations on account of the loss they had sustained, and the operative inferred from this, that business was being transacted as usual.

When the doors were at length opened the operative entered the banking room, and requesting to see Mr. Silby, was ushered into the private office of the president. As he passed through the room he took a passing inventory of the young assistant cashier, Mr. Pearson, who was busily engaged upon his books. He appeared to be a young man of about twenty-four years of age, of a delicate and refined cast of countenance and about medium height. His hair and a small curly mustache were of a light brown shade, and his complexion was as fair as a woman's. The young lady who had been the other victim of the assault was not present, and the detective concluded that she was as yet unable to attend to her duties.

These thoughts and impressions passed through his mind as he walked through the banking room into the office of the president. As he entered this apartment, he found several gentlemen evidently awaiting his appearance, all of whom wore a thoughtful, troubled look, as though they keenly felt the losses they had sustained and were resolved to bear up manfully under their misfortune.

Mr. Silby, the president, a tall, fine-looking gentleman in the prime of life, arose as the detective entered. Manning presented his letter of introduction, and Mr. Silby hastily ran his eyes over the contents, and then extending his hand he gave the detective a most cordial greeting, and introduced him to the other gentlemen present, all of whom received him warmly.

"Take a seat, Mr. Manning," said Mr. Silby, drawing up a chair. "You find us anxiously awaiting your arrival, and prepared to give you any information you desire."

"Thanks," responded the operative, taking the proffered chair. "As I have come here for the purpose of making an examination into this case, I shall require all the information that is possible to obtain."

"Very well," said Mr. Silby. "Now, what do you desire first?"

"A full statement as to how the robbery was committed," answered the detective, promptly.

"Mr. Welton," said Mr. Silby, turning to a gentleman at his right, who had been introduced to the detective as the cashier of the bank, "perhaps you can relate the particulars better than I can."

"Excuse me," interrupted the detective, "but were you present at the time the robbery occurred?"

"No, sir, I was not present," replied Mr. Welton. "Mr. Pearson, our assistant cashier, and Miss Patton, were the only persons in the bank at that time."

"Then," said the detective, "suppose we have Mr. Pearson in at once, and hear the story from him. We always prefer," he added, with a smile, "to receive the particulars of these affairs from eye-witnesses."

The other gentlemen nodded a cordial assent to this proposition, and Mr. Welton arose, and going to the door, requested Mr. Pearson to enter the consulting room.

The young man entered the office, and upon being introduced, greeted the detective with an air of frank earnestness, and signified his readiness to relate all that he knew about the robbery.

He remained standing, and from his statement the facts were elicited which I have given in the preceding chapter. As he finished, he pointed to a scar upon his forehead, which he stated was the result of the blow he received at the time from the robber who attacked him. The wound did not appear to be a very serious one, although the skin had been broken and blood had evidently flowed freely.

"Mr. Pearson," inquired the detective, after the young man had concluded, "do you remember having seen either of those men before?"

The assistant cashier darted a quick glance at the detective, and then answered: "Yes, sir; about three o'clock yesterday afternoon, a well-dressed gentleman came into the bank, carrying a small valise in his hand, which he requested permission to leave here until the next morning. I asked him if it was of any value, and he replied no. Informing him that I would then place it in the office, the man thanked me, and went away. When the two men entered the bank at six o'clock in the evening, I instantly recognized one of them as the man who had called in the afternoon. He was, however, dressed very roughly on the occasion of this last visit, and had evidently changed his clothes for the purpose of escaping detection or recognition."

"Which one of the men attacked you?" now asked the detective.

"The one who left the valise in the afternoon. While the tallest of the two was struggling with Miss Patton, who was screaming loudly, the other one came behind the counter and struck me upon the head with the butt end of his revolver. I became insensible after this, and knew nothing until I found myself in the vault."

"How did you extricate yourself from this dilemma?" inquired Manning.

"Well, sir," began Pearson, and the detective imagined that he noticed a hesitancy in his manner, which was not apparent before, "when I recovered consciousness, I found myself locked up in the vault, with Miss Patton lying beside me. When she recovered, we both shouted loudly for help, and beat with our hands upon the iron doors, in the hope of attracting attention. This failed, and we were nearly desperate. Just then, however, my foot came in contact with some loose silver upon the floor, and on stooping to pick them up, I found that they were ten-cent pieces. Instantly, the idea occurred to me, to attempt to remove the screws which fastened the lock to the inside of the door, and of using one of these coins for the purpose. To my intense joy the screws yielded to my efforts, and in a short time the heavy door swung open, and we were free. I have told you already what followed."

As John Manning jotted these recitals down in his notebook, he could not repress nor account for a feeling of doubtfulness which crept over him at this point. He looked up into the young man's face, but there he saw only the evidence of serious truthfulness, and honest frankness; but still that lingering doubt was upon him and he could not shake it off.

At his request, young Pearson then furnished him with a description of the two men, as nearly as his memory would serve him, and these the detective noted down for future use.

At length, finding that he had obtained all the information which could be afforded him here, he thanked the gentlemen for their assistance, and promised to call again in the course of the day.

"Remember, Mr. Manning," said Mr. Silby, "we rely entirely upon the resources of Mr. Pinkerton's agency, and that we are confident that you will succeed."

"I cannot promise that," returned Manning, "but you may be assured that if success is possible, we will accomplish it."

So saying, he shook hands with the gentlemen, and left the bank. He betook himself at once to the hotel to prepare himself for further action in this investigation.

As the morning was not yet very far advanced, John Manning concluded to pay a visit to Miss Patton, the other eye-witness to, and active participant in the robbery.

Ascertaining the locality of her residence, he walked along the pleasant shaded street, revolving in his mind the various points upon which he had been enlightened during the interview just concluded. Arriving at his destination, he found a neat, cosy little cottage, set in the midst of a bright garden of blooming flowers, the perfume of which filled the morning air. There was an appearance of neatness and beauty and comfort about the place, which at once gave evidence of the refinement of those who dwelt within, and as the detective walked along the graveled path that led to the front door, he found himself involuntarily arranging his shirt-collar, and calling up his best manner for the occasion.

His knock was responded to by a kindly faced, matronly looking lady, whom he instinctively felt was the mother of the young lady. Making his business known, and requesting an interview with Miss Patton, he was ushered into a cool, well-furnished parlor, to await the conveyance of his message and to learn the disposition of the invalid.

In a few minutes the lady reappeared, and stated that although her daughter was still very weak and nervous from the shock she had sustained, she would see him, and requested him to step into her room.

Entering a neatly furnished little chamber, he beheld the young lady reclining upon a couch, looking very pale, but with a pleasant smile of welcome upon her face that at once gave him the courage to proceed with the unpleasant business he had in hand.

Bidding her a polite good morning, he took the seat, which had been placed for him near the bed, and as delicately as possible, stated his business and the reason for his calling upon her. At this point Mrs. Patton excused herself, and retired, with the evident intention of leaving them alone.

Manning quietly and delicately made his inquiries, and the girl answered them in a plain, straightforward manner. Her story corroborated all that had previously been related by young Pearson, and left no doubt in the mind of the detective that the occurrences of the eventful afternoon had been correctly detailed. He could not, however, control the doubtfulness that was impressing him with regard to Eugene Pearson.

"I cannot forbear the thought," said he, when Miss Patton had concluded her story, "that if Mr. Pearson had displayed a reasonable amount of manly bravery, this robbery could not have taken place."

"There is something very strange to me," said the girl, musingly, "about the manner in which Eugene acted, and—there are some things that I cannot understand."

"Would you object to telling me what they are?" said the detective. "Perhaps I can enlighten you."

"Well," responded the girl reluctantly, "I fear that Eugene has not told the entire truth in this matter."

"In what respect?" inquired the detective.

"I would not do anything to injure Mr. Pearson for the world, Mr. Manning, and he may have forgotten the circumstance altogether, but I am sure that I saw one of those robbers on two occasions before this occurred, in the bank and talking to Mr. Pearson."

"Why should he seek to conceal this?" asked the operative.

"That is just what I cannot understand," answered the lady.

"Tell me just what you know, and perhaps I can help you in coming to a correct conclusion."

"I don't like to say anything about this, but still I think it is my duty to do so, and I will tell you all that I know. More than two weeks ago, I returned from my dinner to the bank one day, and I saw this man in the private office with Mr. Pearson; I noticed then that their manner toward each other showed them to be old acquaintances rather than mere strangers. This man left the bank in a few minutes after I came in. He had the manner and appearance of a gentleman, and I did not think anything of it at the time."

"Did Mr. Pearson tell you who he was, or explain his presence there at that time?"

"No, I did not ask anything about him, and he did not mention the matter to me."

"When did you see them together again?"

"That same evening about dusk. I had been making a call upon a friend, and was returning home when I met them walking and conversing together."

"Did Mr. Pearson recognize you on that occasion?" inquired the detective.

"No, sir, he did not seem to notice me at all, and I passed them without speaking."

"You are quite sure about this?"

"Oh, yes, quite sure. I recognized him immediately when he came yesterday afternoon to leave the valise in the bank, and also when he came with the other man when the robbery was committed."

"Do you feel confident that you would be able to identify him, if you were to see him again?"

"I am quite sure that I would," returned the girl confidently; "his features are too indelibly fixed in my mind for me to make any mistake about it."

"Have you said anything to Mr. Pearson about this?"

"Yes, as soon as we were out of the vault, I said to him—'One of those men was the man who left the valise and the same one I saw in the office the other day.'"

"What reply did he make."

"He appeared to be doubtful, and simply said, 'Is that so?'"

"Very well, Miss Patton," said the detective at length, "we will look fully into this matter, but in the meantime, I particularly desire that you will say nothing to anyone about what you have told me today. It is very necessary that a strict silence should be preserved upon this point."

The young lady cheerfully promised compliance with this request, and in a few moments the detective, after thanking her for her kindness in seeing him, arose and took his departure.

As he strolled back to the hotel, he revolved the information he had received carefully in his mind. He had also obtained from Miss Patton a description of the two men, and found that they agreed very nearly with what he had learned from Mr. Pearson. He went to his room immediately, and prepared a report of all that had transpired during the morning, carefully detailing all that he had heard relating to Mr. Pearson's alleged intimacy with one of the robbers, and of the successful attempt he made to extricate himself from the vault, by means of the ten-cent piece. After concluding his relations, he requested the assistance of another operative, in order that they might scour the country round about, in the hope of finding some clues of the escaping robbers.

On the next morning, operative Howard Jackson, a young, active, and extremely intelligent member of my force, arrived at Geneva, and placed himself in communication with John Manning, for the continuance of this investigation.

When Manning's reports were duly received by my son, William A. Pinkerton, the superintendent of my Chicago agency, he gave the matter his most careful and earnest attention, and as he finished their perusal, he formed the opinion that young Pearson was not entirely guiltless of some collusion in this robbery. The more he weighed the various circumstances connected with this case, the more firm did this conclusion become, until at last he experienced a firm conviction that this young man knew more about the matter than he had yet related.

It seemed strange to him that a young, strong, and active man like Pearson should not have manifested even ordinary courage in a crisis like this. He was behind the desk when the attack was made upon Miss Patton at the door, and saw what was transpiring before the second assailant had time to reach him. Even if powerless to defend her, it seemed reasonable that he could have raised an alarm, which would have attracted the attention of the passersby; or, failing in that, he could, at least, have hastily closed the vault doors, and thus have saved the money of the bank. He knew that these doors were open, and that within the vault were nearly thirty thousand dollars, for which he was indirectly responsible. But a moment's time would have sufficed to close these doors and adjust the combination, and yet he made no effort to prevent a robbery which he knew was intended.

The ordinary promptings of manhood would, it was thought, have induced him to make some show of resistance, or to have gone to the rescue of a young and delicate girl; but none of these things did he do, and, if the story related was true, the young man had acted like a base coward at the best, and submitted without a murmur to the outrages that were perpetrated in his presence. Instead of acting like a man, he stood tamely by and allowed a woman to be cruelly beaten, the bank robbed, and the robbers to walk off unmolested and unharmed.

There was another matter which seemed impossible of accomplishment. Pearson had stated that while in the vault he had removed the screws from the lock upon the door with the aid of a ten-cent piece. This idea seemed to be utterly incredible, and prompted by his doubts, William attempted the same feat upon the lock on his office door. After several efforts, in which he exerted his strength to the utmost, he was obliged to desist. The screws utterly defied the efforts to move them, while the coin was bent and twisted out of all shape, by the pressure that it was subjected to.

While he was thus engaged with his thoughts upon this perplexing problem, he was informed that two gentlemen from Geneva desired to speak with him. Signifying his readiness to receive them, two well-dressed gentlemen entered and announced their business.

One of these men was a Mr. Perry, a director of the Geneva bank, and his companion was a Mr. Bartman, a merchant in Newtonsville, a little town situated but a few miles distant from Geneva.

"Mr. Bartman," said Mr. Perry, addressing my son, "has some information to communicate, which I think is important enough to deserve serious consideration, and I have brought him to you."

Mr. Bartman's information proved to be of very decided importance. He stated that he was a merchant, doing business in Newtonsville, and that he was in the habit of purchasing his goods from various traveling salesmen who represented Chicago houses. Among this number was a young man named Newton Edwards, who was in the employ of a large commission house, located on South Water Street, in the city of Chicago. He had known Edwards for some years, and had frequently dealt with him during that period. During the forenoon of the day on which the robbery occurred, he saw Newton Edwards in Newtonsville, but that instead of attempting to sell his goods, that gentleman was apparently seeking to avoid observation. He met him upon the street and familiarly accosted him, but Edwards received his salutations coldly, and did not engage in any conversation. Mr. Bartman thought nothing of this at the time, but in the afternoon, having business in Geneva, he drove over to that place, and, to his surprise, he found Edwards, in company with a strange young man, lingering around the public house in Geneva, apparently having nothing whatever to do. He noticed also, that Edwards was somewhat under the influence of liquor, and that he had effected a complete change in his apparel. A few hours after this he heard of the robbery, and instantly his mind reverted to the strange appearance and actions of Newton Edwards. He endeavored to find him, but, as if in confirmation of his suspicions, both Edwards and his companion had disappeared.

Mr. Bartman gave a full description of Edwards as he appeared that day, and in substantiation of his suspicions, it was found to agree perfectly with that given by both Eugene Pearson and Miss Grace Patton.

Mr. Perry stated that within two hours after the robbery had been discovered, men had been sent out in all directions, in search of the fleeing robbers, but without success. They had only been enabled to learn that two men, carrying a valise between them, had been seen walking along the railroad track in a north-westerly direction from Geneva, but that was all. In the darkness of the night, they had succeeded in eluding their pursuers, and on the following day all traces of them were obscured.

Two things were now to be done at once: to ascertain the antecedents of Eugene Pearson, and to seek the whereabouts of Newton Edwards.

In the meantime operatives Manning and Jackson had been untiring in their efforts to obtain some traces of the robbers. They had found a number of people who recollected seeing two men, answering the description of the suspected thieves, who carried a valise between them, but beyond a certain point all traces of them stopped. It seemed that the ground had opened and swallowed them up, so effectual had been their disappearance.

While thus engaged, operative Manning received instructions to keep a watchful eye upon young Pearson, and also to make quiet and judicious inquiries as to his habits and associates in Geneva.

The result of these inquiries was most favorable to the young man, and under ordinary circumstances would have disarmed suspicion at once. During the progress of this search after truth, operative Manning had preserved the utmost good feeling and cordiality in his dealings with Eugene Pearson, and had succeeded in establishing a friendly intimacy with him that would have allayed any fears the young man might have had as to the opinions entertained by the detectives with regard to himself. Mr. Pearson was very positive that one of the robbers was the same man who had left the valise at the bank during the afternoon, and, after learning that Manning had paid a visit to Miss Patton, he stated his belief that this same person had called at the bank a few weeks before. He could not remember the name he had given at that time, but thought he had inquired as to the financial standing of several of the business men of Geneva. During all these interviews Mr. Pearson displayed the utmost willingness to assist the detectives in their investigation, and with a frankness that was refreshing, answered every question that was put to him as if with the earnest desire of facilitating their labors and contributing to the accomplishment of their success.

The result of these inquiries was not calculated to strengthen the doubts which had been formed of young Pearson's participation in this robbery, and yet the suspicion remained unchanged, and we determined to await developments before yielding our opinions to what seemed to be a pressure of circumstances.

In the meantime, my son William had not been idle in the city. Ascertaining the name of the firm for which Newton Edwards was traveling, and determined to satisfy his mind upon this point, he dispatched an operative to the business house to which he had been referred. The result of this inquiry was that Mowbray, Morton & Co., the firm with which Edwards had at one time been engaged, stated that he had severed his connection with them a short time before, and since then had done nothing for them, but had been traveling for another house on the same street, and they believed he was the junior partner of the firm. Inquiry at this house elicited the information that Edwards had retired from this firm, and had connected himself with a large eastern house, which dealt extensively in fruits and a general line of groceries. At this place, however, several items of information were gleaned which were of importance. The gentlemen connected with this establishment were very well acquainted with Newton Edwards, of whom they spoke in the highest terms. He had been in Chicago during all of the week previous to the robbery, but had left the city on Saturday, stating that he intended to travel through Wisconsin and Minnesota in the interest of the new firm which he represented. He had not been seen since, nor had they heard from him.

Finding that the gentleman who furnished this information was an intimate acquaintance of Edwards, the operative next inquired as to his family connections and his place of residence. On these points he was fully informed, and he cheerfully imparted the desired information. Edwards, it appeared, had been married recently to a lovely and accomplished young lady from one of the outlying towns, and since his marriage had been residing with the husband of his sister, a gentleman named Samuel Andrews, who resided at 29 Logan Place, in Chicago. Edwards also had a brother who was married, and who lived in the city, and the location of this gentleman's residence was also cheerfully furnished by the merchant.

Upon returning with this information, the operative at once reported to my son William, who decided upon an immediate course of action. Directing the operative to inquire for tidings of Edwards at both of the places named, he indited a telegraphic message to the chief of police at Milwaukee and Minneapolis, for the purpose of ascertaining if Edwards had been at either place since leaving the city. He described the man fully, stated the name of the house which he represented, gave the fullest particulars as to his identity, and then requested to be informed if he had made his appearance in either of these cities.

To all these messages the answer was received that Edwards had not, as yet, arrived, although the chief at Milwaukee stated that he had met a friend of Edwards, who informed him that he had received a letter from the young man dated four days prior to the robbery, stating that he would be in Milwaukee in a few days, and that he would be accompanied by his wife. As yet, however, he had not arrived, and nothing further had been heard of him.

This was a corroboration of the first suspicion regarding Newton Edwards, and was convincing of the fact that he had not done as he had informed his friends that he would do. William was convinced, therefore, that he was upon the right track, and impatiently awaited the return of the operative who had been sent to the residences of Edwards's relatives.

The detective delegated for that purpose proceeded to the locality to which he had been directed, where he found a comfortable-looking, well-kept brick dwelling-house, and upon a metal plate upon the door, he noticed the name he was in search of. Ascending the steps, he rang the bell, and shortly afterward was ushered into a handsomely furnished parlor, where he was greeted by a pleasant-faced lady, who announced herself as the sister of Mr. Newton Edwards.

"Is Mr. Edwards residing with you?" inquired the detective.

"Not now," answered the lady. "He was here until Saturday last, when he left, saying that he was going to Milwaukee upon business. I have heard, however, that he was in town on Sunday last, but that I am not sure of."

"Did his wife go with him?" now asked the operative, hoping to obtain an interview with her, if possible.

"No, sir," replied Mrs. Andrews, with an air of sudden coldness and reserve, which was not lost upon the watchful man before her. "Mrs. Edwards left on the same day, in company with her brother, who has taken her to his home; I do not wish to allude to this matter, but I am afraid my brother and his wife do not live happily together."

"Have they separated?" asked the detective, in a tone of solicitude.

After a momentary hesitation, the woman replied, "I am inclined to think they have. Newton has not been himself lately, and has, I am sorry to say, been drinking a great deal. This naturally led to harsh treatment of his wife, and I presume she wrote to her brother, and on last Saturday he came and took her away."

Finding the lady indisposed to furnish further information, the detective took his leave.

At the second place he received much the same information, and concluding that he had exhausted this matter, he started to return to the agency. At this latter place, however, he had casually inquired for the name and residence of Mrs. Edwards's brother, and on learning that, had concluded his visit.

Everything thus far had favored a belief that Edwards was concerned in this robbery. His leaving home a day or two before the act was committed, his quarrel with his wife, his statement made to friends that he was going upon a business trip, which it was evident he had not done, his strange appearance at Newtonsville and Geneva on the day the robbery took place, the fact that his personal appearance agreed perfectly with that given of the robber, by eye-witnesses to that event, and his mysterious disappearance since, all went to prove beyond question that Newton Edwards was the thief, and that decided steps should be taken to discover his whereabouts.

Leaving William to devise a plan to accomplish this much-desired result, we will return to Geneva, and watch the movements of John Manning and Howard Jackson.

In extending their investigations in and around Geneva, operatives Manning and Jackson had discovered numerous items of intelligence corroborative of their previous suspicions. A salesman, connected with a large mercantile house from one of the large cities, furnished the information that on Monday, the day on which the robbery occurred, he had traveled with Edwards as far as Newtonsville, and as he did not see him after leaving that place, he concluded that he must have stopped there. He also stated that Edwards appeared to be unusually cold and reserved, and that he was accompanied by a companion whom he did not introduce to his friends. At Newtonsville it was learned that a man, fully answering the description of Edwards's companion, had visited both of the livery stables in that town, and had attempted to hire a team of horses and a carriage. He had been refused in both instances, for the reasons that he was a stranger, and appeared to be under the influence of liquor. Several people both in Geneva and Newtonsville were found who remembered seeing Edwards, whom they knew—and a companion who was a stranger to them—about these towns on the day of the robbery, and they described their actions as being very peculiar. They had disappeared immediately after that and had not been seen since. If further proofs of the complicity of Edwards were required they could have been procured by the score, and as all traces of their route from Geneva had been lost, William resolved to commence a thorough and systematic process of espionage, which he believed would eventually lead to the discovery of his hiding-place. He thoroughly canvassed the situation and his conclusions were soon found. Newton Edwards had a father and mother—he had brothers and sisters—and in addition to these he had a lovely young wife, from whom he had parted in anger. It was not possible that he could shake himself loose from all these ties of kindred and affection at one blow, and it was reasonably sure that sooner or later he would attempt to correspond with them in some manner. Again, it might be the case that some of his relatives were already aware of his crime, and of the fact that he was hiding from the officers of the law, and it could not be expected that they would voluntarily give information that would lead to his discovery. However grieved and disappointed they might be, however angry they must naturally feel, they could not be expected at such a time as this to turn his accusers, and aid in his capture.

I have known cases in the course of my professional practice, however, when fathers, actuated by what they considered the highest motives, have delivered up their sons to the law, and, though the ordeal was an exceedingly trying and distressing one, they never faltered for a moment in what they considered the performance of their duty. I need not say that such evidences of self-sacrifice were painful to me, and that my feelings were always deeply touched by the mental sufferings of the poor criminals, who in the hour of their sorest need, found themselves deserted by the only friends upon whom they believed they could rely in an emergency which threatened disgrace and servitude.

While this is true, it is equally certain that I have yet to record a single case in which a female relative ever assisted, in any manner, toward the apprehension of a criminal. No power seemed able to force from her a word that would tend to work him injury, and though her heart was breaking, and her love for the lost one had passed away, yet, with a persistence worthy of all admiration, she refused to do aught that would add to the misery of the fallen one, and, if occasion offered, invariably rendered her assistance to secure his escape.

Taking these ideas into consideration, therefore, it would not do to rely at all upon any assistance from the relatives of Edwards, and to advise them of our suspicions and search would naturally only tend to place both him and them upon their guard.

A slower and more laborious operation was therefore necessary. Fully in earnest in his determination to capture these men, and firmly supported by the officials of the bank, who were as resolute as he in their resolve to apprehend the robbers, William at once put this plan into execution.

Operatives were posted to watch the residences of the relatives of Edwards in the city, and instructed to carefully note their actions, particularly in the matter of receiving or posting of any letters. Another operative was despatched to Woodford to note the movements of Mrs. Edwards, the wife of the suspected thief, and to endeavor to obtain some information that would assist us in the chase. It might be possible that this reported quarrel was a mere ruse, to blind the detectives, and to throw them off the scent; and it was important that the truthfulness of this story should be substantiated. At the same time, William decided on no account to lose sight of young Pearson, and directed the operatives at Geneva to maintain a strict watch over his movements, and by no means to permit him to leave town unaccompanied by someone who could note his every action. The young bank clerk, however, gave no cause for any new suspicion. He performed his duties at the bank with unflagging industry and evinced the greatest desire that the thieves might soon be captured. His solicitude for Miss Patton was apparently sincere and unceasing, and he frequently reproached himself for not having acted in a more manly manner at the time the assault was made. So humiliated did he appear at the loss the bank had sustained, and so earnest was he in everything that approached a vigorous and determined chase after the robbers, that he soon became an object of profound sympathy and higher regard to the bank officers and his numerous friends in Geneva.

My son William continued his pursuit of Edwards, and his efforts would reveal he was hiding somewhere in New York state. Our careful scrutiny of his wife's activities bore fruit. Mrs. Edwards had been seen to mail a letter, and one of our operatives, after a serious effort, had obtained a glance at the address. It was as follows:

William Amos,
McDonald, New York.

"That settles it!" William said. "Send at once to McDonald, and my word for it, Edwards will be found."

McDonald, I soon learned, was a little village in the central part of New York, remotely situated, and with no railroad or telegraph facilities of any kind. An excellent hiding-place for a fugitive certainly, particularly, as I suspected, if he had relatives residing there.

Two men were selected for this journey, and their preparations were soon made. That evening they were flying over the ground in the direction of the little hamlet, where they were hopeful of finding the man they were seeking.

As an additional precaution, and fearing that Edwards might not remain in McDonald for any length of time, I telegraphed to my son, Robert A. Pinkerton, at New York City, to also repair, as soon as possible, to that place, and if Edwards was there to arrest him at once, and await the arrival of my operatives from Chicago.

Immediately upon the receipt of this message, Robert left New York City by the earliest train, and without event, arrived at the station nearest to the village of McDonald, which he learned was about twelve miles distant. Here he was obliged to take a stagecoach, and after a long, hot, and fatiguing journey of several hours, he arrived about nightfall at the sleepy little village, which was his point of destination. By making inquiries of the stage-driver in a careless manner, and without exciting any suspicion, he learned that there was a constable at that place, and on arriving, he immediately sought out this important official. From him Robert learned that there was a strange young man stopping with an old farmer about two miles out of the village, who had been there several days, and who was represented as a nephew to the old gentleman. Upon showing him the photograph of Edwards, he recognized it at once, and signified his readiness to render any service in the matter which might be required of him.

After disclosing as much as he deemed advisable to the constable, whose name was Daniel Bascom, Robert gladly accepted his hospitality for the night, and feeling very tired and weary after his hard journey, he retired to rest, and slept the sleep of the just, until he was awakened in the morning by his hospitable entertainer. After partaking of a hearty breakfast, Robert and the village constable matured their plans of operation. As a well-dressed city young gentleman might occasion some curiosity in the village, and as young Edwards might take alarm at the unexpected appearance of a stranger in that retired locality, it was decided to make some change in Robert's apparel. The constable therefore very kindly offered him a suit of his clothing, which as the two men were nearly of the same size, and the articles slightly worn, answered the purpose admirably, and in a few moments Robert was transformed into a good-looking countryman, who was enjoying a short holiday after the labors of harvesting, which were now over.

In company with Mr. Bascom, the constable, Robert sauntered into the village. It was a beautiful morning; the air was delightfully fresh and cool, and the rays of the sun danced and glistened upon the dew-drops which sparkled upon every tree and flower. The feathered songsters filled the air with their sweet melodies, and nature with all its gladsome beauty was spread before him. Such a feeling of rest and thorough enjoyment came over him, that it was with an effort, he was able to shake off the pleasures of the hour, and bring himself to the disagreeable business in hand. After a short walk they approached the general store of the little village, which was the lounging-place of all the farmers for miles around. When they arrived they found a motley gathering assembled to witness the great event of the day in this town, the departure of the stagecoach, and Robert was speedily introduced as a relative of Mr. Bascom, who had come to McDonald to spend a few days.

The mail coach was an important institution in McDonald, and was regarded as the great medium of communication between that place and the great world outside. Every morning at precisely the same hour the coach departed, and every evening with the same regard for punctuality the old time-worn vehicle rolled up before the platform in front of the store, to the intense delight and admiration of the assembled crowd.

Two young men were already seated in the stage, and their luggage was securely stowed away in the boot. The postmaster—the village store-keeper filled that responsible position—was busily engaged in making up the mail, and old Jerry, the fat good-natured old driver, was laughing and joking with the bystanders, as he awaited the hour for departure. As Robert stepped upon the platform he bestowed a hasty, though searching, glance at the two men in the coach, and to his relief found that neither of them was the man he wanted.

Everything being now in readiness, the driver spoke to his steeds, and this time without mishap, the lumbering old vehicle rattled away on its journey. The little crowd gradually dispersed and soon left Robert and the constable alone with the store-keeper.

"I didn't see old Ben Ratcliffe around this morning," said Mr. Bascom to John Todd, the store-keeper.

"No," answered that individual, "he was here last evening, and said if the weather was fine he was going with his nephew over to the lake, fishing."

"That accounts for it, then," said the constable. "I don't think he has ever missed a day for ten years before."

"No, I don't think he has, but that young Mr. Amos, who is stopping here with him, is very fond of fishing, and the old man promised to take him over to Pine Lake this morning, so 'Uncle Ben' missed the mail for once."

After a short conversation with the store-keeper upon general matters, the two men took their leave. It seemed very evident that as yet there was no suspicion on the part of Edwards, as to the discovery of his hiding-place, and here in fancied safety, surrounded by nature in all its beauty, with affectionate relatives, the young burglar was enjoying himself as heartily as though no cares were oppressing him, and no thought of detection ever troubled his mind.

The uncle of young Edwards, it was learned, was a general favorite about the country. A good-natured, honest old farmer, who had lived there from boyhood, and was known to all the farmers and their families for miles around. Even in his old age, for he was long past sixty now, he cherished his old love for gunning and fishing, and held his own right manfully among those who were many years his junior.

It was decided, as a matter of precaution, that they should call at the house of Uncle Ben, in order to ascertain whether he and his nephew had really gone fishing, and to that end the constable harnessed up his horses, and in a few minutes they were on their way to the old farm-house, which stood at the end of a long shady lane leading off from the main road.

Driving up to the gate, the constable alighted and approached the house, while Robert remained seated in the buggy. In a few moments he returned, and stated that Mrs. Ratcliffe, the good farmer's wife, had informed him that her husband and nephew had gone off before daylight to a lake about five miles distant, and they would not return until late in the evening.

It was deemed advisable not to attempt to follow them, as their appearance at the lake might give the young man alarm, and as they were not sure of any particular place to find them, they concluded to quietly await their return. They accordingly drove back to the village, and Robert returned to the constable's house to dinner. In the afternoon the two operatives whom I had sent from Chicago arrived, having been driven over by private conveyance. Without publicly acknowledging them, Robert gave them to understand that he would meet them at the house of the constable, and upon repairing thither they were duly informed of what had taken place, and instructed as to the plans proposed for that evening.

Nothing of any note transpired during the afternoon, and after sundown the party started out upon their errand. Night soon came on, throwing its sable mantle over the earth, the sounds of the busy day were hushed, and all the world seemed wrapped in the tranquil stillness of a summer night. The stars, in countless numbers, were twinkling and sparkling in the blue heavens above, while the new moon, like a silver crescent, shed its soft light upon a scene of rare beauty and quiet loveliness.

Arriving within a short distance of the old farmer's house, the horses and buggy were secreted in a little grove of trees that skirted the main road, and the men stationed themselves in convenient hiding-places along the lane, to await the return of the farmer and his nephew. From the appearance of the farm-house, it was evident that the fishing-party had not yet returned, and they settled themselves down to a patient, silent waiting, which, as the hours wore on, grew painfully tedious and tiresome. At last, long past midnight, and after they had begun to despair of accomplishing the object of their visit, they heard a faint noise, as though footsteps were approaching.

"Hist!" cried Robert, "someone is coming."

They listened intently, and gradually the noises grew louder and more distinct. As they came nearer, the constable distinctly recognized the voice of the old farmer, who was evidently relating some humorous story to his companion, who was laughing heartily. The merry tones of this young man's laugh were as clear and ringing as though he had not a care in the world, and had not committed a crime against the laws of the state. No one, to have heard that hearty, melodious burst of merriment, would have supposed for an instant that it came from the lips of a fugitive from justice.

They were now nearly opposite to the crouching figures by the roadside. The old farmer had evidently reached the climax of his story, for both of them broke out again into a fresh burst of violent laughter that awoke the echoes round about them.

The laugh suddenly died away, the merriment ceased abruptly, as a dark form emerged from the roadside, and the muzzle of a revolver was placed close to the cheek of the young man, while Robert called out menacingly, "Newton Edwards, I want you!"

With an exclamation of pain, the young man dropped his fishing-pole and the bucket of fish he was carrying, while a chill ran through his frame, and he shivered like an aspen in the grasp of the determined detective.

The others had now come forward, and as soon as he could recover from his astonishment, the old farmer cried out, "What does this mean?"

"It means," said Robert coolly, "that we have arrested your nephew for burglary, and that he must go with us."

It was in the gray dawn of the morning when the party arrived at the house of the constable, Daniel Bascom. Here breakfast was prepared, and after full justice had been done to a bountiful repast, an examination of the effects of Newton Edwards was commenced. Ever since his arrest the young man had maintained a rigid silence, not deigning to notice the detectives in any manner whatever. He partook of his breakfast in a dazed, dreamy fashion, scarcely eating anything, and pushing back his plate as though unable to force himself to partake of food. In his satchel was discovered a roll of bank-bills, which on being counted was found to contain a trifle over three thousand five hundred dollars.

Edwards gazed at this money with a greedy, frightened look, like a wild beast at bay, but did not utter a word, as Robert placed it in a large envelope and secured it about his person.

"Will you be kind enough to inform me," said Robert, when this was completed, "how you come to have so much money about you?"

After a moment's hesitation, Edwards replied, doggedly, "Yes, sir, I will. It is the proceeds of the sale of some property that I owned in the west."

"Very well," replied Robert, finding it useless, at present, to attempt to induce him to tell the truth. "You will have ample opportunity to satisfy a court and jury upon that point in a very short time."

Nothing further was said to him until the time arrived for departing, and then the party, with their prisoner, walked into the village in order to take the stage for the railroad station at Birmingham.

Before leaving Mr. Bascom's, however, Robert handsomely remunerated the energetic constable for his valuable assistance, and after thanking him warmly for his active and cordial aid in our behalf, requested his company to the village.

As they approached the store, where the stagecoach was in waiting, they found an unusual crowd awaiting their appearance. The news of the robbery and arrest had by some means become known, and the eager faces of nearly three score of curiosity-seekers greeted them upon their arrival.

The farmers gathered in little groups about the platform, and conversed in low tones, as they furtively regarded with sentiments almost approaching a respectful awe, the unwonted presence of the detectives and their charge. There was an utter absence of the boisterous hilarity which had been manifested on the preceding morning, and one might have thought that they had assembled for the purpose of officiating at a funeral, so thoroughly subdued and solemn did they all appear.

The journey to the railway station was made in due time, and without accident, and the party were speeding on their way to Chicago. Robert forbore to press the young man any further, and let him severely alone during the entire day. During the night they all retired to their sleeping berths, Edwards being securely handcuffed to one of my men, and occupying the same berth with him.

In the morning, Robert noticed a slight change in the demeanor of Edwards, and thought he detected a disposition to converse. He did not encourage him, however, preferring by all means that the advances should be made by the young man himself. Nor did he have long to wait. They procured their breakfast in the dining car, and after the meal was concluded, Robert, without uttering a word, handed Edwards a cigar, which he very gratefully accepted. After sitting quietly smoking for a few moments, he turned to Robert and asked, "Mr. Pinkerton, how did you discover that I was in McDonald?"

"In the same manner in which we have discovered many other things in connection with this robbery," replied Robert. "I may say, however, that the man we came for was William R. Amos; do you know anything about such a person?"

As Robert spoke he gazed scrutinizingly at the face before him, and Edwards winced perceptibly under his glance.

"I can explain that all right," he at length replied, with considerable embarrassment. "I got into some trouble at home with a young lady, and thought it best to leave town for a short time."

"Edwards," said Robert sternly, "falsehood and impudence will not help you in this case, and I wish to hear no more. I have only to say that we have evidence enough against you to insure a conviction, and your only hope lies in making your sentence as light as possible."

"How so?" he asked.

"By telling all you know about this matter. One of your accomplices, we have got dead to rights, and if you won't tell perhaps he will."

"Who have you got?" inquired Edwards, anxiously.

"That I cannot tell you now; our business is with you for the present. I want you to consider this matter carefully. You are a young man yet, and though you have thrown away golden opportunities in the past, you have yet an opportunity to reform your ways, and by assisting the officers of justice in recovering the money which you and your companions have stolen, and in arresting the rest of your associates, you may receive the clemency of the court, and perhaps benefit yourself materially."

Edwards was silent for a long time after this, and it was evident that he was seriously considering the matter. The words of the detective had made an impression upon him, but with the craftiness of an old offender, he was debating a plan by which he might turn his admissions into account for himself. At length he turned to Robert and asked, "Will I be able to escape if I tell what I know?"

"I cannot promise that. But you are aware that the giving of information which leads to the capture of your associates and the recovery of the balance of this money, will work to your advantage very decidedly in the mind of the judge."

"Very well," said Edwards, with a dogged sullenness, "your advice is very good, but I have no confession to make."

"Take your own course," said Robert, carelessly. "My advice was for your own good, and as you don't seem willing to accept it, I have nothing more to say."

Although he had not accomplished very much as yet, Robert was still hopeful of inducing Edwards to unburden himself, but he resolved to attempt nothing further with him until they arrived in Chicago, where he could be managed more successfully by those who were more fully conversant with the facts in the case. He well knew that we already possessed testimony amply sufficient to convict Edwards of participating in the robbery, but what we most desired was to obtain information concerning his partners in the deed. However, he decided to allow him ample time for reflection and said no more to him upon the subject until they reached Chicago, when he was at once conducted to the agency.

In Chicago, a consultation was immediately held to devise the best means to be pursued to induce Edwards to reveal who his partners really were. William at once resolved upon a plan which he was hopeful would lead to good and immediate results. Calling a carriage, he directed the driver to take him to the residence of Edwards's sister, Mrs. Andrews, on Logan Place. On arriving at the house, he found that lady and her daughter at home, and he was immediately ushered into the parlor by the pretty servant, Mary Crilly. Without unnecessary preliminary, William informed the lady that we had succeeded in arresting Edwards for the robbery of the Geneva Bank, and that he was now in custody. He also stated that from information which he had obtained, he was led to believe that his family were perfectly aware of his actions in this matter, if indeed they had not aided him in accomplishing it.

At this point both mother and daughter burst into tears, and sobbingly denied any knowledge of Edwards's crime until after he had committed it, and then they could not act as his accusers. Mrs. Andrews finally urged him to visit Edwards's brother, who resided on Freeman Street, and hinted that he could tell something about the matter, although she asserted he took no part in it, and knew nothing about it until it had been completed.

Taking it for granted that they had told him all they knew about the robbery, William next hurried to the place of business of Edwards's brother, whom he was fortunate enough to find in his office, and disengaged. He at once stated who he was, and what he wanted to know. Mr. Edwards was at first disposed to deny all knowledge of the matter, but on William's informing him of his brother's arrest, and hinting that he had made a partial confession, he changed his mind and became quite communicative.

The brother then stated that for years he had been troubled with Newton's bad habits and extravagances, although he had never known him to commit a crime until the robbery of the bank at Geneva. He remembered hearing his brother boast once when he was intoxicated, that he could get plenty of money without work, but as Newton gambled a great deal, he imagined that he had alluded to that means of obtaining his money.

"Well," said William abruptly, "I want to know what you know about this robbery."

"I will tell you all I know," answered Mr. Edwards. "Some three or four weeks before I heard of this robbery, Newton was at my house, and was intoxicated. He boasted in his maudlin way that he had an opportunity to rob a bank, and that the cashier was a party to the affair, but I attributed all this to the wild utterances of a drunken man, and paid no further attention to it. On the Saturday night before the robbery took place, however, he came to my house during my absence, and had a companion with him, for whom he made a bed upon my parlor floor. In the morning they went away, and I have not seen him since. My wife informed me afterward that Newton, who was drunk at the time, had told her that the man with him was the one that was to help him to rob the bank, and that she had then ordered both of them out of the house. I did not at any time know where the bank was located, nor did I ever seriously entertain the idea of his attempting anything of the kind; but when I heard of the robbery of the Geneva bank, I at once suspected my brother, and although humiliated deeply at the thought, I could not take any step that would tend to bring disgrace and ruin upon my own family."

Without entering into the question of family honor, William inquired, "Do you know the man who was with him at your house, and who was to assist in this robbery?"

"No," answered Mr. Edwards. "I never heard his name, and all that I ever knew of him was that he came from Denver, Colorado."

"Can you describe him?" asked William.

"Yes, I think I can," said Mr. Edwards, and he then gave a description of the man, which agreed perfectly with that of Edwards's companion on the day of the robbery.

Having now obtained all the information that was possible to be gained from this source, William returned to the agency, and entered the room where Edwards was confined. He found the young man sitting with his face buried in his hands and evidently in sore distress.

"Mr. Edwards," said William in his quick, imperious manner, "I have just had an interview with your brother and sister, who have told me all they know about this matter. You will readily see what little hope there is left for you if you persist in keeping from us the information which we desire. Whether you confess or not will make but little difference to us now, as sooner or later your associates will be caught, and your refusal to help us will only make it the harder for you. If you don't confess, Eugene Pearson will."

As William uttered this last sentence Edwards started to his feet, and exclaimed, "My God, you know more than I thought! I will tell what I know."

At last we had succeeded in breaking him down.

———

We had been very careful to keep the fact of Edwards's arrest a profound secret, and as yet, the officers of the bank and the peaceful community at Geneva were in entire ignorance of what had taken place. William had telegraphed to Mr. Silby, stating that he would be in Geneva that night, and requesting him to meet him at the train. About midnight, therefore, when they arrived with their charge, there was no excitement or bustle about the place, and even the wakeful and observant railroad men were unsuspicious of the arrival of one of the robbers. A carriage was procured and the party were rapidly driven to the city hall, where, to the surprise of the officials, Edwards was placed in confinement, charged with being a participant in the robbery of the Geneva bank. Fearing that the information would leak out before morning, and that Eugene Pearson would take fright and endeavor to dispose of his share of the proceeds, it was deemed advisable to go at once to his residence and arrest him.

This was done as speedily and quietly as possible, and before the young man was aware of the danger he was in, he was our prisoner. I will not attempt to depict the grief and anger of the family of this unfortunate young man when the object of our visit was made known; but their resentment of our action was just what might have been expected from people who believed implicitly in the innocence of their child, and regarded any attempt to deprive him of his liberty as an unpardonable outrage.

As respectfully, but as firmly as possible, William stated his determination to arrest Eugene Pearson, and informed them that every opportunity would be afforded him to defend himself, and to remove the stain upon his character when the proper time arrived.

Eugene Pearson was the least disturbed of the party. His coolness was imperturbable. He flatly denied all knowledge of the robbery, and in the strongest terms, assured his weeping and grief-stricken relatives of his innocence.

The arrest, however, was quietly accomplished, and Pearson was soon confined beneath the same roof which sheltered his associate in crime, Newton Edwards.

Early the next morning the town was alive with people, and the greatest excitement prevailed. The news of Eugene Pearson's arrest had spread far and wide, and a universal sentiment of indignation pervaded the whole community. Angry men gathered at the corners of the street, and threats of vengeance against the officers of my agency were loudly uttered. A lawless outrage had been committed by us, and the righteous indignation of an injured community refused to be appeased. The hotel where my men were stopping was besieged by the angry citizens, and our actions were denounced in the most belligerent manner. Eugene Pearson, in their opinion, was above suspicion; he was their ideal of a moral young man, his father was respected everywhere, and the base and unwarranted invasion of their home by my officers was an indignity which they were resolved they would not allow to pass unpunished. As the morning advanced the excitement increased, and several of the boldest of the angry citizens approached William, and in no complimentary terms expressed their contempt, not only for him individually, but for the methods which had been used to ferret out and apprehend men who were innocent of any wrong.

Under ordinary circumstances William would have resented these insults, and that too in a manner that would have convinced them that he was fully able to defend himself; but realizing the importance of coolness and discretion at this critical juncture, he preserved his good humor, and securing their attention for a few moments, he requested them not to be too hasty in their actions. If Eugene Pearson was innocent, he stated, no serious harm had been done the young man; and if he was guilty, as he could prove in a short time, they would deeply regret the course they were now threatening to pursue.

In the meantime he had not been idle in his attempts upon the stoical firmness of Eugene Pearson himself, and at length the young burglar was broken completely down; he confessed his guilt, and promised to conduct the officers to the spot where he had hidden his share of the booty.

The trial was not a protracted one. A jury was speedily empaneled, the low, stern tones of the judge were heard in timely admonition, and the prosecution was commenced. Upon the prisoners being asked to plead to the indictments which had been prepared against them, Mr. Kirkman, a prominent attorney of Geneva, who had been retained to defend the unfortunate young men, arose, and in impressive tones entered a plea of guilty. With the keen perceptions of a true lawyer, he felt that the proofs were too strong to be overcome, and that to attempt to set up any technical defense would only result in greater hardships to his clients.

He, however, made an eloquent and touching appeal for the exercise of judicial clemency. He referred in feeling terms to the youth of the prisoners, to the groups of weeping and stricken relatives, whose prayerful hearts were echoing his appeals. He urged that the evidences of sincere repentance had been manifested by all of the prisoners, and that, as this had been their first offense, the exercise of gentle mercy would be both grand and productive of good results.

His words were not lost even upon the prosecuting attorney, and when Mr. Kirkman had concluded, that gentleman arose, and in a few words echoed the sentiments of the attorney for the defense. He also expressed the conviction that, while justice called loudly for sentence, yet there were elements in this case in which the wisest judgment would be that which partook of the qualities of mercy.

At the conclusion of this request, the judge, with a delicate regard for the tender feelings of the assembled relatives, ordered an adjournment of the court, in order that he might take the merits of the case under advisement, and to enable him to administer such sentence, as, in his best judgment, was demanded under the circumstances. Slowly the immense audience dispersed, and for a few moments the prisoners were allowed to converse with their weeping friends, after which they were again conducted to their cells to await the action of the court.

A few days later they were brought quietly before the judge and their sentences were pronounced. Newton Edwards and Eugene Pearson were each sentenced to an imprisonment of six years on the indictment for burglary.

Thus ended this important case, and the action of the court received the almost universal approbation of the community, while the relatives and nearest friends of the prisoners were compelled to acknowledge its fairness and justice.

FOUR

The American Exchange Bank Robbery

Cleveland Moffett

LATE IN THE AFTERNOON OF FRIDAY, MAY 4, 1888, TWO MESSENGERS left the American Exchange National Bank, at the northeast corner of Cedar Street and Broadway, New York City, and started down the busy thoroughfare for the office of the Adams Express Company, a few blocks distant. They carried between them, each holding one of the handles, a valise made of canvas and leather, in which had just been placed, in the presence of the paying-teller, a package containing forty-one thousand dollars in greenbacks, to be transmitted to the United States Treasury in Washington for redemption.

Although the messengers—Edward S. Crawford and old "Dominie" Earle—were among the bank's most trusted employees, their honesty being considered above suspicion, they were nevertheless followed at a short distance by bank detective McDougal, an old-time police detective, whose snow-white beard and ancient style of dress have long made him a personage of note on Broadway. Detective McDougal followed the messengers, not because he had any fear that they were planning a robbery, but because it is an imperative rule of all great banking institutions that the transfer of large sums of money, even for very short distances, shall be watched over with the most scrupulous care. Each messenger is supposed to act as a check on his fellow, while the detective walking in the rear is a check on both. In such cases all three men are armed, and would use their weapons without hesitation should an attack be made upon them.

The messengers walked on through the hurrying crowd, keeping on the east sidewalk as far as Wall Street, where they turned across, and continued their way on the west sidewalk as far as the Adams Express Company's building, which stands at No. 59 Broadway. Having seen them safely inside the building, the detective turned back to the bank, where his services were required in other matters.

Passing down the large room strewn with boxes and packages ready for shipment, the two messengers turned to the right, and ascended the winding stairs that in those days led to the money department, on the second floor. No one paid much attention to them, as at this busy hour bank messengers were arriving and departing every few minutes. Still, some of the clerks remembered afterward, or thought they did, that the old man, Earle, ascended the stairs more slowly than his more active companion, who went ahead, carrying the valise alone. Both messengers, however, were present at the receiving-window of the money department when the package was taken from the valise and handed to the clerk, who gave a receipt for it in the usual form: "Received from the American Exchange Bank one package marked as containing forty-one thousand dollars, for transfer to Washington," or, at least, so far as has ever been proved, both messengers were present when the package was handed in.

The two messengers, having performed their duty, went away, Earle hurrying to the ferry to catch a train out into New Jersey, where he lived, and Crawford returning to the bank with the empty valise. The valuable package had meantime been ranged behind the heavily wired grating along with dozens of others, some of them containing much larger sums. The clerks in the money department of the Adams Express Company become so accustomed to handling gold, silver, and bank-notes, fortunes done up in bags, boxes, or bundles, that they think little more of this precious merchandise than they might of so much coal or bricks. A quick glance, a touch of the hand, satisfies them that the seals, the wrappings, the labels, the general appearance, of the packages are correct; and having entered them duly on the way-bills and turned them over to the express messenger who is to forward them to their destination, they think no more about them.

In this instance the forty-one-thousand-dollar package, after a brief delay, was locked in one of the small portable safes, a score of which are always lying about in readiness, and was lowered to the basement, where it was loaded on one of the company's wagons. The wagon was then driven to Jersey City, guarded by the messenger in charge, his assistant, and the driver, all three men being armed, and was safely placed aboard the night express for Washington. It is the company's rule that the messenger who starts with a through safe travels with it to its destination, though he has to make a journey of a thousand miles. Sometimes the destination of money under transfer is so remote that the service of several express companies is required; and in that case the messenger of the Adams Company accompanies the money only to the point where it is delivered to the messenger of the next company, and so on.

The next morning, when the package from the American Exchange Bank was delivered in Washington, the experienced Treasury clerk who received it perceived at once, from the condition of the package, that something was wrong. Employees of the Treasury Department seem to gain a new sense, and to be able to distinguish bank-notes from ordinary paper merely by the "feel," even when done up in bundles. Looking at the label mark of forty-one thousand dollars, the clerk shook his head, and called the United States Treasurer, James W. Hyatt, who also saw something suspicious in the package. Mr. Blanchard, the Washington agent of the Adams Express Company, was summoned, and in his presence the package was opened. It was found to contain nothing more valuable than slips of brown straw paper, the coarse variety used by butchers in wrapping up meat, neatly cut to the size of bank-notes. The forty-one thousand dollars were missing.

It was evident that at some point between the bank and the Treasury a bogus package had been substituted for the genuine one. The question was, where and by whom had the substitution been made?

The robbery was discovered at the Treasury in Washington on Saturday morning. The news was telegraphed to New York immediately, and on Saturday afternoon anxious councils were held by the officials of the American Exchange Bank and the Adams Express Company. Inspector Byrnes was notified; the Pinkerton Agency was notified; and urgent despatches were sent to Mr. John Hoey, president of the express company, and to Robert Pinkerton, who were both out of town, that their presence was required immediately in New York. Meanwhile everyone who had had any connection with the stolen package—the paying-teller of the bank, other bank clerks, the messengers, detective McDougal, the receiving-clerks of the Adams Express Company, and the express messenger—was closely examined. Where and how the forty-one thousand dollars had been stolen was important to learn not only in itself, but also to fix responsibility for the sum lost as between the bank and the express company.

Three theories were at once suggested: The bogus package might have been substituted for the genuine one either at the bank, between the bank and the express office, or between the express office and the Treasury. The first assumption threw suspicion on some of the bank employees, the second upon the two bank messengers, the third upon someone in the service of the express company. Both the bank and the express company stoutly maintained the integrity of its own employees.

An examination of the bogus package disclosed some points of significance. Ordinarily, when bank-notes are done up for shipment by an experienced clerk, the bills are pressed together as tightly as possible in small bundles, which are secured with elastic bands, and then wrapped snugly in strong paper, until the whole makes a package almost as hard as a board. Around this package the clerk knots strong twine, melts a drop of sealing-wax over each knot, and stamps it with the bank's seal. The finished package thus presents a neat and trim appearance. But in the present instance the package received at the Treasury was loosely and slovenly wrapped, and the seals seemed to have been put on either in great haste or by an inexperienced hand. Moreover, the label must have been cut from the stolen package and pasted on the other, for the brown paper of a previous wrapping showed plainly in a margin running around the label. The address on the package read:

$41,000.
United States Treasurer,
Washington, D.C.

All this was printed, except the figures "41,000," even the dollar-sign. The figures were in the writing of Mr. Watson, the paying-teller of the bank, whose business it was to oversee the sending of the money. His initials were also marked on the label, with the date of the sending; so that on examining the label Mr. Watson himself was positive that it was genuine.

All this made it tolerably clear that the robbery had not been committed at the bank before the package was intrusted to the two messengers; for no bank clerk would have made up so clumsy a package, and the paying-teller himself, had he been a party to the crime, would not have cut the label written by himself from the genuine package and pasted it on the bogus one; he would simply have written out another label, thus lessening the chances of detection. Furthermore, it was shown by testimony that during the short time between the sealing up of the package in the paying-teller's department and its delivery to Dominie Earle, who took it first, it was constantly under the observation of half a dozen bank employees; so that the work of cutting off the label and pasting it on the bogus package could scarcely have been accomplished then without detection.

Earle and Crawford, the bank messengers, were submitted to repeated examinations; but their statements threw no light upon the mystery. Both stuck persistently to the same story, which was that neither had loosed his hold on the handle of the valise from the moment they left the bank until they had delivered the package through the window of the express company's money department. Accepting these statements as true, it was impossible that the package had been tampered with in this part of its journey; while the assumption that they were not true implied apparently a collusion between the two messengers, which was highly improbable, since Dominie Earle had been a servant of the bank for thirty-five years, and had never in that long term failed in his duty or done anything to arouse distrust. Before entering the bank's employ he had been a preacher, and his whole life seemed to have been one of simplicity and honest dealing.

As for Crawford, who was, indeed, a new man, it was plain that if Dominie told the truth, and had really kept his hold on the valise-handle all the way to the express company's window, his companion, honest or dishonest, would have had no opportunity to cut off the label, paste it on the bogus package, and make the substitution.

Finally came the theory that the money package had been stolen while in the care of the express company. In considering this possibility it became necessary to know exactly what had happened to the package from the moment it was taken through the window of the money department up to the time of its delivery at the Treasury. The package was first receipted for by the head of the money department, Mr. J. C. Young. Having handed the receipt to the bank messengers, he passed the package to his assistant, Mr. Littlefield, who in turn passed it on to another clerk, Mr. Moody, who way-billed it in due form for Washington, and then placed it in the iron safe which was to carry it on its journey. Two or three hours may have elapsed between the receipt of the package and the shipment of the safe, but during this time the package was constantly in view of five or six clerks in the money department, and, unless they were all in collusion, it could scarcely have been stolen by anyone there. As for the express messenger who accompanied the safe on the wagon to the train, and then on the train to Washington, and then on another wagon to the Treasury building, his innocence seemed clearly established, since the safe had been locked and sealed, according to custom, before its delivery to him, and showed no signs of having been tampered with when opened in Washington the following morning by another representative of the express company. The messenger who accompanies a through safe to its destination, indeed, has small chance of getting inside, not only because of the protecting seal, but also because he is never allowed to have the key to the safe or to know its combination. Recently, as a still further safeguard, the Adams Express Company has introduced into its cars an equipment of large burglar-proof and fire-proof safes, especially as a guard against train robbers, who found it comparatively easy to break open the small safes once in use. In the present instance, of course, there was no question of train robbers.

One important fact stood out plain and uncontrovertible: that a responsible clerk in the money department of the Adams Express Company had receipted for a package supposed to contain forty-one thousand dollars intrusted to the company by the bank. This threw the responsibility on the company, at least until it could be shown that the package as delivered contained brown paper, and not bank-notes. In accordance with their usual policy of promptness and liberality, the Adams people paid over to the American Exchange Bank the sum of forty-one thousand dollars, and said no more about it. But their silence did not mean inactivity. Their instructions to their detectives in this case, as in all similar cases, were to spare neither time nor expense, but to continue the investigation until the thieves had been detected and brought to punishment, or until the last possibility of clearing up the mystery had certainly expired.

Hastening to New York in response to the telegram sent him, Robert Pinkerton examined the evidence already collected by his representative, and then himself questioned all persons in any way concerned in the handling of the money. Mr. Pinkerton, after his investigation, was not so sure as some persons were that the package had been stolen by employees of the express company. He inclined rather to the opinion that, in the rush of business in the express office, the false package, badly made up though it was, might have been passed by one of the clerks. This conclusion turned his suspicions first toward the two bank messengers. Of these he was not long in deciding Dominie Earle to be, in all probability, innocent. While he had known of instances where old men, after years of unimpeachable life, had suddenly turned to crime, he knew such cases to be infrequent, and he decided that Earle's was not one of them. Of the innocence of the other messenger, Crawford, he was not so sure. He began a careful study of his record.

Edward Sturgis Crawford at this time was about twenty-seven years old, a man of medium height, a decided blond, with large blue eyes, and of a rather effeminate type. He went scrupulously dressed, had white hands with carefully manicured nails, parted his hair in the middle, and altogether was somewhat of a dandy. He had entered the bank on the recommendation of a wealthy New-Yorker, a young man about town, who, strange to say, had made Crawford's acquaintance, and indeed struck up quite a friendship with him, while the latter was serving in the humble capacity of conductor on a Broadway car. This was about a year before the time of the robbery. Thus far Crawford had attended to his work satisfactorily, doing nothing to arouse suspicion, unless it was indulging a tendency to extravagance in dress. His salary was but forty-two dollars a month, and yet he permitted himself such luxuries as silk underclothes, fine patent-leather shoes, and other apparel to correspond. Pushing back further into Crawford's record, Mr. Pinkerton learned that he had grown up in the town of Hancock, New York, where he had been accused of stealing sixty dollars from his employer and afterward of perpetrating a fraud upon an insurance company. Putting all these facts together, Mr. Pinkerton decided that, in spite of a perfectly self-possessed manner and the good opinion of his employers, Crawford would stand further watching. His general conduct subsequent to the robbery was, however, such as to convince everyone, except the dogged detective, that he was innocent of this crime. In vain did "shadows" follow him night and day, week after week; they discovered nothing. He retained his place in the bank, doing the humble duties of messenger with the same regularity as before, and living apparently in perfect content with the small salary he was drawing. His expenses were lightened, it is true, by an arrangement voluntarily offered by his friend, the young man about town, who invited him to live in his own home on Thirty-eighth Street, whereby not only was he saved the ordinary outlay for lodgings, but many comforts and luxuries were afforded him that would otherwise have been beyond his reach.

Thus three months went by with no result; then four, five, six months; and, finally, all but a year. Then, suddenly, in April, 1889, Crawford took his departure for Central America, giving out to his friends that he was going there to assume the management of a banana plantation of sixty thousand acres, owned by his wealthy friend and benefactor.

Before Crawford sailed, however, the "shadows" had informed Mr. Pinkerton of Crawford's intention, and asked instructions. Should they arrest the man before he took flight, or should they let him go? Mr. Pinkerton realized that he was dealing with a man who, if guilty, was a criminal of unusual cleverness and cunning. His arrest would probably accomplish nothing, and might spoil everything. There was little likelihood that the stolen money would be found on Crawford's person; he would probably arrange some safer way for its transmission. Perhaps it had gone ahead of him to Central America weeks before.

"We'll let him go," said Mr. Pinkerton, with a grim smile. "Only we'll have someone go with him."

The Pinkerton representative employed to shadow Crawford on the voyage sent word, by the first mail after their arrival in Central America, that the young man had rarely left his state-room, and that whenever forced to do so had employed a colored servant to stand on guard so that no one could go inside.

Nothing more occurred, however, to justify the suspicion against Crawford until the early part of 1890, when the persistent efforts of the detectives were rewarded by an important discovery. It was then that Robert Pinkerton learned that Crawford had told a deliberate lie when examined before the bank officials in regard to his family relations in New York. He had stated that his only relative in New York was a brother, Marvin Crawford, who was then driving a streetcar on the Bleecker Street line. Now it came to the knowledge of Mr. Pinkerton that Crawford had in the city three married aunts and several cousins. The reason for Crawford's having concealed this fact was presently brought to light through the testimony of one of the aunts, who, having been induced to speak, not without difficulty, stated that on Sunday, May 6, 1888, two days after the robbery, her nephew had called at her house, and given her a package which he said contained gloves, and which he wished her to keep for him. It was about this time that the papers contained the first news of the robbery, and, her suspicions having been aroused, she picked a hole in the paper covering of the package large enough to let her see that there was money inside. Somewhat disturbed, she took the package to her husband, who opened it and found that it contained two thousand dollars in banknotes. Realizing the importance of this discovery, the husband told his wife that when Crawford came back to claim the package she should refer him to him, which she did.

Some days later, on learning from his aunt that she had spoken to her husband about the package, Crawford became greatly excited, and told her she had made a dreadful mistake. A stormy scene followed with his uncle, in which the latter positively refused to render him the money until he was satisfied that Crawford was its rightful possessor. A few days later Crawford's young friend, the man about town, called on the uncle, and stated that the money in the package belonged to him and must be surrendered. The uncle was still obdurate; and when Crawford and his friend became violent in manner, he remarked that if they made any more trouble he would deliver the package of money to the Adams Express Company and let the company decide to whom it belonged. This brought the angry claimants to their senses, and Crawford's friend left the house and never returned. Finally Crawford's uncle compromised the contention by giving his nephew five hundred dollars out of the two thousand, and retaining the balance himself, in payment, one must suppose, for his silence. At any rate, he kept fifteen hundred dollars, and also a receipt in Crawford's handwriting for the five hundred dollars paid to him.

Other members of the family recalled the fact that a few days after the robbery Crawford had left in his aunt's store-room a valise, which he had subsequently called for and taken away. None of them had seen the contents of the valise, but they remembered that Crawford on the second visit had remained alone in the store-room for quite a time, perhaps twenty minutes, and after his departure they found there a rubber band like those used at the bank. The detectives also discovered that on the 15th of May, 1888, eleven days after the robbery, Crawford had rented a safety-deposit box at a bank in the Fifth Avenue Hotel building, under the name of Eugene Holt. On the 18th of May he had exchanged this box for a larger one. During the following months he made several visits to the box, but for what purpose, was not known.

On presenting this accumulated evidence to the Adams Express Company, along with his own deductions, Robert Pinkerton was not long in convincing his employers that the situation required in Central America the presence of some more adroit detective than had yet been sent there. The difficulty of the case was heightened by the fact that Crawford had established himself in British Honduras, and that the extradition treaty between the United States and England did not then, as it does now, provide for the surrender of criminals guilty of such offenses as that which Crawford was believed to have committed. Crawford could be arrested, therefore, only by being gotten into another country by some clever maneuver. The man best capable of carrying out such a maneuver was Robert Pinkerton himself; and, accordingly, the express company, despite the very considerable expense involved, and fully aware that the result must be uncertain, authorized Mr. Pinkerton to go personally in pursuit of Crawford.

Mr. Pinkerton arrived at Balize, the capital of British Honduras, on February 17, 1890, nearly two years after the date of the robbery. There he learned that Crawford's plantation was about ninety miles down the coast, a little back of Punta Gorda. Punta Gorda lies near the line separating British Honduras from Guatemala, and is not more than a hundred miles from Spanish Honduras, or Honduras proper, directly across the Gulf of Honduras.

Difficulties confronted Mr. Pinkerton from the very start. People were dying about him every day of yellow fever, and when he started for Punta Gorda on a little steamer, the engineer came aboard looking as yellow as saffron, and immediately began to vomit, so that he had to be taken ashore. Then the engine broke down several times on the voyage, and the heat was insufferable.

As the boat steamed slowly into Punta Gorda it passed a small steam craft loaded with bananas. "Look," said one of the passengers to Mr. Pinkerton, not aware of the nature of Mr. Pinkerton's mission, "there goes Crawford's launch now."

Landing at once, the detective waited for the launch to come to shore, which it presently did. The first man to come off was Marvin Crawford, whom Mr. Pinkerton recognized from a description, although he had never seen him. Then he saw Edward Crawford step off, dressed smartly in a white helmet hat, a red sash, a fine plaited linen shirt, blue trousers, patent-leather shoes, and so on. Mr. Pinkerton approached and held out his hand.

"I don't remember you," said Crawford; but his face went white.

"You used to know me in New York when I examined you before the bank officials," said the detective, pleasantly.

Crawford smiled in a sickly way and said, "Oh, yes; I remember you now."

Mr. Pinkerton explained that he had traveled five thousand miles to talk with him about the stolen money package. Crawford expressed willingness to furnish any information he could, and invited Mr. Pinkerton to go up to his plantation, where they could talk the matter over more comfortably. Seeing that his best course was to humor Crawford, Mr. Pinkerton consented, though realizing that he thus put himself in Crawford's power. They went aboard Crawford's launch and steamed up the river, a very narrow, winding stream, arched quite over through most of its length by the thick tropical foliage, and in some parts so deep that no soundings had yet found bottom. The plantation was entirely inaccessible by land on account of impassable swamps, and the crooked course of the river made it a journey of twenty-three miles from Punta Gorda, although in a straight line it was only six miles away.

Mr. Pinkerton was surprised at the unpretentious character of the house, which was built of cane and palm stocks and roofed with palm branches. Originally it had been one large room, but it was now divided by muslin sheeting into two rooms, one at either end, with a hall in the middle. Almost the first thing Mr. Pinkerton noticed on entering was a fire-proof safe standing in the hall. It was of medium size and seemed to be new. He knew he was powerless, under the laws of the country, to search the safe, but he made up his mind that while he was in the house he would keep his eyes as much as possible upon it. That night he did not sleep for watching. But Crawford did not go near the safe until the next morning, when he went to get out some account-books. While the door was open Mr. Pinkerton saw only a small bag of silver inside, but he felt sure from Crawford's manner that there was a larger amount of money there.

Mr. Pinkerton remained at the plantation for forty-eight hours. On the second day he had a long interview with Crawford, questioning him in the greatest detail as to his connection with the robbery. Crawford persisted in denying that he had had any connection with it, or had any knowledge as to what had become of the stolen money. Argue as he would, Mr. Pinkerton could not beat down the stubbornness of his denials. All direct approaches failing, at last he tried indirection. He spoke of Burke, the absconding State treasurer of Louisiana, who, along with a number of other American law-breakers, had fled to Central America. "Burke had a level head, hadn't he?" said he.

"How do you mean?" asked Crawford.

"Why, in going to Spanish Honduras. You know the United States has no extradition treaty there under which we could bring back a man who has absconded for embezzlement or grand larceny. Burke is as safe there as if he owned the whole country."

"Is that so?" said Crawford, looking significantly at his brother Marvin, who was present.

"Yes," said Mr. Pinkerton, "it is. I only wish the fellow would come up here into British Honduras; then we might do something with him."

Here the subject was dropped.

Next Mr. Pinkerton exhibited to Crawford a sealed letter written by James G. Blaine and addressed to the chief magistrate of British Honduras, pointing to the seals of the State Department to assure Crawford of the letter's genuineness, and hinting mysteriously at the use he proposed making of this document and at the probable effect that would follow its delivery.

With this the interview closed, and Mr. Pinkerton announced his intention of going back to Punta Gorda. Crawford had practically told him to do his worst, and he had not concealed his intention of doing it. Nevertheless their relations continued outwardly pleasant, and Mr. Pinkerton was treated with the hospitality that is usual in tropical countries. He saw no sign of any disposition on the part of either of the Crawfords to do him harm, but he kept his revolvers always ready, and gave them no chance to catch him napping.

Toward evening of the second day Crawford and his brother got the launch ready, and took Mr. Pinkerton down the river back to Punta Gorda, where they said good-bye. At parting Crawford made a brave show of treating the whole matter lightly. "I may see you in New York in a couple of months," he said to the detective as they shook hands.

"If you see me in New York," said Mr. Pinkerton, "you will see yourself under arrest."

On landing, Mr. Pinkerton proceeded, with all the obviousness possible, to call at the house of the British magistrate, which was so situated that Crawford from the launch could not fail to see him enter. This seems to have confirmed the impression he had been striving to create, that British Honduras, though in truth a perfect refuge for a criminal like

Crawford, was none. Crawford, apparently thoroughly frightened, and thinking he had not an hour to lose, steamed back in all haste to his plantation, gathered together, as subsequently appeared, his money and other valuables, and then, under cover of night, dropped down the river again, put out to sea forthwith, and crossed the Bay of Honduras to Puerto Cortés, in Spanish Honduras, the country of all Central America in which Mr. Pinkerton preferred to have him. In short, Mr. Pinkerton's stratagem had worked perfectly.

Mr. Pinkerton's reason for wishing to get Crawford into Spanish Honduras was not because the treaty arrangements were more favorable there than in British Honduras, but because the Pinkerton Agency enjoyed unusual personal relations with the Honduras government. Several years before, when President Bogram had in contemplation the federation of Central American States under one government, he had applied to the Pinkerton Agency for reliable detectives for secret-service work. In consequence of this the present head of the Honduras secret force was no other than a former Pinkerton employee who had been recommended by the New York office to the Honduras government, and upon whom Mr. Pinkerton knew he could rely absolutely. Another man equally disposed to favor him was Mr. Bert Cecil, a member of the cabinet, and at the head of the telegraph service, and thus in a position to render most valuable service in the apprehension of Crawford.

As soon as Mr. Pinkerton learned of Crawford's flight, he hurried in pursuit, crossing the bay to Livingston, in Guatemala. In so doing he risked his life, first by putting out to sea in a little dory, and then by trusting his safety to a treacherous Carib boatman, who, when they were several miles out, evinced a strong disposition to take possession of the detective's overcoat, in order, as he explained with a cunning look, to turn its silk lining into a pair of trousers. At this, Mr. Pinkerton carelessly produced his revolver, which had a quieting effect upon the fellow, and the voyage was completed in safety. But soon after landing Mr. Pinkerton suffered an attack of fever, and being warned by the doctors to return to a Northern latitude, he got the government machinery in motion for the apprehension of Crawford, had photographs of the former bank messenger broadcast through the country, and then, having cabled the New York bureau to send responsible detectives to take his place, he sailed for New Orleans.

Mr. Pinkerton was succeeded in Central America by detective George H. Hotchkiss, one of the best men in the country, who arrived in Balize on the 18th of March. A telegram from Pinkerton's former employee, now chief of the secret police in Honduras, informed him that Crawford had been seen in San Pedro, Spanish Honduras, on the previous Saturday, and was being closely pursued by Spanish soldiers accompanied by Pinkerton men. Hotchkiss sailed at once for Puerto Cortés, where he learned from the American vice-consul, Dr. Ruez, that Crawford had left San Pedro hastily the previous Monday night. On further investigation the detective discovered that a San Francisco bully and former prize-fighter, "Mike" Neiland, had called at Crawford's boarding-house on Monday, and warned him that detectives were pursuing him from Puerto Cortés on a hand-car. Neiland had pretended to be Crawford's friend, and said he would keep him out of the hands of the detectives. Crawford, very much frightened, grabbed up some of his luggage and left the house with Neiland. It was generally believed that Neiland had designs on Crawford's money, and would not hesitate to kill him, if need were, in order to get it.

Hotchkiss immediately requested Mr. Bert Cecil, at Tegucigalpa, the capital, to cover all telegraphic points, and, if possible, have Crawford and his companion arrested on some trivial charge. The day after he reached San Pedro, on March 22, he received a telegram saying that Crawford and Neiland had been arrested and taken before the governor at Santa Barbara. They had been searched, and about thirty-two thousand dollars had been found on Crawford's person. The money was in old and worn bills that in every way resembled those in the stolen package. Whether they were the identical bills or not it was impossible to say, as the bank had not recorded the numbers.

On receipt of this news, Hotchkiss, accompanied by Jack Hall, a guide, set out across the country for Santa Barbara. The journey was accomplished, but only after the most terrible suffering and many privations and dangers. Moreover, the fever got its deadly clutches upon detective Hotchkiss; and when he had finally dragged himself into Santa Barbara, he cabled the New York office: "Crawford and money held for extradition. Am sick. Cannot remain. Coming on steamer Tuesday. My associate takes charge."

Before sailing for New Orleans detective Hotchkiss had an interview with Crawford, in the presence of the Spanish officials, and obtained from him a written confession of his guilt. While admitting that he had been a party to the robbery, the absconder tried to lessen his own crime by declaring that the plan to plunder the bank had been suggested to him by two men, named Brown and Bowen, whom he had met accidentally on a railway-train in New York, and with whom he had afterward become very friendly. These men had taken him to Brown's house on Thirty-eighth Street, somewhere between Eighth and Ninth Avenues (Crawford could not locate the place more precisely), and introduced him to a fine-looking woman presented as Mrs. Brown, who was also in the conspiracy. They told him that he was earning very little money for a man in such a responsible position, and that he might easily make a fortune if he would put his interests in their hands and be guided by their advice.

The outcome of several conversations was a plan to get possession of a valuable money package on some day when Crawford should know a large sum was to be sent away from the bank. He claimed that on the day of the robbery one of his fellow-conspirators, Bowen, followed behind himself and Earle after they entered the Adams express offices, and managed to substitute a bogus package for the real one while the two messengers were going up the stairs. He did not make this attempt until he saw the bank detective McDougal turn back up Broadway. Crawford said that he managed it so as to precede Earle in going up the stairs, which gave Bowen, who was standing at the first turn, in the shadow, an opportunity to open the satchel and quickly make the substitution. Crawford declared that the conspirators gave him only twenty-five hundred dollars as his share of the booty, although promising him more. This sum he put in two envelopes and sent to his aunt, the one to whom he afterward intrusted the package supposed to contain gloves.

Crawford stated further that Brown and Bowen, having been forced to flee the country, sent him word from Paris, some time later, in a letter written by Mrs. Brown, that the greater part of the stolen money had been buried in a flower-bed in the southeast corner of a yard on West

Thirty-eighth Street, and asked him to dig it up and send it to them. A remarkable fact in this connection is that the yard referred to on West Thirty-eighth Street belonged to the house of the friend and benefactor with whom Crawford was living at the time of the robbery.

Crawford claimed to have carried out these instructions, and deposited the package of money taken from the flower-bed in the safe deposit vaults in the Fifth Avenue Hotel building, where, as a matter of fact, he was known to have rented a box. He gave as his reason for not sending the money to Paris that he was in trouble himself, being under constant surveillance, and thought it best to keep the money secreted for the time. He admitted that he had carried this money with him to Honduras, and that it was the same found on his person by the detectives. By his description of Brown and Bowen, the former was a man about twenty-five years old, of slight build and light complexion, while the latter was ten years older, two or three inches taller, with a sandy mustache and very fat hands. Mrs. Brown Crawford described as about twenty-five years old, a blonde, with regular features. He had no idea what had become of these people since he left America, having had no further communication with them. None of the alleged conspirators has ever been found, and they are believed to be purely mythical.

Detective Hotchkiss also had an interview with "Mike" Neiland, Crawford's companion in flight, who described his first meeting with Crawford at his boarding-house in San Pedro, and acknowledged that he had deliberately frightened Crawford into running away by his story of the pursuing detectives. He described their adventures and hardships in trying to escape over the rough country, the difficulties they experienced in buying mules, their sufferings from exposure in the swamps, and finally their capture by the soldiers. Neiland said that Crawford gave him three thousand dollars in fifty-dollar bills, and also allowed him to carry, a part of the time, a large package wrapped in oil-cloth paper and sewed up tightly. Crawford had told him to throw this package away rather than let anyone capture it; for, he said, it contained money which would send him to prison if found upon him.

As they pushed along in their flight, Crawford declared repeatedly that he would put an end to his life rather than be taken prisoner; and when the soldiers surrounded them he drew his revolver and tried to blow his brains out. One of the soldiers, however, was too quick for him, and struck the weapon out of his hand. After the capture Crawford vainly tried to bribe the guards to let him escape, offering them as much as ten thousand dollars. When the large package was opened, it was found to contain bundles of bills sewed together with black thread, and with about a dozen rubber bands wrapped around them, and a stout covering of buckskin under the oiled paper. The money amounted to thirty-two thousand five hundred dollars, all in United States bills—fives, tens, twenties, fifties, and hundreds, but mostly fives. Ultimately the money was returned to the American Exchange Bank.

When organizing the pursuit of Crawford, detective Hotchkiss had arranged with the Honduras government that any letters and telegrams that might come addressed to the absconder should be delivered to him. Several letters were thus secured from the young man about town in New York who had befriended Crawford so constantly in the past, and who seemed now disposed to stand by him even in adversity and disgrace. The letters contained counsel and reproaches, and seemed to indicate that relations of unusual familiarity had existed between the two men. Besides these letters, two cablegrams were intercepted from the same source, both being sent through an intermediary. The first was dated March 15, 1890, and read: "Tell Crawford go back. Papers bluff. No treaty exists." The second, sent two days later, read: "Inform Crawford will meet him in Puerto Cortés."

It is needless to say that the young man did not carry out his intention of joining Crawford in Honduras, for the same mail which would have brought him Crawford's reply carried the startling news that his protégé and friend was under arrest in Santa Barbara, a self-confessed bank robber.

The government of Honduras consented, thanks to their friendly relations with the Pinkertons, to deliver Crawford over to one of the representatives of the agency, and superintendent E. S. Gaylor, who had meantime replaced detective Hotchkiss, took him in charge. A guard of Spanish soldiers brought the prisoner to Puerto Cortés, where he was placed in a hotel pending his transfer to a vessel sailing for the United

States. Superintendent Gaylor himself was present to see that everything was managed properly, and he was seconded in his oversight by the former Pinkerton employee, the head of the secret police in Honduras. The final arrangements had been made, the government having taken advantage of a law authorizing the expulsion of "pernicious foreigners" in order to get rid of Crawford. The superintendent had actually taken passage for himself and Crawford, and selected berths, on an American vessel that was to sail on the morning of May 2, 1890; but the night before Crawford made his escape from the hotel, going without the money, which remained in the detective's keeping. How he escaped is still a matter of conjecture. The hotel stood on the water's edge, and from a balcony to which Crawford had access he may have managed to spring down to a wall built on piles. From there he may have reached the hotel yard at the back, and escaped over one of the picket fences that separated the hotel from the adjoining property. There is also a possibility that the Spanish soldiers were bribed; but this has never been proved, and is scarcely probable, as Crawford at the time of his escape had not more than seventy-five dollars in Honduras bills in his possession.

During the following days and weeks untiring efforts were made to recapture him. The swamps were searched for miles, and soldiers were sent out in all directions. Mr. Gaylor believed that Crawford succeeded in making his escape into Guatemala, which was only thirty miles distant. He was undoubtedly assisted in his escape by the fact that people in the surrounding region sympathized strongly with him and would have done anything in their power to conceal him from his pursuers. At any rate, the man was never recovered.

Seven years have passed since Crawford's escape, and all this time he has been left undisturbed in Central America, where he has been frequently seen by people who know him, and where he seems to be thriving. At last accounts he and his brother were engaged in business on one of the islands in the Mosquito Reservation of Nicaragua, where they were regarded as dangerous men by the government, likely to incite revolution. So strong was this feeling on the part of the Nicaraguan officials that some years ago advances were made to the United States government to have Crawford surrendered, the Nicaraguan officials declaring that they would gladly give him up if a demand for his extradition was made by the proper authorities in Washington. For some reason the demand has never been made, and probably never will be.

Immediately after Crawford had made confession, the American Exchange Bank, realizing that there was no longer any doubt that the robbery was committed by one of its employees, voluntarily refunded to the Adams Express Company the forty-one thousand dollars that had previously been paid to it by the company, together with interest thereon for two years, and a large part of the expenses. Therefore the only complainant in the case now available would be the bank officials, who, for some reason, have seen fit to let the matter drop.

Mr. Pinkerton's theory of the way in which this robbery was committed is that Crawford had an accomplice who had previously prepared the bogus package, and who, by previous appointment, was standing on the stairs in the express office when the two messengers arrived. It has always been a question in Mr. Pinkerton's mind whether the old man Dominie Earle told the exact truth in his testimony before the bank officials. Not that he suspected Earle of having been implicated in the crime, but he has wondered whether Earle might not have been simply negligent to the extent of leaving Crawford in sole possession of the valise at some time after they entered the office. There is no doubt that Earle was very anxious to catch a four-o'clock train at one of the New Jersey ferries, in order to get home early. He may, in his haste, have allowed Crawford to go upstairs with the valise unaccompanied.

This would explain how Crawford found opportunity to open the valise and make substitution of the bogus for the genuine package. Assuming that the accomplice was standing at a turn of the stairs, which are winding and rather dusky, it is perfectly conceivable that such a change of packages might have been effected with scarcely a moment's delay.

But consenting that Earle told the exact truth, he admitted that he lingered behind Crawford a little in ascending the stairs, and in so doing he may have furnished sufficient opportunity for the substitution. An old man going up rather steep stairs naturally bends his head forward to relieve the ascent, and in such position he might fail to see what a man close in front of him even was doing. The trouble with this theory is that it supposes the label on the bogus package to have been a forgery.

There is still another theory suggested by Mr. Pinkerton to account for the presence of the bogus money package in the valise when the two messengers reached the counter of the receiving department. It is that Crawford's confederate had provided himself with a second valise, similar in all respects to the one used by the bank, and that in this had been placed the bogus package with a forged label, making the substitution a matter of merely changing valises, which could have been accomplished in a second. It has also been suggested that Crawford might have managed the whole scheme himself, by having prepared a valise like the one he carried daily, arranged with two compartments, in one of which was placed the genuine package received from the paying-teller at the bank, while out of the other compartment was taken at the express office a bogus package previously placed there. What makes it the more reasonable to suppose that Crawford accomplished the theft single-handed is the fact that when arrested in Honduras the bulk of the stolen money was found on his person, while it was known that, in addition to the thirty-two thousand dollars then recovered, he had previously spent considerable sums in various ways. His voyage, for instance, must have been expensive; and it was found that he had given at various times to members of his family sums ranging from twenty to fifty dollars. This would have left out of the original forty-one thousand dollars a very meager remuneration for a confederate.

Perhaps the most reasonable explanation of the robbery lies in the assumption that Dominie Earle, honest, but simple-minded, did not go upstairs at all with Crawford, but left him at the foot of the stairs, influenced by his eagerness to get home. Granting this supposition, what would have been easier than for Crawford, left alone at the foot of the stairs, to have turned back with the valise and gone into the back room of some neighboring saloon, or other convenient place, where he could manipulate the label and substitute the bogus package? There is reason to think that the bogus package had been prepared weeks before, which would have accounted in a measure for its worn and slovenly appearance. The time occupied in doing all this need not have been over fifteen minutes, which would not have been noticed at the bank, especially as the robbery occurred after banking hours. It is highly improbable, however, that Crawford could have accomplished the substitution on the stairs of the express office; for, while these are winding and somewhat in the shadow, they are by no means dark, and are plainly in view of clerks and officials who are constantly passing. Besides that, Crawford could not have carried the dummy package concealed about his person without attracting attention, for the original package was quite bulky, being about twenty inches long, twenty inches wide, and fourteen inches thick. The bogus package was not quite so thick, and more oblong, but could not easily have been hidden under a man's coat. Finally, even supposing Crawford did carry the bogus package with him in some manner, he would never have dared to expose himself to almost certain detection by cutting off the label from the genuine package, pasting it on the bogus package, placing the latter in the valise, and hiding the genuine one in his clothes—and doing all this on the busy stairs of an express office where at that hour of the day a dozen men are going up and down every minute.

The sum of all these theories is, however, that, in spite of the fact that the author of the robbery is known and the bulk of the money has been recovered, the manner of the robbery is to this day a mystery.

FIVE

The Last Good Heist

Tim White, Randall Richard, and Wayne Worcester

DEUCE IS DEPRESSED. HE IS CONVINCED THAT COMING TO RHODE Island is the worst move he has made in years, and he's got a few bad ones to pick from. He's batting zero on both of the jobs he's taken. First, hitting Sciarra, though he's just as glad that didn't work out because he hasn't killed anyone before. Then there was the fiasco at the coin shop, which should have gone like clockwork.

How could he know Lanoue would blow up on him? He figures Lanoue is his biggest liability, but he sort of likes the old guy. He's funny, and he doesn't put up with much crap from anybody. Thing is, he just never seems to stay on the same track for too long, kind of flits from one thing to another, sort of in control, sort of not. So over the weekend, Deuce takes him aside and starts selling him on the notion that as driver of the getaway van, Lanoue has the key role in the heist, more important, in fact, than anybody else's.

"Everything you do," Deuce says, "is going to make the difference between us pulling off this job or getting caught with our pants down." He has Lanoue drive the route to and from Bonded Vault more than a dozen times, every time repeatedly going over the details of the guy's job.

Deuce tells him flatly and forcefully, "When everyone's in the truck, you're the boss. You call the shots. There's no talking." He reminds Lanoue to make sure the men put on their coveralls and masks before they leave the van, and he says they must walk to the building in pairs about a minute apart so as not to attract attention. He warns Lanoue to stay alert and, if he sees anything really suspicious, to come in and get him.

The getaway should be simple too. Lanoue is to help load everything into the van then drive the men to their three cars, which will have been parked nearby in different spots around the block. Then he is to drive slowly back to the hideout.

Lanoue laps it up, and Deuce is convinced the old man will be okay. With Lanoue more or less neutralized, Deuce tries to relax a little.

The next day, Monday, August 11, Ouimette stops by, tells the crew they will hit Bonded Vault first thing Wednesday morning, August 13, and gives them five hundred dollars. Deuce and Byrnes go shopping for the tools they'll need for the break-in—a few crowbars; a couple of power drills with the hardest bits available; long, heavy-duty extension cords; and sets of dark worker's coveralls. They go out of state, to stores in New London and Groton, Connecticut, figuring that by changing the venues they will throw police investigators off their scent.

Back at the hideout, Deuce fills toolboxes for the crew and goes over the plan he and Chucky came up with. He reminds everyone that if they need to speak with one another on the job, they are to use the name "Harry." That's everyone's name, "Harry." If they can shut up altogether, that's even better.

Lanoue, in his stolen van, is to pick up the men as they drop off their three cars, then drive everyone to Cranston Street. He'll park the van down the road just out of sight of the building. When he sees the first of the men come out to the curb with a full bag, he will ease the vehicle up the street and stop in front of the building. Until then, Lanoue is to simply sit, watch, and wait.

On August 12, the day before the heist, Ouimette tells Flynn and Deuce the score will have to wait a day because somebody higher up the food chain needs time to get his machine gun out of one of the safe deposit boxes.

"It'd bring too much heat if it got left behind," Ouimette says.

Deuce lets loose with a string of obscenities. He doesn't believe the machine gun story. Except for Byrnes, everybody involved in the robbery has a rap sheet you could wallpaper a small room with. They get caught with cap pistols, it's all over. And now it's time to worry about a machine gun?

He figures somebody's moving valuable goods to safety. He has been on edge anyway, and now he is seething, his mind racing. He feels as though he's about to explode again when Byrnes bursts into the house.

"We just blew the truck," he announces. "We were cleaning it out, and some cop in the neighborhood spotted us standing next to it. If the cop remembers, he'll be able to make us when they find the truck after the score."

The men agree to steal a new van. The task goes to Walter Ouimette. They have to wait another day anyway, thanks to the supposed machine gun problem. As soon as everyone leaves, Deuce tries a final time to talk Chucky out of the job. He might as well have struck up a conversation with a gravestone.

Exasperated, Deuce calls a cab and announces to Chucky that he's going out to buy some Chinese chicken wings.

Thirty minutes later, at Ming Garden, a popular Chinese restaurant on Kennedy Plaza in downtown Providence, Deuce asks for a double order of chicken wings and sits down to wait. Ten minutes later, order in hand, he walks outside and signals another cab. He climbs in the back, and the taxi heads out. The muffler is loud enough to announce the Second Coming. Less than a mile from Flynn's hideout, the cab is stopped by East Providence police officers. Turns out, the taxi's taillights don't work either; the cops spotted that even before they could hear the car.

Deuce cracks open the rear door, letting out a scrumptious aroma cloud of soy and ginger. He tells the two patrolmen that if it's all the same to them, he'd just as soon walk home with his chicken wings; no hard feelings. He says his kids are waiting for him and they're hungry. He puts one foot on the pavement and starts to get out of the cab.

"Stay right there, sir," one of the cops says. "Get back in the vehicle, please."

Deuce winces but obliges.

The patrolman sneers at the cab and tells the driver curtly, "What a piece of junk. I should order you off the road."

"No," says the other man, a patrol sergeant. "Just give him a citation. This guy's family's waiting for supper."

Deuce mutters his thanks to the cops. He exhales and sinks back into the car seat. He has lost his appetite. He leaves the double order of chicken wings on the kitchen table and tells Chucky he needs a good night's sleep.

"All I got to say is, if things don't go any better tomorrow, Charles, we're royally fucked."

"It'll be fine, Deuce," Chucky says. "We're going to get rich."

———

At precisely 8:00 a.m. a man named Sam Levine opens his Bonded Vault. The door to it is a massive, foot-thick slab of molded stainless steel weighing seven tons, fourteen thousand pounds. It would take high explosives to go through it. He dials the lock combination, and perfectly machined tumblers turn. The doors unlock. Furs worth hundreds of thousands of dollars hang on racks inside, and just beyond is an inner sanctum, a rectangle about the size of the average ranch house living room. It contains about 150 safe deposit boxes of varying sizes, most very large.

As Levine returns to his office around the corner, a dark green panel van pulls up to the curb out of sight and down the street. Traffic is slight. There are no pedestrians. The air in the closed van is stifling, hot, and there's not nearly enough of it for the comfort of eight men. Lanoue is driving. Deuce is beside him. Chucky, Tillinghast, Danese, Tarzian, Macaskill, and Byrnes are packed in behind them.

They have parked three cars at prearranged sites around the block and joined everyone else in the van, so now it holds eight men. They are in an ugly mood, nervous and growing more short-tempered by the second. Even Deuce, though calm is what he's paid for. He sits in relative silence, as though alone. The other men are big or wide, some both, except for Macaskill, who is skinny and tall. They are not built for tight places or quick wardrobe changes. Their dark worker's coveralls, masks, and the tools they bought with John Ouimette's five hundred dollars cover the floor.

One of the men falls into another while trying to fit into a jumpsuit. The guy responds with a hard push. One push begets another, and then another. Every move is punctuated by a loud obscenity. In moments the men are pushing and shoving each other into the walls, which makes the van rock and lurch erratically from side to side.

The fighting enrages Lanoue. He has been assured that he is the boss of the van. No talking, he had told the men; not a word, not a goddamned solitary word. And here they are, cursing and shouting and making the van jerk around like a four-wheeled advertisement for trouble.

He tries to outshout them. "Do what the hell I fucking tell you, hey."

The men decline.

"Shut the fuck up," says one.

"Yeah, you little French fuck. Who the fuck you think you are?"

"Shut the fuck up," orders another.

"Hey, you the boss now, you little shit?"

This greatly displeases Lanoue, so he shouts even louder.

"You miserable sons of bitches, you . . ."

Deuce has had enough.

"Knock it off! All of you. Jesus H. Christ! Knock it off, or I swear to God I'll kill somebody."

As far as anyone knows, Deuce has never shot anybody, nor has he killed anyone, but that doesn't mean he couldn't, and it certainly doesn't mean he wouldn't.

The men don't really give a damn. At least three of them have killed before and would again without hesitation. Two of them are especially good at it. But what they all know for sure, and not from watching B-grade movies, is that when somebody carrying a gun gets really pissed off in close quarters, there are only two choices: Kill him or do what he says. As options go, the former isn't viable, what with Deuce being Chucky's appointed leader and all, so, if only for the moment, the men quiet down.

Deuce is wishing he were safely back in prison where things are predictable enough to make uncertainty something to fear. What you don't know can kill you. In his gut, he worries that what he doesn't know about this job could turn it into a mass suicide.

He still would dearly like to leave the entire crew to its own inevitable destruction, but the prospect of a big score is just too much to pass up. Wealth trumps all. Deuce knows he is in it for the distance now. He twists halfway around in his seat and turns to Chucky. Flynn is staring straight ahead. He's wide-eyed, tight-lipped, and wound tighter than a hangman's noose.

"I'll see you in thirty seconds," Deuce says.

Chucky nods sharply just once.

Deuce moves, opens the door of the van, and steps out into the muggy heat of the August morning.

Cranston Street is still quiet. Deuce tries to roll the tension out of his shoulders. He rocks his head from side to side, like a boxer loosening up. From behind blue-tinted sunglasses, he surveys the street then walks straight toward Bonded Vault. He's wearing a new light-gray suit and carrying a leather valise under his right arm, tightly, because the revolver Chucky gave him is inside. Deuce doesn't look threatening, just intent, all business; but as he walks toward the building, he is nervous, his mind racing, running through everything that has brought him to this, the unlikeliest of places, looking to score big.

He's thinking that maybe, just maybe, this is *the* job, the one every crook longs for but never gets. His mind races. What if . . .? What if, when all is said and done, he has been born just for this one gig and it turns out to be gigantic? Why not dream a little?

He disregards the "Closed for Vacation" sign and opens the front door to the office. The room is washed in sunlight and bright fluorescent overhead light. Deuce steps up to the counter. Normally, fifteen people would be working, but with vacation there are only five. The owner is Sam Levine. He looks up from his desk and gives Deuce a look that's somewhere between condescension and boredom, as if to ask, "Can nobody read the sign?"

"Can I help you?" Levine asks.

Deuce pays him no attention. He puts his valise on the counter and opens it. He pulls a slip of paper from the breast pocket of his suit and studies it. He has the names of some mobbed-up guys whose deposit boxes Ouimette has said not to miss: Jerome Geller, the Bingo Man, Babe Kowal, Mike Ross.

Deuce squints at the piece of paper and, feigning difficulty, tries to softly read the names aloud. Levine grimaces with annoyance and leaves his desk. He walks over to the counter, leans forward to read the note, and Deuce quickly pushes the barrel of his revolver into the little man's nose.

"Touch any alarm button, and I'll blow your head off," Deuce says.

Levine turns white and starts shaking. "You don't know how bad this is, what you are doing," he says.

"Where's the alarm?" Deuce asks softly.

Levine slowly and unsteadily raises an arm and points toward a button midway up the far wall.

"Who else is in the building?"

Levine says there are four other people. His brother Hyman and his sister-in-law Rosalind are at their desks in smaller offices off the corridor. His brother Abraham and the firm's attractive young secretary and apprentice furrier, Barbara Oliva, are about to move a rack of furs through the massive door of the vault.

Deuce orders Sam Levine to call everyone into the office, one at a time. First Hyman, then Rosalind and Abraham. Barbara Oliva hears her name but thinks Sam is mistaken and probably wants only his brother. She turns back to get another rack of furs. Suddenly, Deuce is right beside her.

"Oh, no," Deuce says. "You too."

"Why?" she asks.

Deuce answers with his handgun. He points it straight at her. "Because I said so."

The .38 is only inches from the young woman's face, so she can't help but look straight at it. Without taking her eyes from the revolver, she asks softly, "Are those real bullets in that gun?"

"Are you a fucking comedian?"

Oliva's first thought is that she will not live to see her children again, and that this man with the gun is going to be the reason. She is scared and angry in parts approximately equal. She moves her gaze from the revolver to the man holding it. With only a slight tremor in her voice she says, "I've seen guns before. Get that goddamned thing out of my face."

At that instant, before Deuce can say anything or exercise his preference, which would be to slap the pretty blonde across the face, he catches movement on the periphery of his vision. Through the office window he sees Chucky walking quickly toward the building, mask in hand.

Deuce growls at Oliva and, using his gun as a pointer, herds her into the cluster of hostages. Chucky comes through the door struggling with his nylon stocking mask. Oliva notices him and stares straight at him. Chucky moves down the corridor out of sight for an instant then returns, his mask in place and gun in hand.

The two crooks seat their five captives in a semicircle of chairs. Deuce hands out flimsy pillowcases and tells everyone but Sam Levine to put them over their heads. Chucky is looking in every direction at once, taking in the entire office in short darting glances.

The first two-man team should have arrived from the van by now. Two minutes pass. Then another. And another. Deuce and Chucky look at each other. It is the first punch of panic. They wait.

Inside the van, there's mayhem. In fact, there is mutiny. Mitch Lanoue is inching the vehicle along the curb of Cranston Street. The nose of the van is in plain sight from the office window. Deuce and Chucky see it creeping along and realize what's happening. The job is going bad fast. There will be blood. Deuce can see it in Chucky's eyes.

Flynn catches Oliva staring at him. He says to Deuce, "You tell her not to look at me or I'm going to blow her fucking head off."

Oliva needs no prompting. She turns her gaze straight down at the floor. Deuce lowers the gun and adjusts the pillowcase over her head. She is slightly claustrophobic. She gasps and starts to shake. "Please don't make me wear this," she says.

"You have to," Deuce replies.

Outside, Lanoue is a split second from hitting the gas pedal when Joe Danese's anger at the situation rolls through him and blows out like a clap of thunder.

"Crazy Joe" pulls out a hidden snub-nosed .38 and shouts, "Stop. Stop the van. You motherfuckers are going in right now. I'll kill every one of you if you don't fucking move. Get out. Do it. Now!"

The men throw open the doors of the van and tumble onto the pavement, even as the vehicle is stopping. They leave the doors wide open and Lanoue nearly hysterical. He jumps from the van, runs around slamming the doors shut, calling out, "You goddamned sons of bitches, you! Fucking know-nothing assholes. *Sacré bleu!*"

The five men are bogged down with their duffels, a suitcase, an oversize bag, toolboxes, and crowbars. They're stumbling and banging into one another. They all hit the front door at once. They look like the Three Stooges all trying to get through a narrow doorway at the same time. After more swearing and pushing, they manage to get through. They pass the door in single file, each man peering into the office.

Deuce glowers at them; Chucky stares, his eyes like bullets. He's rigid with anger. His arm is extended as straight as a railroad directional aimed at the vault. The masked men look quickly away as they pass.

Deuce turns back to his captives.

"Sam, keep your eyes on the floor," he tells Levine.

Barbara Oliva is weeping softly.

Flynn lifts the hood above her eyes again.

He asks if she's okay.

"I . . . I'm all right," Oliva says.

She looks out into the room again before Deuce lowers the flimsy pillowcase.

Chucky heads for the inner sanctum where the safe deposit boxes are. Minutes later, banging and the sound of electric drills drift out of Bonded Vault.

The biggest heist as of this date in US history finally is under way.

———

Deuce looks at Sam Levine and is glad he didn't make him wear a pillowcase. The old man's color is bad, ranging from gray to white and almost a sickly yellow-green. Deuce needs him free should unexpected business arrive. Now, especially with the rising heat of the morning, Deuce thinks Sam might have died with his head inside a pillowcase. Levine is leaning against the edge of his desk, shaking his head, his eyes fixed on the floor, and he keeps repeating, "You don't know the trouble you bring me." Over and over.

Deuce worries that if he doesn't help him take his mind off the predicament he's in, Sam will either get sick all over the place or have a heart attack. The last thing Deuce wants is for anybody to die on this gig, at least not accidentally. But what to say? What to do? Calm him down, Deuce decides. So he says, "I realize you're upset, Sam, but you know, this is a hell of a way for me to make a living too."

Levine squints at the gunman, terminally perplexed and feeling all the worse for it.

Suddenly the glass front door opens with a bang.

Levine jumps to his feet. The other hostages are startled. Oliva whimpers. Deuce twists toward the door and moves his trigger finger inside the guard of his revolver.

In rushes Lanoue. In a stage whisper that probably can be heard all over the building, he tells Deuce he believes someone has been watching him. The gunman peers out the door and sees a derelict weaving along the sidewalk, straight down the street but more than a block away.

"That son of a bitch couldn't even crawl this far," Deuce shouts. "Goddammit, Harry, get back out there and do your fucking job."

Lanoue turns and leaves. Deuce watches Lanoue through the window as he scrambles toward the van, then he turns back to the hostages. This time the problem is Hyman Levine. He appears to be doing worse than Sam; his breathing is labored. He's sweating profusely.

"Lift your pillowcase up above your nose," the gunman says. "That should help."

Deuce reassures the hostages that everything is okay and will stay that way if they keep doing just as they are told.

"Don't abuse and you won't lose," he tells them calmly.

Then he shrugs, as though embarrassed that he couldn't come up with anything snappier.

❦

Again, Deuce catches movement beyond the window. He spots a very old man approaching the front door, a lighted cigarette dangling from his lips. Where the hell is Lanoue this time? Deuce rushes over to greet the visitor as he comes in. The gunman sticks his .38 in the old man's face. "Be quiet and you won't get hurt," Deuce says. The cigarette jiggles a little and there's a puff of smoke, but the man says nothing.

The newcomer has the distinction of being older by far than anyone else in the building. He looks to be somewhere between ninety and a casket. He blinks several times. Smoke drifts from his cigarette. Deuce gently tugs it away from the old guy's mouth, drops the butt on the floor, and grinds it out with his shoe. He guides his guest to a seat beside the other hostages and puts a pillowcase over the old man's head. The latest arrival is Max Gellerman of Warwick, Rhode Island. He is Sam Levine's uncle. Sam Levine doesn't acknowledge Gellerman in any way; Gellerman returns the favor.

A lot of noise is coming from the men deep inside the vault. First it's the high-speed drills and a lot of swearing. The name Harry emanates repeatedly. It is attached to more cursing over and over and over, because the high-speed drilling is going slow. In fact, the men are burning and breaking case-hardened steel drill bits and making no real progress at all.

In frustration, Tarzian jams the flat end of his crowbar behind the edge of the cast-iron collar of the big lock on one of the safe deposit boxes then pulls down hard and quick. Cast iron is strong but brittle. The collar splits in two and falls to the floor with the lock still attached. The door is open. The box inside is pulled to the floor. The sound of its fall is akin to the drop of a manhole cover, and it resonates to shouts of amazement.

There are more men than crowbars, but more than enough internal boxes to be dumped and scoured. One crash follows another. The noise of the locks and then the boxes falling to the floor is broken only by more shouts and hoots and hollers. The men move fast, but they can't stay ahead of the boxes' contents. They do their best to snatch what's most obviously of value. If it is green or glitters, it goes.

Minutes later, Chucky appears at the door to the main office. His mask is perched atop his head and he's steadying himself against the casing. He is drenched in sweat. His eyes are wide and glazed over. His lips, normally thin and tight, betraying no emotion, are curled into a grin so broad and silly it looks like something he borrowed for a Halloween party.

"Harry," he says to Deuce, "you got to see this. It's the fucking jackpot."

Chucky takes Deuce's place while the gunman briefly visits the vault. When Deuce returns to trade places, he's wearing the same silly grin.

The haul is not what John Ouimette promised. It is unbelievably bigger and better. In adventure movies, when pirates finally uncover hidden treasure, the floor of the cave usually is covered in glowing gold and silver coins, jewel-encrusted goblets, sparkling gems, and mounds of jewelry. That's what Deuce and Chucky see. Little wonder they both are dumbstruck.

The heist takes from seventy-five to ninety minutes. The men empty 146 safe deposit boxes. They leave two boxes in the corner unscathed because they didn't have room enough to leverage their crowbars.

"Time to go, Harry," Chucky says. "We got enough"—words Deuce thought nobody would ever hear Chucky say.

— —

Chucky and Danese are the first to leave the building. They are strong men and what any fool would call motivated, and they have all they can do to carry the loot. They hoist it into the van and return for more. Chucky is a little miffed with Danese because, though he did save the day by forcing the nervous crew out of the van and into action, he didn't bring as many satchels and duffels as they could have used, or enough to match the money Chucky gave him. Danese probably gambled it away, Chucky figures.

On the other hand, Chucky says years later, "Who knew there was so much to take?" He has known about the operation for three years, and he has always been certain it would be a good score, but it was not his to make—not without permission. It would be disrespectful, and no doubt suicidal, to act otherwise. He later tells friends that there was so much in those safe deposit boxes, the entire crew could have spent the day trying to empty them, and even then they might not have been able to finish the job.

One of the crew brings out a big green duffle bag crammed with so much loot that he has to drag it. The others who follow do the same. Out of the vault, down the hallway, and out the front door to the sidewalk, where he props it upright against the reopened doors of the van, then bends, lifts, and heaves the bag aboard, sweating and straining.

The dragging and straining and bending and lifting are repeated until all but two of the duffle bags have been muscled aboard. The big van sags under the load. Two remaining satchels go into Byrnes's Chevrolet Monte Carlo.

The van moves off so the loot can be transferred to the other three cars. There are only minutes left now.

The first man into Bonded Vault is the last man out, so it's time for Deuce to wrap things up. He turns to his hostages, tells them he has taken Sam Levine's driver's license so he'll know where to find him if they don't all follow his instructions now.

Deuce was going to just lock everyone in the vault, but Sam Levine said closing the vault door before the programmed end of the business day would trigger the silent alarm, partly a precaution against theft and partly for safety's sake.

Deuce asks his captives if they need to use the bathroom. The pillow-cases all nod quickly and in unison.

"Good," he says, "'cause you're all going."

Then he marches his six captives into a tiny toilet stall adjoining the main office. Deuce squeezes everyone inside, shuts the door, and jams a chair under the doorknob.

He leaves the building quickly but not at a run. Byrnes is sitting in his black Monte Carlo at the curb. The car travels only a short distance when Deuce tells Byrnes the car seems to be dogging it. The front of the vehicle is nosed sharply upward, and its rear bumper is only inches off the roadway.

Byrnes looks at him and says, "It's all that weight in the trunk. The silver bars are in there."

"Oh, yeah," Deuce says.

He throws his head back and laughs aloud for the first time all morning.

"The bars of fucking *silver* are in the trunk!" he screams, pounding the dashboard. "I hear ya! I hear ya!"

For Barbara Oliva, this is one of the worst moments of all, as bad as when the pillowcase went over her head. All six people are crunched together and waiting to die inside a funky room the size of an ill-used closet. The room is so small, one person can stand in the middle and touch every wall. For two wellproportioned women to be crushed together against four old men is an indignity in itself.

Oliva never believes that Deuce isn't going to kill them. She fully expects that at any moment, bullets will come tearing through the hollow door and partitioned walls and she will spend her last moments on earth bleeding to death beside a filthy toilet, her blood mingling with the body fluids of five other people, people she works with. They are friends supposedly, but what has been their very first concern? What are they most worried about? What they should report to the police.

"I can't breathe," says one of them.

"Don't talk. You'll use up air."

Silence.

"I don't hear anybody outside."

More silence.

"Kick at the door. Kick at the bottom of the door. Rattle the knob hard."

A few superheated minutes later, the chair that Deuce had wedged under the knob falls to the floor, and the captives fall out into the room.

They go to the cooler and drink all the water they can.

Abraham, Hyman, and Sam start working their way through the mounds of valuables that have been left behind—and there is a lot. The floor of the inner sanctum is covered nearly wall to wall with what the thieves have passed up: mounds and mounds of gold and silver coins; loose, brilliantly colored gems; handguns; gold chalices, some inset with jewels; elegant high-end jewelry, much of it still in individual presentation cases; stock books; and albums of collectors' postage stamps.

They pick up jewelry by the armload and use a shovel to scoop up some of the gold and silver coins scattered all over the inner room of the vault. They stash the valuables in barrels and boxes and push them well out of sight. They grab and empty random containers, stuff valuables in them, and carry them upstairs.

All the while, the brothers are arguing among themselves over what to tell the police and when.

Some people who see the ravaged vault report that apart from the crooks' abandoned tools and bent and broken pry bars, the floor still is literally knee-deep in abandoned treasure by the time police arrive. Others say it is ankle-deep. Barbara Oliva was one of the few to see it.

"It was closer to knee-deep," she says. "What they left behind was so incredible," she said, "it's impossible to imagine what they took."

Minutes tick by, and still the Levines have still not called the police. They are dithering, confused, disoriented; more than that, they are quite simply terrified. They do not want to call the police. Their bickering continues. They keep stalling and arguing, and the longer they delay, the angrier Barbara Oliva becomes.

She is already seething for having had a loaded .38 stuck in her face. When she can't take the Levines' dallying and debating any longer, she marches over to the wall of the main office and presses the button that triggers an alarm at Rhode Island Electric Protection Co. In minutes police sirens rise into the thick, superheated haze of the morning, and Sam Levine goes silent. His complexion is still grayish white, and he glares at Oliva until the police arrive, but he has no choice but to explain what happened.

He delivers a straightforward account to police. It would have been helpful to know when the safe deposit box operation was set up and who uses it, but Levine doesn't volunteer the information and the police don't ask because, on the face of it, there's nothing illegal going on.

Besides, the police are content to let Levine stew over how he and his brothers, in less than ninety minutes in the heat of a summer morning, have suddenly managed to lose untold valuables carefully entrusted to their safekeeping.

They are quick to notice when Patriarca's shadow passes over his victims. The hint of Mafia action tends to induce amnesia or stupidity among otherwise intelligent people. They forget. They don't hear things. They know nothing. And the Levines are looking like a chorus of those answers.

"Providence police called me the day of the robbery," says Albert E. DeRobbio, then-assistant attorney general, decades after the heist. "And they asked what to do.

"I said, 'Did you do the fingerprinting, talk to the owners and get their statements?'

"They said they did, so I said, 'Well, did you secure the premises?'

"They said they did. So I said, 'I don't think you've got any further obligation in this case,' so they closed it up and left.

"God knows what happened after that. But it was some time before anybody even claimed any losses. I couldn't put it before the grand jury because nobody stepped up to say what had been stolen. Technically, we didn't even really have a robbery."

Chucky returns to the hideout first and parks behind the house so no activity will be visible from Golf Avenue. He has a couple of big bags bulging with loot. He jumps from the car and pushes open a bedroom window on the first floor. He tips the bags through the window and climbs through after them. The rest of the crew arrives sporadically. They park out of sight near Chucky and pass the loot to him through the window.

Sometime later, John Ouimette pulls up out front of the house in his jet-black Lincoln Continental Mark IV and walks in on bedlam. The treasure is all indoors, and the men are drenched in sweat. The house is hot and airless. Some of the men have stripped to the waist. They are ecstatic but as jumpy as a roomful of ferrets and hurrying sharply, almost without direction. They are hooting and hollering and backslapping and hugging one another.

There is about as much organization to the divvying process as there is honor among thieves. Each of the men tries to keep an eye on the others while daring his own sleight of hand. Gold coins slip away by the handful. Big diamond rings drop into pants pockets. Dazzling, glittering jewels get tucked into ankle socks. Somebody is always checking the windows; all they'd need is for a mail carrier to arrive.

The crooks throw as much of the cash on the twin bed as will fit. All the rest of the loot spills deep across the floor in mounds of gold;

necklaces; rings; coins; jewelry boxes; silver; bracelets; and diamond, emerald, and ruby clusters. The volume is extraordinary.

The men begin sorting the cash by throwing matching denominations and marked stacks into big plastic laundry baskets. Byrnes is sent off to a local market to get two dozen large brown paper bags.

Macaskill uses a calculator to follow the cash count as best he can. He doesn't include armloads of piddling one- and five-dollar bills, just the tens, twenties, fifties, and hundreds. After five thousand dollars is set aside for Walter Ouimette, who stole the vans in addition to chauffeuring Deuce from Boston to East Providence, the tally of cash is $704,000.

That means each of eleven men—Deuce, Chucky, Danese, Byrnes, Tillinghast, Lanoue, Tarzian, Macaskill, John Ouimette, his managing brother Gerard, and their silent patron, Raymond L. S. Patriarca Jr.— should collect sixty-four thousand dollars, not bad for less than ninety minutes of work, at least $873 a minute.

For delivery, the bills are packed tightly in the grocery bags that Byrnes got. The men double the bags for reinforcement. Wouldn't want to drop one in public and have to explain why you're walking around with all of those bundles of dreams.

*   *

Around noon, there's a loud banging on the front door of Chucky's hideout. In unison befitting a cartoon, the men dive at the windows. Venetian blinds are snapped shut. Chucky walks slowly to the front door and opens it a crack, holding a revolver behind his back.

A workman is standing on the front steps. "Here to take down the storm windows," the guy says. "Landlord sent us down."

"Yeah," Chucky says. "Okay." Behind him, the entire house exhales. Then the counting resumes, but quietly.

If the same cash robbery were possible today, each of the eleven men would take home nearly $288,000. Little wonder that the folding money had more immediate appeal than the hard glittery stuff. The men stop to admire the sheer grandeur and outrageous heft of fourteen large solid silver ingots, but they're content to bag it up with the rest of the swag and hand it all over to Byrnes and Danese. Byrnes says he will bury it so they can fence it all later.

Nobody gives either the loot or the men in charge of it much more thought. There's no grand plan, no well-orchestrated scheme that will reunite them with the fenced proceeds of their morning's work. Everyone is preoccupied with grabbing his share of cash and putting Rhode Island in the rearview mirror. Danese and Macaskill also take bags for Lanoue and Tarzian, who already have left to dispose of the van.

By early afternoon, only Deuce, Chucky, and Ellen are left in the house. Deuce says good-bye and starts to gather his share. He is about to call a taxi. He's a luxury junkie, and the sooner he's at it the better. "Time to go have some fun with this," he says. "This is what it's all about, right?"

Chucky and Ellen tell him to hold up; he should savor the time. That's their plan, their reason for being. They are in love, after all, and this is the fling of a lifetime. They talk in earnest about their plans. Naturally, they want to get out of town, and they know that as soon as the cops understand how big a job this was, there will be plenty of heat, but who will it come from? They can't exactly complain to their parish pastor now, can they?

For that matter, who are the cops going to look for? Not them. At least at first, everything will point to *Il Padrino,* just because it always does, but the police won't have anything that ties the heist directly to either him or his son, Junior.

Sooner or later, the Old Man will do what he always does: Deny any knowledge, complain that the cops and reporters have been making him a scapegoat for years, insist that he's just an honest businessman, and then tell them all to fuck off. It's his script, all but patented.

Figuring they have a little time, Deuce, Chucky, and Ellen settle on Las Vegas as their destination, and they will go by way of New York City first thing in the morning. Where to stay? The Plaza is nice? Why the hell not?

They check into a suite of rooms and give the bellman a tip he can tell his grandchildren about. After a good night's sleep and a long, leisurely breakfast, the three set out to do some serious shopping. Deuce is very happy. Buy what you want. Money's no object. What could be better? What's life for, if it isn't this?

———

Deuce goes shopping and buys the most expensive clothes he can find, not because he needs them but simply because he can. Ellen goes clothes shopping on her own. Chucky goes poking around in jewelry stores.

Two days after the heist, the trio boards a direct flight from New York to Las Vegas. Chucky and Ellen are lovebird happy and seated side by side. Deuce is a short distance away next to some guy who talks from takeoff to landing about what a great place Las Vegas is.

Deuce gleans one important fact from him: The best hotel in the entire city is the MGM Grand. It's right there on The Strip, South Las Vegas Boulevard—that preposterous three-mile mecca of glamour, high-rolling glitz, and neon glow that mobster Bugsy Segal and his friends raised up out of the hot desert sand.

The trio gets in a cab at the airport and Deuce casually tells the driver, "MGM Grand." Chucky and Ellen do a double take in surprise. Deuce just looks at them blankly. "It's the best in Vegas." That's one of the reason's Chucky holds Deuce in such high esteem; he always seems to know these things. It's as though he has access to a part of the world Chucky knows nothing about.

The taxi parks in the MGM Grand's porte cochere, and Deuce strides up to the front desk.

"All we have is a suite," the clerk tells him.

"Good. That's just what I want," Deuce says flatly, "a nice suite."

A young bellhop loads their luggage onto a gleaming brass cart and escorts them to a spacious three-room suite. He moves swiftly all around the suite, proudly showing off every accouterment and appurtenance. He says if they need anything, anything at all, just call the front desk and ask for him by name: Ricky Purcell. Deuce tips him one hundred dollars.

Ellen and Chucky have packed thousands of dollars in a valise and don't want to leave it in their hotel room. Deuce volunteers that the hotel has its own safe deposit boxes that guests may use. Chucky is surprised. Deuce is about to take the money downstairs when Chucky takes him aside.

Chucky has a problem. His brow is furrowed, and he looks a little sheepish, which is completely out of character. He says he spent $4,600 of his cash on an engagement ring for Ellen and wants to ask her to marry him, but he wants Deuce's advice on the best way to go about it.

Deuce doubts that Chucky actually bought the ring, but he gives Chucky his best all-knowing smile and says, "I'll take care of it. Give me the ring."

Deuce puts the valise full of cash in a hotel safe deposit box and goes looking for Purcell, who is in the lobby. Clearly it is time for the grand gesture, the kind of suavity that only a would-be high-roller like Deuce could pull off. He gives Purcell the ring, tells him to hook it carefully to the neck of a very good bottle of champagne and bring it up to the suite with one dozen long-stemmed red roses when Ellen returns from shopping. He gives the bellman another couple of hundred dollars for the errand.

Ellen is bowled over. Chucky is happy. He loves Ellen, and he's proud as all hell to have handled the proposal with flair; it's one more reason he and Deuce are so close: Deuce always knows such good stuff.

━ ⌁

With the two lovebirds accounted for, Deuce sets his sights on finding a woman of his own. He isn't about to waste time wining and dining. This is Las Vegas, after all. You want the company of a woman, you buy it.

He picks a likely candidate from one of the continuously updated catalogs that are everywhere in the hotels. He calls the phone number listed for an attractive young brunette and, sure enough, in less time than it takes to invent a story about who he is and what he's doing in town, not that anyone would care, he's got himself a three-hundred-dollar woman.

She is as pretty as advertised, but she no sooner comes to the door than another woman shows up, a friend of a croupier Deuce had spoken with earlier. He had asked the guy if he personally could recommend a sweet young thing. He said he could, but Deuce didn't expect action this fast.

The croupier's friend, actually his prostitute wife's friend, is a knockout. She is younger than the girl from the catalog, in her early twenties, five feet two inches tall and slender. She's well built, with big green eyes and a melt-your-heart smile, and she says her name is Karyne Sponheim.

Deuce says his name is Dennis Allen. He is dazzled. With the other woman in the room behind him, he explains his situation, peels three hundred-dollar bills from a roll in his pocket, and hands them to Karyne, who smiles and leaves.

The next day she is still a vivid memory, so Deuce sends Purcell to find her, which he does. Karyne is no unplucked flower blossom. She is a hooker, but she hasn't been at it long enough to look hard or jaded; quite the opposite. She's bubbly, intensely and eternally interested in whatever Deuce has to say, and she is as enthusiastic about sex as he is. The gunman from Lowell has found his heart's desire.

Karyne falls for Deuce about as hard and fast as he falls for her. The pay-as-you-go sex ends nearly as fast as it starts. The two quickly become inseparable, and so Deuce and Karyne and Chucky and Ellen settle down to wring all the fun they can out of the one city in America with the loudest, brassiest boast that its specialty is fun of any and every kind.

***

In the capital cities of many states, the exposure and ransacking of a secret Mafia depository might be something of an embarrassment; not so in Providence, at least not in any terribly obvious way. Mayor Vincent A. "Buddy" Cianci Jr. downplays it, as any chief executive would. He points out that despite all the talk of goods worth millions being stolen, no one actually has claimed extraordinary losses. He's right, of course, but his nay-saying is just damage control. The truth is, he is angry. Cianci is a proud man and proudly Italian. He sees *La Cosa Nostra* as a blight, and he campaigned on an anticrime pledge. Worst of all, a caper of Bonded Vault's magnitude is not soon forgotten, and that tarnishes the city he loves.

The FBI gets involved in the investigation early. Figuring that goods this glittery are too hot to fence quickly in this country, agents try tracing the stolen jewelry through a team of contacts in Bern, Switzerland, and Bonn, Germany, but get nowhere. This is unfortunate, because the two police commands that will have to unravel the brazen robbery, the Rhode

Island State Police and the Providence Police Department, do not have a history of cooperating with each other.

The state police are run by superintendent Col. Walter E. Stone, an uncompromising law enforcement legend, one of several high-ranking and widely respected cops who first testified in Congress to the existence of organized crime in America.

Stone's troopers are carefully selected, bright, well paid, highly trained, blade-straight, by the book, and paramilitary. They wear jodhpur uniforms of slate-gray whipcord with red piping and trim black ties; Sam Browne belts; three-quarter-length coats; wide, flat-brimmed Stetsons; and lace-up, knee-high brown leather boots. They drive big-mill Ford Interceptor LTDs the color of burnished silver, and they do not routinely trust cops from lesser Rhode Island departments, which is to say, all thirty-eight of them.

Providence police, under the blustering but savvy control of lame-duck Col. Walter A. McQueeney, appear lackluster by comparison, but not for lack of some tough, hard-working and intelligent cops. They just don't like the state police.

Providence cops wear standard-issue chocolate brown uniforms with matching caps, the same design as those worn by most every other cop in the land. They joke that it takes the average Rhode Island State Police trooper three hours to get dressed, and they routinely dismiss them as peacocks, glory hounds, and AAA with a badge.

Cianci, looking back over forty years, still smiles. "Cops are just trying to climb the ladder like everyone else, and there's always a lot of angling and jealousy in the ranks. So, yeah, when the state police are involved it can be a problem. But from about the level of captain on up, where the bigger cases are handled, look out. They'll do anything and everything they can to get a good collar, even if it means cooperating."

From the beginning, the police labor with the presumption that no heist as big as the Bonded Vault job goes down without someone some-where knowing something about it, so first comes the sorting, grinding, and sifting—the routine procedural work, statements from witnesses, reviews, re-interviews, follow-ups, interview comparisons, team briefings, and consultations behind closed doors. And then detectives turn to their most reliable weapons: rats and snitches, the little guys, the hangers-on who suck up to the bigger guys, the ones who ingratiate themselves to even bigger guys, who throw them crumbs for jobs and whose livelihoods depend on knowing the streets and who is calling which shots when, where, and why.

The trick is to convince the guy that it's in his best interest to tell what he knows. Sounds simple. In fact, it is leagues away from that. It is not the kind of thing anyone just sits down one day to do. It's what good detectives accomplish very gradually over a long period of time, learning who is important to whom and under what circumstances, steadily building small networks of well-placed informers, manipulating systems of rewards, favors, and blind spots, some little, some not so little, but all geared to developing the pressure it takes to make the rat release critical information when it is needed the most.

What matters most is that all of the pressure is brought to bear on the right man. In a very real sense, the guy with the best rat wins.

———

The day after the robbery, Sam Levine petitions the superior court to put Bonded Vault in receivership, thereby relinquishing responsibility for any of the valuables the robbers left behind. The fate of what remains is put in the hands of Thomas R. DiLuglio of Johnston, a tough lawyer who two years hence will become the lieutenant governor of Rhode Island.

This amounts to the Levines saying, "You've got a problem with what you had in those boxes? You take it up with him."

The list of box holders is leaked to the press. The effect is a lot like turning over a rock and watching all the little critters scurry in search of new darkness in which to prosper. At least one in every five names has a recognizable link to organized crime, and the likelihood is that a good many of the other names are merely fakes or shells on loan from friends or relatives.

The Internal Revenue Service quickly puts a lien on all the "unidentifiable and unclaimed" valuables the robbers left behind and asks the court to freeze all the company's assets until it can be determined how they should be distributed.

The IRS is looking for assets belonging to a host of box holders in whom the government has a special interest:

William A. and Mildred A. Lamphere of Cranston, a coin dealer and his wife, who the agency asserts owes the government nearly $691,000 in back taxes.

Frank "Babe" Kowal, under indictment for possession of stolen goods, has access to four boxes under an assumed name.

Eugene Carlino, indicted for tax evasion after an investigation by the IRS and the Organized Crime Racketeering Strike Force, has four boxes in his own name and access to four others under an assumed name.

Matthew Levine, indicted by the same two government agencies, has access to at least two boxes under the name of a real estate company with which he was associated.

Raymond Lyons, a professional gambler under investigation by a special federal grand jury looking into organized gambling in Rhode Island, has access to three boxes in his wife's maiden name.

One of the box holders is William Marrapese, whose life term in prison for murder was recently reduced after he testified for the government in a related case; he has access to four boxes in the names of two people who could not be reached for comment.

One of the box holders is Frederick Carrozza, whose address is listed as 168 Atwells Avenue, the location of Raymond L. S. Patriarca's National Cigarette Service Co. and Coin-O-Matic Distributors. Patriarca was a partner with the late Philip Carrozza, Frederick Carozza's father. Patriarca and the younger Carrozza deny having any mutual business interests.

Most everyone else on the list of box holders has "no comment" for reporters, which is of course a damning kind of comment in itself. It's also one of Rhode Island's most popular responses when the circumstances are untoward or embarrassing, right up there with "I don't know nothing."

For about two weeks, Karyne and Ellen and Chucky and Deuce roll through Las Vegas as though they're spending their last weeks on earth. As their personal concierge Purcell gets them great seats at some of the best shows in town. There's no shortage to pick from. The Righteous Brothers draw crowds, Diana Ross even more. Joan Rivers always is a hit. So is Liberace. Dean Martin. Even Jerry Lewis for a brief stint. Sammy Davis Jr. is a favorite, and Elvis, even on the slide, always fills the room. There are choices of great magic shows where live animals disappear faster than liquor and ten-dollar bills. Karyne and Deuce have their pictures taken as they celebrate and enjoy long, lavish meals. He buys clothes for himself, and for her he buys gifts galore, mostly clothes and jewelry.

Deuce thinks it's only appropriate that he give Ellen and Chucky an engagement present, so he fills a shoebox full of cash, gives it to Purcell, and tells him to go buy a nice car, a convertible. Purcell returns with a flashy silver Lincoln convertible. Chucky loves it.

In between the shows and dinners and the constant drinking, Deuce and Chucky are gambling. In the casinos there are no windows and no clocks. Time stops so that the workaday world, with all its achingly quotidian worries, does not interrupt the fun. Deuce is doing pretty well at the blackjack tables; nothing big, but he's at least winning more than he's losing.

Chucky, on the other hand, is shooting craps and losing big. Ellen can't pry him away from the tables, and she's frightened. At one point he throws the dice for twenty-four hours straight, and they are cold all the way; he couldn't warm them up if he set fire to his bankroll. He borrows some money from Deuce so he can keep playing.

Ellen is distraught. She tells Deuce in a teary-eyed, frustrated rush that Chucky has even gone through the stacks of five-hundred-dollar bills that he had. She might as well have dumped a bucket of ice water over Deuce's head. He is stunned, not so much by news of the loss, but because he had no idea that Chucky, whose highest professed ideal always has been loyalty, apparently cut everybody, including his best friend, out of what had to have been a lot of additional cash from the heist—tens of thousands of dollars more at least. Deuce figures Chucky must have set it aside right after the robbery, before everyone got back to the hideout. It's not that Deuce might not have done the same thing if he'd had the chance; he is a thief, after all. It's just that this secret little sleight of hand somehow feels sort of personal; it hurts, but he shakes it off.

Ellen is frantic over Chucky's losses, and she says she wants to go home; they argue. He goes back to the craps tables. Deuce follows him, watches him lose more money, talks him into taking a break, and then convinces him that Ellen is right. Chucky's on a losing streak that can't be broken. Next day, the couple flies home.

———

Las Vegas can wear down the most devoted of revelers after a while, so Deuce arranges for Purcell to take him and Karyne on a sightseeing tour of California. Karyne is disappointed. She knows California well and is eager to show Deuce all there is to see. "Why didn't you ask me?" So he does. Purcell stays in Las Vegas, and Deuce and Karyne go to San Francisco and take in the sights for several days. Then they drive—Karyne always behind the wheel—leisurely down through Big Sur and along the spectacular California coast. They head toward Los Angeles, tour Hollywood, and stop when they reach Beverly Hills. Where to stay? The famed Beverly Hills Hotel, of course.

Deuce's eyes light up when he sees the lobby. There is a boutique on one side, a small jewelry store on the other. He figures the window jewelry alone is good for five million dollars, and the place is run by just one person. Despite his best instincts, he rents a room, and he and Karyne get comfortable in a cabana by the pool.

He spots David Hartman, host of ABC's *Good Morning America*, and quite by accident ends up being introduced to famed author Harold Robbins and a few retired actresses. So many famous people are paged almost one after another that Deuce starts to feel as though his head is on a swivel looking for celebrities.

Deuce and Karyne are tourists too. They pop into a few shops on Rodeo Drive for some baubles, take day trips to Disneyland, and do some gambling at a racetrack outside of San Diego.

Partly out of his warped sixth sense and partly out of plain old curiosity, Deuce calls a guy near Rhode Island who knows him by one of the several aliases he contrived over the years and asks what's going on.

Deuce tells him he's out in California vacationing but figures he'll be back pretty soon. He likes the fall, the changing leaves and all, even when he's looking at them through steel bars, because he knows Christmas is coming. He feels it in his bones. It's only September, but his homing instinct is keen.

His friend tells him that about a month ago there was this big robbery at some fur storage place in Providence that turned out to have tons of loot nobody knew about. He says it's been all over the papers and even on TV. The word is millions of bucks walked out of the place. Some of Raymond's guys probably. It's odd though. The cops are after some guy named Dussault. You'd have thought they'd be hunting an Italian.

———

Deuce isn't exactly shocked that he is wanted by the police, but he is surprised that he has been identified so quickly. Jail is always a prospect. When he pulls a job, he never wears a disguise or a mask, partly because they are always a pain in the neck and can get in your way, and partly because they seem stupid. Somebody sees you going into a jewelry store wearing a mask, it's a safe bet they'll get a quick grasp of the situation. As for identifying him, well, eyewitness accounts and descriptions are notoriously unreliable; any cop will tell you that. So Deuce just goes in fast and hard, orders people not to look at him, and hopes for the best. Half the time, it works pretty well; on the other hand, half is just about as much of his life as he has spent in jail.

Still, he is saddened a bit. The past few weeks have been the time of his life, and he'd just as soon see this run with Karyne stretch a good distance into the future. He goes back to the cabana in a more somber mood but does his best to hide it from his girlfriend, which works for a while. But over the next couple of days, he starts drinking more than usual, which is a lot, and that darkens his mood. He and Karyne argue over some minor thing; he explodes in anger, grabs her by the neck, and throws her across the bed, calling her a miserable little cunt and other obscene and unkind things too numerous to mention. This isn't the Dennis she knows; it's somebody else, and she is afraid of him.

Deuce packs his bags. Karyne is distraught and in tears. Dennis is about to leave her over what? Some stupid little argument? It makes no sense. When she says so, Deuce only gets angrier and calls her more obscene names. He calls Purcell and hires him to drive him to Los Angeles International Airport. Deuce is going back to Rhode Island. It'll be like hiding the pearl in a fishbowl, a plain-sight place no one will think to look. He'll find Chucky; they'll figure out what to do.

By the time the silver Lincoln pulls into the airport, Deuce has calmed down a bit, thought things over. He bought the car for Chucky. How's he going to get it to him? And what about all of the stuff he bought? He takes a deep breath, goes to a telephone, and calls Karyne, who is still in the hotel room sobbing. He apologizes until he runs out of appropriate words. She agrees to pack up the rest of their bags and meet him in a lounge at the airport.

When they meet, he apologizes again, tells her what he does for a living, and that the police back East are looking for him. His voice jitters when he says everything just fell in on him all of a sudden and that's why he blew up at her. Karyne by now is composed and relatively unfazed; no schoolgirl she. He's still her Denny, and they are still a couple. Karyne says, in fact, that she loves Deuce; he says he loves her too.

Deuce buys Purcell a ride back to Las Vegas, and he and Karyne head east, this time as fugitive tourists. They visit the Grand Canyon, Old Faithful at Yellowstone National Park, then Mount Rushmore and the Badlands of South Dakota, all the more majestic from the front seat of a convertible. Deuce calls Chucky several times, partly because more than ever now he wants to know what's going on, and partly because his money is running out and he'd like some more of what he's certain was a job that netted more than his sixty-four-thousand-dollar share.

Deuce says he wants another hundred thousand dollars. Chucky says he'll see what he can do, but it's clear something is amiss. Chucky sounds cautious and, in fact, a little stiff, almost wary, but he agrees to meet Deuce at a motel at O'Hare International Airport in Chicago.

Two days later, Chucky checks into a room at the hotel. Karyne waits in the hotel lounge while Deuce goes up to Flynn's room. Chucky is there. So is Skippy Byrnes.

Deuce barely acknowledges Byrnes and gets quickly to the point. Did Chucky bring him the money? Flynn hands over about $8,500. He says the guys took up a collection for him, and now they're trying to fence the Bonded Vault loot in one big deal; that's likely to take some time.

Deuce says nothing. The silence is uncomfortable.

"Did you leave any fingerprints behind?" Chucky asks.

"What? Nah," Deuce says, "you know me better than that."

"Well," Chucky says, "that thing that you touched . . ."

During the robbery, Deuce asked Sam Levine if he had an office cash box. Levine said he did. Deuce said, let's have it. The gray steel box contained petty cash, a couple of hundred dollars, no more. Deuce took it, and all the while was careful to handle the box only by its edges.

"Remember I had to wipe that thing 'cause you left prints all over it?" Chucky says.

Deuce is irked. "Hey, wait a minute. You know me better than that. I didn't leave no fingerprints behind there. What the hell's the story? What's happening?"

"The cops say they got your prints."

"That's bullshit and you know it, Chucky. They're making that up because somebody must have fingered me, and they're covering for him. Some son of a bitch ratted me out."

Six

The Crude Map and the Buried Treasure

John W. Cook

"I<small>T'S</small> <small>NO USE, PARD; THE JIG IS UP, AND</small> I'<small>M GOIN' ACROSS THE RANGE</small> mighty shortly."

The speaker was John Reynolds—miner, gambler, rebel guerrilla, stage robber, and cut-throat—as reckless a daredevil as ever met his just deserts in the whole West. The person addressed was his partner in crime, Albert Brown, a desperado like himself, a man hardened to scenes of bloodshed and death, yet he brushed a tear from his eye as he turned to get a drink of water for the dying man.

"If we could only have got to Denver, we'd have been all right," continued Reynolds. "I've got over $60,000 buried not fifty miles from there in the mountains, and I could go right to the spot where Jim and me buried it in 1864. But there's no use in me wastin' breath, for I'm to the end of my rope now, an' I'll tell you just where it is, so that you can go an' get it after you've planted me deep enough so the coyotes won't dig me up an' gnaw my bones."

The dying man was sinking rapidly, but he went on: "Jim an' me buried it the morning before the fight at the grove on Geneva Gulch. You go up above there a little ways and find where one of our horses mired down in a swamp. On up at the head of the gulch we turned to the right and followed the mountain around a little farther, an' just above the head of Deer Creek we found an old prospect hole at about timber line. There was $40,000 in greenbacks, wrapped in silk oil cloth, an' three cans of gold dust. We filled the mouth of the hole up with stones, an' ten steps below there stuck a butcher knife into a tree about four feet from the ground an' broke the handle off, an' left it pointing to the mouth of the hole."

Reynolds fell back exhausted, and asked Brown for a pencil, so that he could draw him a map. Brown had no pencil, but breaking open a cartridge he mixed the powder with some water, and as soon as Reynolds had revived a little he drew a rude map of the locality on the back of an old letter. Cautioning Brown to remember his directions, he fell back upon his rude couch, and in a few minutes was dead.

Brown set to work to digging a grave in the dirt floor of the dugout, and having no tools but a sharp stick, spent two days at the work. He placed Reynolds's body in the shallow grave, covering it up carefully, then carried stones and put over it in accordance with his agreement. As soon as Brown completed his task, he secured his horses and started for Denver. While he is on his way thither, we will improve the opportunity to relate the history of the boldest band of robbers, and indeed, the only party of rebel guerrillas that ever invaded Colorado, of which John Reynolds, whose death we have just chronicled, was the last surviving member. Before beginning the recital of our story proper, it might be well to give a hasty sketch of the conditions prevailing in Colorado at the time our story opens.

The population of Denver in 1861 was decidedly cosmopolitan. The mining excitement had attracted hither men of almost every nationality, profession, and occupation on the globe. On the question of secession, then the theme on every tongue, the people seemed pretty evenly divided. The Unionists, however, seized upon the opportunity, and enlisting several companies of militia, were soon masters of the situation. All suspects were then called up to take the oath of allegiance. Those who refused to do this were thrown into jail. Among those arrested were two brothers, James and John Reynolds. They belonged to a large class of men just upon the borderland of crime, working in the mines, driving bull teams, steering for gambling houses, in fact, turning their hands to whatever offered. Jack Robinson, a guard at the jail, was a fitting companion for them, although he had not fallen under suspicion. One night while he was on guard, a large party of suspects, known as the McKee party, broke jail and made their escape, probably through the connivance of Robinson.

At any rate he carried food and supplies to them while they were concealed about the city, and when they went south to join the rebel army, Robinson went with them.

Early in 1864, James Reynolds, who was beginning to tire of the restraints of military life, little irksome as they were among the irregulars under the Confederate flag in northern Texas, found himself at the head of a company of fifty men, among whom were his brother, John, and Jack Robinson. Then, too, Reynolds had an ambition to be a second Quantrell, to be a freebooter, going where he pleased and plundering all who were not strong enough to resist. He believed that with his company he could imitate Quantrell's famous raid on Lawrence, overrun all southern Colorado and burn and sack the city of Denver, where he had been imprisoned. The majority of his men were Texans, and they did not relish the idea of a 500-mile raid through a hostile country, so that when he got ready to start, in April, 1864, he found that but twenty-two of his men would stay with him.

Nothing daunted, he resolved to push forward with this small band, fully believing that he could get plenty of recruits in the mines, where rebel sympathizers had been plentiful enough a few years before. In this, as we shall learn later, he was badly disappointed, never securing a single recruit. His friend, Col. McKee, gave them a pass through to Belknap, and taking only a few rations they pushed on through the Confederate lines. Once through the lines they rode swiftly westward toward the Spanish peaks—grim beacons in an ocean of sand. When they ran out of food they killed their pack animals, and thus managed to subsist until they struck the Santa Fe trail.

They encountered a band of hostile Indians, but defeated them without loss. A little further along the trail they met a wagon train which Reynolds decided was too strong to be attacked, so he traded a horse for some provisions. A few miles further up the trail they struck a Mexican train, which they attacked and captured. Here they made a rich haul, securing $40,000 in currency, $6,000 in drafts, and about $2,000 in coin. Taking arms, ammunition, provisions, and such mules as they wanted, they proceeded northward, leaving the Mexicans to get along as best they could. A great deal of dissatisfaction had arisen among the members of the band on account of Jim Reynolds taking possession of most of the money himself. A portion of the gang sided in with Reynolds's theory that the captain should have charge of the surplus funds, since he proposed to arm and equip recruits as soon as they reached Colorado. Accordingly fourteen of the party quit the gang and rode back toward Texas.

The little party now consisted of but nine men: James Reynolds, John Reynolds, Jack Robinson, Tom Knight, Owen Singletary, John Babbitt, Jake Stowe, John Andrews, and Tom Halliman. That night they held a council of war. It was decided to push on to Pueblo, then up the Arkansas into the rich placer mining districts of the South park. Here they felt confident of securing not only much plunder, but enough recruits to swoop down on Denver. They cached a lot of their heavy plunder, consisting of extra guns, ammunition, and several hundred dollars of silver coin, which was too heavy to be carried easily. Resting their horses, they moved on toward Pueblo. Crossing the Arkansas at that place they rode on up the river to where Cañon City now stands, where they went into camp. A man named Bradley kept a store where the city now stands, and Reynolds dispatched several of the gang with plenty of money to purchase clothing, provisions, and whisky. He did not go near Bradley himself, as he feared that gentleman would recognize him, and Reynolds was not yet ready for trouble. After having secured their supplies they pushed on to Current Creek. Finding there plenty of grass and water for their horses, they decided to camp several days for rest and recuperation.

After holding another council they decided it would be better to push on to California Gulch (the present site of Leadville) in small squads so as not to excite suspicion. After looking over the gulch for a day or two they decided that the Buckskin and Mosquito camps offered better opportunities for plunder. Accordingly the band reunited and came back down the Arkansas, entering South park below Fairplay. They stopped for the night at Guireaud's ranch, and Capt. Reynolds had a long talk with Guireaud, with whom he seemed to be acquainted. He wrote several letters to friends at Fairplay, and the next morning inquired of Guireaud what time the coach left Buckskin, as he wanted to beat it to McLaughlin's ranch to mail his letters.

They at once set out for the ranch, which is ten miles from Fairplay. On the road, Capt. Reynolds halted his men and informed them that he proposed to rob the coach at McLaughlin's. When they reached the creek below the ranch, they met McLaughlin and Maj. Demere, and took them prisoners. McLaughlin was riding a very fine horse, and Capt. Reynolds at once suggested that they swap. McLaughlin demurred, but got down when Reynolds and several other members of the party drew their guns. Reaching the ranch the party dismounted and put out a picket. McLaughlin treated the men to some whisky and ordered his wife to prepare dinner for the gang.

When the coach drew up, Reynolds stepped out and commanded the driver, Abe Williamson, and Billy McClelland, the superintendent of the stage line, who occupied the seat with the driver, to throw up their hands, one of his men stepping in front of the horses at the same time.

Their hands went up promptly, and after being disarmed by another of the gang, Reynolds ordered them to get down, at the same time demanding their money. Williamson resented the idea of his having any money, saying that it was the first time in all his travels that a stage driver had ever been accused of having any of the long and needful green about his person. But his talk didn't go with the bandits, and after searching him carefully they found fifteen cents, which they took. Williamson's eyes scowled hatred, and as will be learned later, he finally took an awful revenge for the outrage.

They "shook down" McClellan with much better results, securing $400 in money and a valuable chronometer balance gold watch. They then turned their attention to the express trunk, there being no passengers on this trip. Halliman secured an axe to break it open, when McClellan offered him the key. Reynolds refused the key, venturing the opinion that they could soon get into it without the key. Breaking it open they took out $6,000 worth of gold dust and $2,000 worth of gold amalgam that John W. Smith was sending to the East, it being the first taken from the Orphan Boy mine, as well as the first run from the stamp mill erected in Mosquito Gulch. Capt. Reynolds then ordered Halliman to cut open the mail bags, passing him his dirk for the purpose. They tore open the letters, taking what money they contained, which was considerable, as nearly all the letters contained ten- and twenty-dollar bills, which the miners were sending back to their friends in the East. The haul amounted to $10,000 in all, a much smaller sum than the coach usually carried out.

After having secured all the valuables, Capt. Reynolds ordered his men to destroy the coach, saying that he wanted to damage the United States government as much as possible. His men at once went to work to chopping the spokes out of the wheels. They ate the dinner prepared by Mrs. McLaughlin, and Capt. Reynolds then announced his determination to go on to the Michigan ranch and secure the stage stock which were kept there. Before leaving, he said to McClellan and the other captives, that if they attempted to follow the bandits they would be killed, and that the best thing they could do would be to remain quietly at the ranch for a day or two, adding that they were only the advance guard of 1,500 Texas Rangers who were raiding up the park, saying also that 2,500 more Confederate troops were on their way north and had probably reached Denver by that time.

They then rode away, leaving the settlers dumbfounded by the news. There had long been rumors of such a raid, and there being neither telegraph nor railroad, they had no means of verifying the reports. McClellan at once announced his determination to alarm the mining camps of their danger, and although his friends endeavored to dissuade him from his hazardous trip, he mounted a mule and followed the robbers. He rode through Hamilton, Tarryall, and Fairplay, spreading the news and warning out citizens and miners, arriving in due time at Buckskin. From there he sent runners to California Gulch and other camps. McClellan himself stayed in the saddle almost night and day for over a week, and in that time had the whole country aroused. His energy and determined fearlessness probably saved many lives and thousands of dollars worth of property.

Active measures were now taken for the capture of the guerrillas. Armed bodies of miners and ranchmen started on their trail. Col. Chivington sent troops from Denver to guard coaches and to assist in the capture. Gen. Cook, at that time chief of government detectives for the department of Colorado, accompanied the troops, and was soon on the trail of the marauders. The news that a band of armed guerrillas was scouring the country was dispatched by courier to Central City, and all the camps in that vicinity were notified. Even south of the divide, at Pueblo and Cañon, companies were organized, and it was but a question of a few days at least when the band would be wiped out. Indeed, if there had been 4,000 of them as Reynolds had reported, instead of a little band of nine, they would have been gobbled up in short order.

Reaching the Michigan house the guerrillas took the stage horses and robbed the men who kept the station. Going on they passed the Kenosha house, stopping at various ranches and taking whatever they wanted, and robbing everybody they met. Passing Parmelee's and Haight's, they camped near the deserted St. Louis house, and at daybreak moved on to the Omaha house for breakfast. Besides refusing to pay for their meal, they robbed all the travelers camped around the station except an Irishman hauling freight to Georgia Gulch. He gave them the pass word and grips of the Knights of the Golden Circle, and was allowed to go on unmolested. While here they found out that large bodies of citizens were in pursuit, and they decided to move off the main road; so after leaving the Omaha house they turned off and went up Deer Creek to the range. Just after they had gotten off the road into the timber a posse of twenty-two mounted men passed up the road toward the Omaha house. After a while they saw another party evidently following their trail. Capt. Reynolds took a spyglass, and finding that there were but eighteen of them decided to fight. He strung his men out in single file in order to make a plain trail, and after going about a mile, doubled back and ambushed his men at the side of the trail. Fortunately for the pursuing party, they turned back before they were in gunshot of the guerrillas. Whether they scented danger, or were tired of following what they thought was a cold trail, is not known, but it was probably the latter, as the Reynolds gang was not molested that day nor the next, although with the aid of his glass Reynolds saw scouting parties scouring the mountains in every direction. He saw that they were likely to be captured and resolved to scatter the band in order to escape, hoping to be able to rendezvous away down near the Greenhorn.

Capt. Reynolds decided that it would be prudent to conceal the greater portion of their spoils until the excitement had died down somewhat. Calling his brother, John, they passed up the little creek that ran by their camp until they reached its head. Elk Creek also heads near there.

They found a prospect hole which they thought would answer their purpose. Capt. Reynolds took from his saddle-bags $40,000 in currency and three cans full of gold dust, about $63,000 in all, leaving one large can of gold dust and considerable currency to be divided among the band before separating. They wrapped the currency up in a piece of silk oil cloth and put it and the cans back in the hole about the length of a man's body. Returning to the camp, Capt. Reynolds told his men that there were no pursuers in sight, and announced his determination to disperse the band temporarily, as he believed there was no chance of escape if they remained together. He described the place of rendezvous mentioned, and told them that it would be safe to move on down to a grove of large trees on Geneva Gulch, a short distance below, and camp for dinner, as there was no one in sight. They went on down and camped, and turned their horses loose to graze while dinner was being gotten.

Two of the men were getting dinner, and the others were gathered around Capt. Reynolds, who was busily dividing the remaining money and gold dust among them, when suddenly a dozen guns cracked from behind some large rocks about 220 yards from the outlaws' camp. Owen Singletary fell dead, and Capt. Reynolds, who was at that moment dipping gold dust from a can with a spoon, was wounded in the arm. The outlaws at once broke for the brush, a few even leaving their horses.

The attacking party, which consisted of twelve or fifteen men from Gold Run under the leadership of Jack Sparks, had crawled around the mountain unobserved until they reached the rocks, and then fired a volley into the robber band. When the robbers took to the brush, they went down to their camp and secured several horses, the can of gold dust, the amalgam that was taken from the coach at McLaughlin's, Billy McClellan's watch, and a lot of arms, etc. It was coming on night, and after searching the gulches for a while in vain, they cut off Singletary's head, which they took to Fairplay as a trophy of the fight. This was July 31, 1864.

The next day Halliman was captured at the Nineteen-mile ranch, and they kept picking up the guerrillas one or two at a time until the Thirty-nine-mile ranch was reached. John Reynolds and Jake Stowe, who were traveling together, were pursued clear across the Arkansas River, but they finally escaped, although Stowe was severely wounded.

The remainder of the party were brought from Fairplay to Denver under a heavy guard and placed in jail. They were given a sham trial, and as it could not be proven that they had taken life they were sentenced to imprisonment for life, although a great many of the citizens thought they richly deserved hanging. While the party were in jail in Denver, Gen. Cook had a long talk with Jim Reynolds, the captain, and tried to find out from him what disposition had been made of all the money and valuables the robbers were known to have captured, knowing that they must have concealed it somewhere, since they had but little when captured. Reynolds refused to tell, saying that it was "safe enough," and afterwards adding they had "sent it home."

About the first week in September the Third Colorado cavalry, commanded by Col. Chivington, was ordered out against the Indians. Capt. Cree, of Company A, was directed to take the six prisoners from the county jail to Fort Lyon for "safe keeping," and to shoot every one of them if "they made any attempt to escape." The prisoners knew that they would be shot if the soldiers could find the slightest pretext for so doing. The troop was composed of citizens of Denver and vicinity, some of whom had suffered from the depredations of the gang. One man they particularly feared was Sergt. Abe Williamson, who, it will be remembered, drove the coach which they robbed at McLaughlin's. As they left the jail, Jim Reynolds called out to Gen. Cook, who stood near watching the procession start, "Good-bye, Dave; this is the end of us." He did not know how soon his prediction was to be fulfilled.

The first night out they camped eight miles from Denver, on Cherry Creek. The prisoners were given an opportunity to escape, but they knew better than to try it. The next day the troops moved on to Russelville, where they camped for the night. Again the prisoners were given a chance to escape, but were afraid to try it.

The next morning they were turned over to a new guard, under command of Sergt. Williamson. They were marched about five miles from camp, and halted near an abandoned log cabin. Williamson now told the prisoners that they were to be shot; that they had violated not only the civil but the military law, and that he had orders for their execution. Capt. Reynolds pleaded with him to spare their lives, reminding him of the time when the robbers had him in their power and left him unharmed. Williamson's only reply was the brutal retort that they "had better use what little time they still had on earth to make their peace with their Maker." They were then blindfolded, the soldiers stepped back ten paces, and Sergt. Williamson gave the order, "Make ready!" "Ready!" "Aim!" "Fire!" The sight of six unarmed, blindfolded, manacled prisoners being stood up in a row to be shot down like dogs unnerved the soldiers, and at the command to fire they raised their pieces and fired over the prisoners, so that but one man was killed, Capt. Reynolds, and he was at the head of the line opposite Williamson. Williamson remarked that they were "mighty poor shots," and ordered them to reload. Then several of the men flatly announced that they would not be parties to any such cold-blooded murder, and threw down their guns, while two or three fired over their heads again at the second fire, but Williamson killed his second man. Seeing that he had to do all the killing himself, Williamson began cursing the cowardice of his men, and taking a gun from one of them, shot his third man. At this juncture, one of his men spoke up and said he would help Williamson finish the sickening job. Suiting the action to the word, he raised his gun and fired, and the fourth man fell dead. Then he weakened, and Williamson was obliged to finish the other two with his revolver. The irons were then removed from the prisoners, and their bodies were left on the prairie to be devoured by the coyotes. Williamson and his men rejoined their command and proceeded on to Fort Lyon, with Williamson evidently rejoicing in the consciousness of duty well done.

Several hours afterward one of the prisoners, John Andrews, recovered consciousness. Although shot through the breast, he managed to crawl to the cabin and dress his wound as best he could. He found a quantity of dried buffalo meat, left there by the former occupants, upon which he managed to subsist for several days, crawling to a spring nearby for water. About a week later, Andrews, who had recovered wonderfully, hailed a horseman who was passing, and asked him to carry a note to a friend in the suburbs of Denver. The stranger agreed to do this, and Andrews eagerly awaited the coming of his friend, taking the precaution, however, to secrete himself near the cabin for fear the stranger might betray him. On the third day a covered wagon drove up to the cabin, and he was delighted to hear the voice of his friend calling him. His friend, who was J. N. Cochran, concealed him in the wagon, and taking him home, secured medical attendance, and by careful nursing soon had him restored to health and his wounds entirely healed. While staying with Cochran, Andrews related to him the history of the guerrilla band as it is given here, with the exception of the story of the buried treasure, which neither he nor any of the other members of the band, except Jim and John Reynolds, knew anything about.

When he had fully recovered, Andrews decided to make an effort to find John Reynolds and Stowe, who, he thought, had probably gone south to Santa Fe. Cochran gave him a horse, and leaving Denver under cover of darkness, he rode southward. Reaching Santa Fe, he soon found Reynolds and Stowe, and the three survivors decided to go up on the Cimarron, where they had cached a lot of silver and other plunder taken from the Mexican wagon train on the way out from Texas. Their horses giving out, they attacked a Mexican ranch to get fresh ones. During the fight Stowe was killed, but Reynolds and Andrews succeeded in getting a couple of fresh horses and making their escape. They rode on to the Cimarron, and found the stuff they had hidden, and then started back over the old trail for Texas. The second day out, they were overtaken by a posse of Mexicans from the ranch where they had stolen the horses, and after a running fight of two or three miles, Andrews was killed. Reynolds escaped down the dry bed of a small arroyo, and finally succeeded in eluding his pursuers. Returning to Santa Fe, he changed his name to Will Wallace, and lived there and in small towns in that vicinity for several years, making a living as a gambler. Tiring of the monotony of this kind of a life, Reynolds formed a partnership with another desperado by the name of Albert Brown, and again started out in the holdup business. They soon made that country too hot to hold them, and in October, 1871, they started toward Denver.

When near the Mexican town of Taos, they attempted to steal fresh horses from a ranch one night, and Reynolds was mortally wounded by two Mexicans, who were guarding the corral. Brown killed both of them, and throwing Reynolds across his horse, carried him for several miles. At length he found an abandoned dugout near a little stream. Leaving his wounded comrade there, he set out to conceal their horses after having made Reynolds as comfortable as possible. He found a little valley where there was plenty of grass and water, about two miles up the cañon. Leaving his horses there, he hastened back to the dugout, where he found Reynolds in a dying condition, and the conversation related in the first chapter of this story took place.

Brown pushed on northward to Pueblo, intending to push his way along the Arkansas on up into the park, but found that the snow was already too deep. Returning to Pueblo, he pushed on to Denver. He stayed there all winter, selling his horses and living upon the proceeds. When spring came he was broke, but had by chance made the acquaintance of J. N. Cochran, who had befriended John Andrews, one of the gang, years before. Finding that Cochran already knew a great deal about the gang, and needing someone who had money enough to prosecute the search, he decided to take Cochran into his confidence. Cochran was an old '58 pioneer, and had been all over the region where the treasure was hidden, and knowing that Brown, who had never been in Colorado before, could not possibly have made so accurate a map of the locality himself, agreed to fit out an outfit to search for the treasure. They took the map drawn by Reynolds while dying, and followed the directions very carefully, going into the park by the stage road over Kenosha hill, then following the road down the South Platte to Geneva Gulch, a small stream flowing into the Platte. Pursuing their way up the gulch, they were surprised at the absence of timber, except young groves of "quaking asp," which had apparently grown up within a few years. They soon found that a terrible forest fire had swept over the entire region only a short time after the outlaws were captured, destroying all landmarks so far as timber was concerned.

They searched for several days, finding an old white hat, supposed to be Singletary's, near where they supposed the battle to have taken place, and above there some distance a swamp, in which the bones of a horse were found, but they could not find any signs of a cave. Running out of provisions they returned to Denver, and after outfitting once more returned to the search, this time going in by way of Hepburn's ranch. They found the skeleton of a man, minus the head (which is preserved in a jar of alcohol at Fairplay), supposed to be the remains of Owen Singletary.

They searched carefully over all the territory shown on the map, but failed to find the treasure cave. Cochran finally gave up the search, and he and Brown returned again to Denver.

Brown afterward induced two other men to go with him on a third expedition, which proved as fruitless as the other two trips. On their return, Brown and his companions, one of whom was named Bevens and the other an unknown man, held up the coach near Morrison and secured about $3,000. Brown loafed around Denver until his money was all gone, when he stole a team of mules from a man in West Denver, and skipped out, but was captured with the mules in Jefferson County by Marshal Hopkins. Brown was brought to Denver and put in jail, while Gen. Cook was serving his second term as sheriff. When Sheriff Willoughby took charge in 1873, Brown slipped away from the jailer and concealed himself until he had an opportunity to escape. He went to Cheyenne, and from there to Laramie City, where he was killed in a drunken row.

Gen. Cook secured Brown's map, and a full account of the outlaw's career substantially as given here, and although he has had many opportunities to sell it to parties who wished to hunt for the treasure, he declined all of them, preferring rather to wait for the publication of this work. There is no question but that the treasure is still hidden in the mountain, and, although the topography of the country has been changed somewhat in the last thirty-three years by forest fires, floods, and snow-slides, some-one may yet be fortunate enough to find it.

Seven

The Amazing Mr. Leslie

J. North Conway

GEORGE LESLIE BOWED SLIGHTLY AS IF BEING INTRODUCED TO ROYALTY while graciously shaking Fisk's hand in a hearty, congratulatory way. As in everything he did, Leslie's gesture was deliberate and rehearsed. It was not done solely for Fisk and his guests. He had practiced his outward behavior as if preparing for a part in a play, and perhaps George Leslie did indeed see himself as the leading man in some lavish production of his own creation. He would spend hours standing before the full-length mirror in his hotel room, practicing his bow, his handshake, and his intriguing smile.

Each bow had its purpose—always to show respect, of course, but also to indicate his level of admiration and respect for the person he was being introduced to. A slight bow, more of a tip of his head than anything else, was reserved for those he was not enamored of. A more pronounced bow, bending slightly at his waist with his shoulders thrust a bit forward, was used for those he was interested in becoming acquainted with but had yet to discover why or how. The last bow in his repertoire, a full-blown flourishing bow at the waist, was strictly reserved for the cream of the crop, and Jubilee Jim Fisk was surely one of New York City's finest.

Leslie also took great pains to practice his handshake by using a pincushion and standing in front the mirror. The faint, barely recognizable handshake, limp in nature, was once again reserved for the general populace. It was a handshake that said, "Yes, I am required to do this, but I have no interest in continuing any relationship with you." The indents in the pincushion would be hardly noticeable. His second handshake, reserved for those he was inclined toward knowing better, was a tighter, firmer handshake—not overly aggressive, but sincere and memorable, one that was sure to let the person know that he was indeed pleased to be in his or her company and would like to continue the relationship. The pincushion would show the clear definition of his palm and fingers. Lastly, reserved, once again, for the cream of the crop, like Fisk and others whom he greatly admired or in some way wished to emulate, he had practiced a hearty, lasting, congratulatory, and overly animated handshake that clearly conveyed his great admiration and respect. In this case, the pincushion he practiced on would show the effect of his crushing grip.

For the ladies he was introduced to, he had developed a single sweeping gesture that he had practiced endlessly to perfection. This and only this modus operandi applied to every woman, young or old, rich or poor, beautiful or homely. He would bow with great enthusiasm, as if greeting a long-lost friend, cup the woman's hand gently in his, as if not so much holding her hand as balancing it delicately on his own, and with the slightest brush of his lips, he would kiss her hand and then gently remove his own, leaving the woman's hand floating in space. The kiss was always brief and appropriate but tinged with a certain sense of mystery. Rising up from his bow and from kissing the woman's hand in this gentlemanly way, he would maintain deep and penetrating eye contact with the woman, as if judging her response to his ovation. It usually sent hearts aflutter, exactly the reaction he was looking for.

His smile too was practiced to perfection, often many times before going out in public. A slight parting of his lips beneath his dark trimmed mustache was reserved for the general public. A broader, more expansive grin, where he bared his pearly white teeth, was awarded to those he would like to get to know better. And a wide, open-mouthed smile that stretched lines in his cheeks—sometimes referred to as smiling from ear to ear—was saved for royalty like Jubilee Jim. Being introduced to Fisk at Delmonico's, Leslie pulled out all the stops. Smiling ear to ear, he bowed deeply and shook Fisk's hand heartily.

Leslie was introduced as a successful architect from Cincinnati, the son of a wealthy Toledo beer magnate. Even before being introduced to the other two people dining with Fisk, Ned Stokes and Josie Mansfield, Leslie congratulated Fisk on his new theatrical venture, the Grand Opera House. Leslie noted that Pike's Opera House—which had been refurbished by Fisk and renamed the Grand Opera House—had been built by a Cincinnati man, Samuel N. Pike. Leslie lavished praise on Fisk for what he had accomplished, making the opera house the most majestic theatrical venue in the entire city. Fisk was not beyond flattery when it came to the theater, and he beamed with pride upon hearing Leslie's unsolicited assessment of the place. His plump cheeks grew rosy red with delight. Fisk immediately offered Leslie free tickets to his newest production, an extravagant musical performance called *The Twelve Temptations*.

Fisk took an immediate liking to the gentlemanly George Leslie after their brief encounter at Delmonico's. Fisk subsequently sent Leslie an invitation to join him at a private party to be held at 79 Clinton Street, the home of Marm Mandelbaum. The invitation intrigued Leslie. He had heard of Fredericka Mandelbaum from friends, and was well aware that she was known as the biggest fence in the city. Whatever Jim Fisk was doing associating with the likes of her was beyond him, but Leslie was more than happy to attend. Perhaps Mandelbaum could open a few of the doors that Leslie was hoping to step through. Since he had abandoned all thought of plying his trade as an architect, and since he didn't really know what he wanted to do with the rest of his newfound life in New York City, he thought meeting Marm Mandelbaum might be a step in the right direction, since he had come to New York City intent on beginning a new career—a life of crime.

It wasn't losing the money that bothered Leslie, although the two hundred dollars that had been in his wallet was a lot of money by anyone's standards. And it wasn't losing his personal papers that were also in the wallet; he could always replace them. It was the little, round metal plate—the prototype of his invention—that was irreplaceable. He had been working on it for three years and had yet to test it out. Somewhere in one of his many notebooks he had sketches of it. But these notebooks, along with the rest of his possessions, were still in transit, coming by train from Cincinnati to

New York. Losing this small mechanical device would be a major setback for him. Among his many other talents, George Leslie had an uncanny mechanical ability. His invention, a little tin wheel that he had sarcastically dubbed "the little joker," might take a year or more to duplicate. It had been stolen when someone picked his pocket at the train station.

Leslie had left Delmonico's restaurant feeling on top of the world. He had met the infamous Jubilee Jim Fisk; he'd received free tickets to the Grand Opera House performance of the sold-out show, *The Twelve Temptations*; and he'd also received a personal invitation by Fisk to attend the next dinner party at Marm Mandelbaum's.

Fredericka "Marm" Mandelbaum, acknowledged by almost everyone as "The Queen of the Underworld," was also known for throwing some of the most lavish parties in the city, where she entertained many of New York's wealthiest socialites, including businessmen, lawyers, judges, and politicians. Word was that you really hadn't made it in New York City if you hadn't been to one of Marm's exclusive soirees. She was definitely someone Leslie wanted to meet.

⸺ ❦ ⸺

Along with being a time of great industrialization in the country, 1869 was also a time of great inventions, both large and small. Thomas Edison created his first invention, the electric vote counter, which could instantly record votes. It was intended to be used in congressional elections, but members of the United States House of Representatives rejected it. He also invented the stock ticker that year, an electrical mechanism that would keep investors updated on their stock-market dealings.

Ives McGaffey invented the first vacuum cleaner, a "sweeping machine" that cleaned rugs. Inventor Sylvester H. Roper built the first steam-powered motorcycle. The first typewriter was invented and patented by Christopher Sholes, Samuel Soule, and Carlos Glidden. In George Leslie's home state of Ohio, W. F. Semple invented chewing gum.

All of these inventions in some way revolutionized life in America. Not to be outdone by any of these extraordinary devices, George Leslie also tried his capable hand at inventing. His invention would also revolutionize a certain aspect of American life, specifically banking—more specifically, bank robbing. If he was correct, Leslie was certain that his "little joker" would turn bank robbing into a modern science, no longer requiring holdups, guns, dynamite, or any other previously used, time-consuming apparatus.

In 1862, Linus Yale Jr. invented the modern combination lock. Almost everyone believed that the new combination locks were burglarproof. What they hadn't counted on was something as inventive as George Leslie's little joker. It was a simple device: a small tin wheel with a wire attached to it that would fit inside the combination knob of any bank safe. All anyone had to do was take off the dial knob of a bank lock and place the little joker on the inside of the dial. Then, after carefully replacing the knob, it could be left there undetected. When bank officials opened the vault the next day during regular business hours, Leslie's little joker, still concealed under the safe's knob, would record where the tumblers stopped by making a series of deep cuts in the tin wheel. The deepest cuts in the wheel would show the actual numbers of the combination. Although it wouldn't record the exact order of the numbers in the combination, it would only be a matter of trying several different combinations before the safe would open. Leslie was sure of it.

A bank robber could then sneak back into the bank, remove the knob, and examine the marks in the tin plate. All the robber had to do was figure out the exact order in which the stops were used. Using the device *did* require a robber to break into a bank twice—once to place the contraption inside the dial of the vault, and a second time to retrieve it—and not many robbers had the aptitude or patience to perform such a tricky endeavor. It would take a very special kind of person to accomplish the undertaking, someone with brains, patience, and nerves of steel. George Leslie saw himself as that person.

The little joker eliminated the need to use dynamite to blow open a vault. Robbers often blew up more than just the vault door when pulling off a bank heist. Hundreds of times robbers used too much dynamite and ended up blowing up all the cash, securities, and other valuables inside— or worse, injuring themselves. And of course, the blast from using dynamite drew attention and caused panic, leading to many failed robbery attempts.

The little joker also eliminated the need for long and laborious safe-cracking techniques used by many robbers—turning the dial this way and that to determine the right sequence of combination clicks. Safecracking took hours and it wasn't foolproof. Leslie was sure that his device was the safest, most effective way of robbing a bank. No bank vault would be safe from it.

The most popular method of safecracking was to simply steal the entire safe and move it to a place where it could be taken apart in a leisurely fashion. However, banks and other financial institutions were now investing in huge, complex steel vaults, so moving a safe was no longer an option. Most robbers were forced to use one of four techniques: lock manipulation to determine the combination, screwing the vault, drilling it, or blowing up the vault using either gunpowder or dynamite. None of these methods were expedient.

Lock manipulation required skill and time. The robber would try a series of possible combinations, listening to the tumblers through a stethoscope to determine the exact location where the tumblers stopped. The process could take an inordinate amount of time, and depending upon the number of tumbler stops, it would require the robber to try hundreds, if not thousands, of possible combinations.

Screwing the vault required the robber to drill a hole into the door plate and then tap a thread through it where a heavy machine bolt would be inserted and used to slowly unscrew the door bolts. This was also time-consuming, depending on the thickness of the door. It also required the robber to use dozens of drill bits that would be chewed up in the process.

Drilling required the robber to have access to engineering drawings of the vault's bolt mechanism, and then locating a point on the safe door to drill through. A screwdriver was then shoved through the opening and maneuvered to free the bolts. This process bypassed the vault's combination lock completely. It was also a lengthy process, and without the vault's engineering schematic showing the exact workings of the lock, there was no way of telling where the correct spot was to begin drilling.

Finally, bank robbers could resort to using either gunpowder or dynamite to blow up the safe. Although faster than any of the other three methods, it was fraught with danger. Too little gunpowder and the lock would not be blown. Too much dynamite, and not only would the vault door be blown off its hinges, but the contents of the safe could also be blown to smithereens. In the worst-case scenario, the robbers could blow themselves up as well. The explosion caused by using either gunpowder or dynamite always attracted attention.

But these methods were all a bank robber had to work with, except for the mythical device that some robbers had unsuccessfully tried to create. It would let the robber know exactly what the vault combination was so that the vault could be opened quickly, safely, and without drawing attention to the crime. Many criminals had tried to perfect such a device but none had succeeded; that is, not until George Leslie put his mind to it.

The Mandelbaums may have lived in meager surroundings on the upper floor of the Clinton Street address, but Marm's guests experienced only luxury in the lavishly furnished back portion of the building, where she did all of her entertaining. As she had accumulated wealth and stature in the criminal community, she gained a certain notoriety in the legitimate world. She became adept at living in both worlds, learning how to deftly balance between the legitimate world and the underbelly of the criminal one.

Although Mandelbaum was the leading criminal fence in New York City, she was, by her own account, still a lady. She had exquisite taste and manners and was an avid admirer of intelligence and sophistication. She wouldn't tolerate foul language around her, especially at her dinner parties. She expected everyone, especially the rough trade she surrounded herself with, to be on their best behavior when they were in her company. Those that couldn't abide by these rules were seldom allowed to do business with her. She was constantly trying to improve the lagging social graces of her criminal friends, imploring them to read and aspire to proper etiquette and good manners.

Her parties were considered the highlight of the city's social season, where thieves and thugs would mix freely with businessmen and politicians. Many of these legitimate guests ironically had homes and businesses that had probably been robbed by the very crook sitting next to them at the lavish banquet table Mandelbaum always set. Still, no one who was anyone in New York City could resist an invitation to one of her parties. George Leslie was no exception.

Leslie arrived at his first dinner party at Marm's wearing his best attire: a Highland frock coat, an elegant Wyatt striped shirt with a string tie, wool tailcoat pants, and a Farrington vest, with its high-cut, notched collar—the kind so many businessmen in New York City were wearing at the time. He wore a black Victorian top hat and white formal gloves and carried a cane, a hardwood staff topped with a shiny brass three-knob crown.

Leslie had the carriage drop him off at the front door of Mandelbaum's store on Clinton Street. He held a package under his arm. The store was dark. He strode to the door and knocked loudly, but there was no answer. He was sure he had the right date and the right address. He knocked again and finally heard someone coming.

Mandelbaum's teenage son Julius, fair-haired and slim, opened the door and let him in. Behind Julius stood Herman Stroude, Mandelbaum's part-time clerk and full-time bodyguard. Muscular and tall, he towered over Leslie, who was himself at least six feet tall. Stroude was bald, wore a gold earring in his ear, and had a bushy black mustache. Julius reluctantly made eye contact with Leslie as he explained that he'd been invited to the party by Jim Fisk. He gave Julius one of his cards. Stroude took the card and went upstairs to verify Leslie's story with Jubilee Jim, who was already enjoying the gala event with Josie Mansfield. When Stroude returned a few minutes later he whispered something to Julius.

Julius led the dandified Leslie through the darkened store to a long corridor, up several flights of stairs, and into a huge, brilliantly lit dining room, filled with a bustling, noisy crowd. Guests were laughing, chatting, and eating while a piano player off in the corner played a rousing version of "Little Brown Jug." It was one of the most popular songs in 1869, played in respectable saloons and dance halls throughout the city, as well as being a musical staple in the city's so-called "free and easies," the more disreputable drinking establishments that provided music as well as prostitutes. These large riotous taverns proliferated throughout the New York

City slums. "Little Brown Jug" was written by Joseph Eastburn Winner, the brother of another popular composer during the same period, Septimus Winner. Septimus's songs "Listen to the Mockingbird" and "Oh, Where Has My Little Dog Gone" were both popular dance hall and tavern favorites.

Mandelbaum's dining room was spacious, elegant, and comfortable, with plush carpets of red and gold and an assortment of formal dining tables and chairs, as well as upholstered couches and high-back leather chairs. The room featured a coffered ceiling and hand-carved woodwork, including an ornate fireplace and bookcases. Huge pocket doors separated the two parlor sections. The windows were covered with luminously embroidered silk drapes along with carved wooden shutters that concealed guests from prying eyes. The ceilings rose nearly twelve feet high, where the cut-glass chandeliers hung at a lower level, in keeping with the practice during the Gilded Age, when lighting needed to be closer to arm's reach for quick replacement.

More than sixty guests dined at the many tastefully set, Chippendale-style mahogany tables with matching chairs, each of which had a shaped crest with acanthus carving on it. Mandelbaum, who was too huge to fit comfortably into one of the chairs, was seated on an embroidered, cushioned bench. All the tables were covered with ornate linen tablecloths and decorated with gold candelabras. The walls were covered with paintings, some framed, some not. The elaborate decor of the dining room was abundant with Victorian elegance and whimsy, all of it stolen from some of the best homes and offices throughout the city and country. Mandelbaum had exquisite taste in stolen property.

Guests dined on lamb and sliced ham that was provided at the party by "Piano" Charlie Bullard. Bullard was a former butcher who now focused on his talent for safecracking. However, when called upon, he still provided the best cuts of meat for Marm's parties. Bullard was also a trained pianist, able to perform the most intricate piano concertos. He was known throughout the underworld for having the most sensitive fingers in the safecracking business. No bank safe tumbler was safe from Bullard's nimble fingertips. Bullard often entertained Marm's dinner guests, playing anything from Beethoven to the most popular songs of the day on the white, baby grand piano that adorned Marm's lavish dining room. It was Bullard who was playing the rollicking version of "Little Brown Jug" as Leslie entered the room.

As Leslie stepped out of the dark hallway into the crowded, gaily lit, and festive dining room, George Leslie knew he had arrived—in more ways than one.

That evening at Marm's party, Leslie paid his respects to Fisk, thanking him profusely for inviting him. Fisk told Leslie that Marm was anxious to meet him, advising him to introduce himself to her, posthaste. He did what Fisk suggested and made his way over to Marm's table straightaway.

Mandelbaum was busy holding court in a far corner of the busy dining room. When Leslie introduced himself, Mandelbaum's otherwise downward-curved mouth turned into a smile. Marm asked Shang Draper to move down so that Leslie could sit next to her, a place of honor by anyone's account. The request annoyed Draper, who had become, or so he imagined, second in command to Mandelbaum. He didn't like the idea of having anyone take his place next to Marm, either physically or figuratively. Nonetheless, Draper grudgingly moved over and Leslie sat down next to Mandelbaum.

Leslie immediately thanked Mandelbaum for the invitation to the dinner party, and especially for helping to retrieve his stolen wallet. Leslie had learned from Sheriff O'Brien, to whom Leslie had paid a handsome reward, that he owed his gratitude to Marm. It was only through her efforts that the wallet had been returned, almost intact—sans the two hundred dollars, of course. Leslie had only been concerned with the return of his little joker, which was now sitting safely in the Fifth Avenue Hotel's safe, along with many of his other precious possessions.

Mandelbaum took an immediate liking to George Leslie. Perhaps it was his good looks, or his manners. Perhaps it was because Marm always prided herself on being a good judge of character, and she sensed that the handsome, well-mannered gentleman from Cincinnati had a larcenous heart. In fact, being a good judge of character, she knew he did.

Once Leslie was seated comfortably next to Marm, she clapped her hands and a young boy maneuvered through the noisy crowd, carrying a tray of wineglasses. Leslie recognized the boy immediately. It was the young pickpocket from the train station. Along with his many other attributes, Leslie was also gifted with a near-photographic memory. He could look at something or someone for the briefest time and recall the person or place in the minutest detail.

The pickpocket—who was called Johnny Irving—had a shock of blond hair and wide blue eyes. He wasn't dressed in the rags he'd been wearing earlier at the train station; instead, he now sported a white shirt, black vest, and bowtie. Leslie politely took a glass of wine and handed it graciously to Marm. He then took one for himself, all the while keeping his eyes fixed on Irving, who grew more uncomfortable by the minute. Leslie asked after the boy's younger sister. Irving pretended not to understand. Marm intervened, asking if Leslie knew the boy. Leslie explained how he had run into the boy and his sister at the train station. Marm told him that she made every attempt to care for the poor orphaned street children by finding them work. She boasted of running a small school for them on Grand Street. Leslie had heard all about the "school" she ran.

Leslie was bright enough to realize that it was Irving who had stolen his wallet that day at the train station, and that he worked for Marm as one of her many criminals in training. It was the only way he could have gotten his wallet back nearly intact. Irving had stolen it and dutifully returned it to his teacher and benefactor, Marm Mandelbaum. It made perfect sense. Still, Leslie had to wonder, of all the possibly hundreds of wallets stolen by Mandelbaum's cadre of young pickpockets, why had his been so readily returned to him? Sheriff O'Brien had only been the go-between. It was Marm who'd had the wallet and Marm who returned it to him. It was a puzzle to Leslie.

With Irving still standing in front of them, Leslie quickly brought up the issue of the stolen wallet. He again thanked Mandelbaum for returning it to him. Marm took no credit for finding the wallet, explaining that it had been all Sheriff O'Brien's doing. She explained that the wallet had simply and miraculously come into her possession when someone, she could not remember who, had brought it into her store claiming that they had found it. It was pure coincidence as far as she was concerned. God, she told him, worked in mysterious ways. So did Marm Mandelbaum, Leslie suspected.

It was just too bad that he'd lost his one hundred dollars, Marm said. Leslie winked at Irving, who looked as though he was about to drop his tray and bolt at any second. Both Leslie and little Johnny Irving knew that his wallet had contained *two* hundred dollars. For one brief moment the knowledge of that fact struck a tenuous bond between Leslie and Irving.

Marm waved Irving off. Before he could make his getaway, Leslie reached into his pocket and handed him a silver dollar, commending the boy for his fine service. Irving looked at Marm before taking Leslie's tip. She nodded approvingly and Johnny Irving snatched the silver dollar and tucked it safely away, no doubt relieved that Leslie hadn't revealed his deception to Mandelbaum.

Irving's secret was safe with Leslie. Based on what the police officer had told him, Leslie knew that Mandelbaum's little pickpockets only received a small percentage of what they stole for her. There was, of course, no honor among thieves. Irving must have returned only half of what was in Leslie's wallet. The rest he must have kept for himself and his sister. *Enterprising boy*, Leslie thought.

After Irving left, Leslie explained that he didn't care so much about the money; it was the contents of the wallet that mattered most to him. Some of it was irreplaceable, he said. Marm understood completely. Of all the people in the world who might have appreciated what it was George Leslie was trying to perfect—the Holy Grail for bank robbers—Marm Mandelbaum was at the top of the list. Leslie wasn't the first to try to create a device that could be used to surreptitiously uncover the combination to any bank safe. And now that Marm knew he had a safecracking instrument tucked away in his wallet, she was anxious to find out why. This handsome young man from Cincinnati didn't look or act like any of her other employees. For the first part of the evening, Mandelbaum would not let Leslie leave her side, much to the chagrin of her other criminal guests, always eager to bask in her ample limelight and good favor.

Red Leary tapped Leslie on the shoulder. He pointed to Marm, who was standing on the other side of the room, waiting for him. Leslie bid Tilden and Fisk good-bye. Stokes now sat sullenly beside Mansfield. Leslie saw no reason to engage him further. He headed across the room to where Marm was waiting to take him downstairs to the storefront, the only place they could talk privately. Leslie graciously took the arm of his hostess as she led him out of the brightly lit room into the dark corridor and down the stairs.

Although Marm was taken by the gentlemanly Leslie, she was nobody's fool. She needed to test him to be sure he wasn't an agent for the police or the Pinkerton detectives. Mandelbaum had enough money to bribe police and politicians in order to stay one step ahead of the law, but the uncompromising Pinkerton detectives were different. They were incorruptible, which made them dangerous to Mandelbaum and her criminal empire.

The Pinkerton Detective Agency was started in 1852 by Allan Pinkerton, a deputy sheriff in Chicago. It quickly grew to become the vanguard of criminal detection, known for its high moral standards and relentless pursuit of criminals. It was reportedly the prototype for the Federal Bureau of Investigation. During the Civil War, Allan Pinkerton was the head of the Union secret service, responsible for spying on the Confederacy. The agency was also given the job of guarding President Abraham Lincoln. Their slogan was "We Never Sleep," and the sign that hung over their offices in Chicago depicted a huge, black-and-white, wide-open eye. This logo led to the term "private eye."

In later years, the Pinkerton Detective Agency became known as an instrument of big business, acknowledged more for squashing union riots and strikes than for pursuing criminals. Notably, in 1875, the Pinkertons infiltrated and crushed the Molly Maguires, a secret coal miners' organization in Schuylkill County, Pennsylvania. They also broke up the strike of the iron and steel workers' union at Andrew Carnegie's Homestead plant in Pittsburgh. But before their image was forever tarnished by their link to big business and efforts to suppress the burgeoning labor movement in America, the Pinkerton Detective Agency, under the leadership of Allan Pinkerton and later, his two sons, Robert and William, was engaged in the pursuit of known criminal gangs and most conspicu-ously, Marm Mandelbaum. They were a dangerous force to be reckoned with, and Mandelbaum was not about to take any chances. She had to be sure that George Leslie was not a Pinkerton agent sent to infiltrate her operation.

Alone downstairs in the dingy storefront, far from the gaiety upstairs and from prying eyes, Mandelbaum confronted Leslie. She wanted to know what he was doing with something like the little joker in his wallet. Although she didn't know Leslie's name for his invention, she certainly knew what the contraption was supposed to be used for. She had seen similar devices before, dozens of times, and she had seen them all fail to produce the desired result—miraculously opening up a bank safe. She laid her cards on the table: She knew what he had in his wallet; what she wanted to know now was why someone of Leslie's upbringing, education, and social standing would have such a device.

Leslie gave it to her straight. He wanted to rob banks, and his little joker would help him do it. He explained to her how it worked and how it would revolutionize bank robbing. Mandelbaum had heard it all before. Leslie explained he'd tested it on his own safe and it worked like a charm. Mandelbaum still wasn't convinced. There was a big difference between using the device on a safe he had in his room, with all the time in the world to fiddle with it, and actually using it in a real bank robbery where you potentially had someone breathing down your neck. Leslie agreed. He told her that was why he wanted her to give him a chance to prove it to her.

Mandelbaum feigned surprise. Whatever made him think she knew anything about robbing banks? She stared at him suspiciously, complain-ing that the rich food and wine had upset her stomach. Leslie played along, boasting that if she was looking for somebody to rob a bank, he was the man to do it. He provided a litany of his qualifications, explaining that he had been gifted with a photographic memory. That, along with his understanding of architectural design, allowed him to practically memo-rize the layout of any building after seeing it only briefly.

She agreed that this was an amazing ability, to be able to size up any room or building so quickly, a gift that must be helpful in his career as an architect. Helpful in perhaps other careers as well, Leslie told her—including robbing banks.

Mandelbaum wanted to know why he wanted to rob a bank. It was dangerous, and if he was caught he could spend years in prison. Leslie assured her that he would never get caught, and that his device would take all the danger out of robbing a bank. There would be no need for laborious safecracking, no need for dynamite or any other explosives, and no need for guns or weapons of any kind. He said he had it down to a science.

He still hadn't answered her question about his motive for robbing a bank. He already appeared to be fairly wealthy. He didn't need the money, did he? It was easy enough to answer. People like Jubilee Jim Fisk robbed everyone—banks, trains, other Wall Street brokers, even the government. And Boss Tweed and his political machine—well, they robbed the city blind. The Carnegies, Belmonts, and Vanderbilts, they all robbed from each other and called it good business. And they all put their money in banks for safekeeping. He just wanted to eliminate the middleman, Leslie explained. If all the robber barons put their money in banks, he would just rob the bank. It made perfect sense to him.

It was beginning to make perfect sense to Mandelbaum as well. Still, no matter how taken she was with this handsome young gentleman, she was a shrewd businesswoman, and an even shrewder criminal. No matter how much she liked him, his loyalty had to be tested—and it would be, soon enough.

Leslie spent much of the remainder of the evening seated in the chair of honor next to Mandelbaum, an act that prompted some speculation and a great deal of envy, especially from Marm's criminal cohorts at the party. Across from Leslie was Max Shinburn, a German-born criminal whose expertise was burglary and safecracking. He was also one of Mandelbaum's favorites because of his gentlemanly demeanor. Shinburn liked to be referred to as "The Baron." He had spent some of his ill-gotten gains buying a title of royalty in Monaco. He and Leslie hit it off famously.

During dinner the guests drank an array of fine sparkling wines from Victorian etched wineglasses, but after the meal they were treated to a variety of mixed drinks prepared by New York City's most famous mixologist, Jerry Thomas. Thomas was the principal bartender at the

Metropolitan Hotel, on the corner of Broadway and Prince Street. He was known as the city's premier bartender, popular among all the best "club men" and widely known for his famous mixed drink inventions, including the "Martinez," a drink wrongly described as the original martini. Thomas's Martinez was made with sweetened gin, red vermouth, maraschino liqueur, and bitters.

Seeing the attention Marm paid to the stranger infuriated Shang Draper, who didn't take lightly to some tinhorn from Cincinnati cutting in on his turf. Draper worked closely with Mandelbaum, using her as both a fence for stolen property as well as a financial resource for bank robberies. He didn't know who Leslie was or what role he might play in the ongoing business of New York City crime, especially as far as his association with Marm was concerned, but he wasn't about to let anyone come between him and his dealings with Marm, especially not the handsome, sophisticated George Leslie. Draper, who had grown up in the horrific Five Points, had a suspicious mind, and worse, an abiding hatred of the upper class.

Another underworld thug who was not pleased with Leslie's encroachment of Mandelbaum was Johnny "The Mick" Walsh, the leader of the notorious Walsh Gang in the Bowery section of the city. Walsh's violent gangland tactics, including shakedowns of businesspeople and immigrants for protection money, dominated the Bowery. Walsh was no friend of Shang Draper's; he was looking to expand his criminal operations throughout the city, and Draper stood firmly in his way. The two gang leaders had been engaged in a long-running feud, and their gangs had fought turf wars in a series of bloody knife fights and gun battles, with neither gang besting the other. A successful albeit shaky peace had been brokered by Mandelbaum, who saw the feud as bad for business. The truce between Draper and Walsh would be shattered many years later during a bloody shootout at Shang Draper's saloon in 1883, with Draper finally getting the best of "The Mick."

Leslie left the dinner party with private invitations extended to him from three people: Mandelbaum, who wanted to discuss his little joker in more detail; Josie Mansfield, who gave him the dates that Fisk would be in Washington; and exotic beauty Black Lena Kleinschmidt, who, despite

Mandelbaum's orders, had found a way to arrange a secret rendezvous with Leslie.

All in all, it had been a very productive evening for George Leslie.

———

Mandelbaum organized a gang for the bank job and put Leslie in charge. She felt he could now concentrate his full attention on what was most important: the robbery of the Ocean National Bank.

The old adage "One man's floor is another man's ceiling" wasn't lost on George Leslie as he prepared to undertake his first bank heist. It was more important for Leslie to know whose ceiling was another's floor as he planned his intricate robbery of the Ocean National Bank. The robbery was one part planning and another part hocus-pocus, but it was all sheer criminal genius.

George Leslie pulled off his first bank heist in June 1869, a few short months after his introduction to Marm Mandelbaum. Mandelbaum supplied Leslie with a handpicked gang of her best and most trusted associates, including Johnny Dobbs, Billy Porter, Jimmy Hope, Gilbert Yost, Red Leary, and Shang Draper. Leslie's gang robbed the Ocean National Bank located at the corner of Greenwich and Fulton Streets, getting away with close to $800,000, an unprecedented amount of cash. The take in the Ocean Bank robbery would have been even higher if Leslie hadn't decided that they would only take what they could carry, and only those items—cash, checks, and jewelry—that were untraceable. He saw no point in stealing bank certificates that could only be cashed at the bank itself, or gold that would weigh them down. Leslie was particular about what he wanted to steal and how he wanted to steal it, which branded him among other criminals he was working with as a prima donna. Prima donna or not, this was his first heist, but would by no means be his last.

It was the largest take of any bank job in the city's history up and until then, and it was pulled off without firing a shot or blowing open the bank safe. Leslie's little joker did all the work. Although Mandelbaum financed the operation at a cost of $3,000, it was Leslie who masterminded the caper. Leslie had clearly demonstrated his amazing knack for planning and pulling off successful, not to mention highly rewarding, bank robberies. It was the beginning of a great career in crime for George Leslie, and an opportunity afforded him solely by Marm Mandelbaum, a fact that Leslie never forgot. Throughout his reign as "the King of Bank Robbers," the title that was later given to him by friends in the criminal world, as well as New York City police officials and newspaper reporters, Leslie paid tribute to Mandelbaum either through a direct percentage from every bank job he pulled or by laundering stolen securities and other valuables through her, whether she'd financed the caper or not. This relationship would last throughout his short life.

Shang Draper had not been so keen on Leslie, seeing him as a challenger to his own lofty position within the crime world, and especially with Marm. He would later come to see Leslie as a threat to someone even more important to him—his wife, Babe Irving.

Planning for the Ocean National Bank heist took three months, much to the chagrin of Draper and the others, who wanted to simply break into the bank vault and blow up the safe. This wasn't what Leslie had in mind and, over almost everyone's objections, Marm put the novice bank robber Leslie in charge of the whole operation. Leslie promised her the biggest payday in criminal history, and he wasn't far off the mark. It would take another nine years before Leslie tried to make good on his promise by pulling off the greatest heist in American history, the robbery of nearly $3 million from the Manhattan Savings Institution on October 27, 1878.

Leslie put Mandelbaum's financial backing to good use, providing his gang with the best burglary tools available, bribing several officials, drawing up a full set of plans for the bank's layout, and actually constructing a room identical to the one inside the Ocean National Bank in one of the many empty warehouses Mandelbaum owned. In the end he needed to borrow another $1,000 in cash from Mandelbaum to rent office space. Although it sounded strange to her, Mandelbaum complied. She had complete trust in Leslie, even though he was a novice in the criminal world. She knew true criminal talent when she saw it, and George Leslie had the quickest criminal mind she had ever witnessed. Besides, she knew that Leslie was good for any amount of money she put up to finance the bank job.

No one had ever gone to the extent Leslie did in planning a bank robbery. At the vacant warehouse, Leslie rehearsed with the gang how the entire operation would work—like clockwork, with each member of the gang performing a specific function at a specific time. He had all the gang study the blueprints and drilled into them the step-by-step process they would take during the robbery. Leslie timed each of the steps so that everything would be done within split seconds. Timing was every-thing as far as Leslie was concerned. Leslie also reenacted the bank heist over and over, throwing in various possibilities and forecasting alternative measures. He even had the gang reenact the robbery in the dark in case something happened to the lighting inside the bank.

Draper and the others weren't accustomed to Leslie's style of lengthy, meticulous planning. They were more adept at blowing things up and taking what they could grab. Leslie wanted a more sophisticated opera-tion, one that he could export to other gangs in the city and across the country—for an advisor's fee, of course. The Ocean National Bank job would be not only his trial run but also his initiation into the New York City crime world. Leslie passed his test with flying colors, not to mention the nearly $800,000 payday in stolen cash, securities, and precious jewelry.

To pull off the bank job, Leslie deposited a large sum of his own money into the Ocean National Bank. This gave him ample opportunity in the months leading up to the heist to visit the institution in the guise of a new depositor. He withdrew his money prior to the robbery. Leslie's many visits to the bank yielded invaluable information, not to mention an in with the bank president. The grounds of the bank were scrutinized until every square inch of the building was known to Leslie. He memorized and then committed to paper the entire layout of the bank, which was located on the first floor of a five-story brownstone. With his knowledge of architecture and his photographic memory, Leslie was able to draw up blueprints of the bank's interior and the outside surroundings that would have put even the most knowledgeable architect to shame. The plans were used to build the replica of the bank where he and the gang rehearsed.

Dining with the bank president and others associated with the bank and its operations, Leslie, who was readily accepted into upper-crust soci-ety, was able to learn the name of the company that had built the bank's safe. Leslie did this under the pretense of verifying that the safe where he was depositing his money was indeed one of the best around. He said that as an architect, he would know a good safe from a bad one, and wanted to see for himself what kind of product the safe maker was known for. He was able to ingratiate himself with the Yale locksmith responsible for the bank's safe. The locksmith boasted that the lock was impenetrable. It had been tested time and time again, and no one had been able to pick the lock. The safe had even been exhibited in Paris where a bevy of international locksmiths had all tried their hands at picking the lock but had failed.

Leslie wasn't about to leave anything to chance. With the information he had obtained from the locksmith, Leslie was able to make the necessary adjustments to the little joker—specifically, to accommodate the size and shape of the dial on the Ocean National Bank safe. Yale lock or not, nothing was safe from the little joker.

Once inserted inside the safe's dial, the joker would duplicate where the tumblers stopped after it was opened and secured several times. Of course, there was the matter of breaking into the bank so that he could remove the dial on the safe, place the joker inside, and then replace the dial so no one was the wiser. That meant he and the gang had to break into the bank twice: once to insert the joker, and once again to remove it, determine the safe combination, and then actually open the safe. With the safe combination known, it would just be a matter of having a skilled safecracker like Johnny Dobbs, one of the best in the business, try any of the various combinations that showed up on the joker to open the safe. This all seemed too elaborate for most of the gang, but that didn't matter; Mandelbaum had designated Leslie as the boss of the operation, and they all fell into line—most of them, anyway.

Draper remained skeptical of Leslie's plan and his motives. He had already secretly ordered Red Leary, the strongman and muscle behind the gang, to be ready to "take care of" Leslie if he did anything stupid. Draper was sure that the dandified Leslie, with no known experience in robbing banks, would fail miserably. If indeed Leslie was a spy, sent by the Pinkertons to infiltrate Mandelbaum's operation, then Draper, with Red Leary's help, would make sure Leslie never lived to tell about it.

Leary told Draper he was ready to take care of Leslie if and when the bank job went south on them. In fact, Leary had no such intentions. Leary knew which side his bread was buttered on, and it was Marm Mandelbaum who was doing the spreading. If she said Leslie was in charge, then Leslie was in charge. Leary was working for Marm, not Draper, and took orders only from her. And her orders were to do whatever George Leslie wanted him to do—even if he told him to kill Draper. Leary was a company man, and the company was Marm Mandelbaum as far as he was concerned.

The most difficult part of the whole operation was trying to introduce one of the gang into the confidence of the bank. The problem was twofold: First, it had to be someone that the bank trusted to hire in some humble capacity. Leslie needed someone on the inside who could let them into the bank after hours to place the joker inside the dial of the safe and then let him in again to retrieve it. The inside man had to be someone Leslie trusted implicitly, because that person would hold Leslie's career—if not his life—in his hands. It also had to be someone the bank would never suspect. Breaking into the bank once was hard enough. Doing it two times was, in most people's estimation, impossible.

But Leslie knew just the man for the job—a boy, actually: Johnny Irving, the young pickpocket. Leslie knew that he had established an unspoken bond with Irving ever since he chose not to reveal to Mandelbaum that Irving had stolen from her. Using his newfound connections at the bank, Leslie was able to persuade the bank president to hire Johnny Irving, who with his blond hair and sad blue eyes looked his angelic best, to sweep up the bank after hours. It was perfect. Leslie now had his trustworthy inside man.

Besides having an inside man in Johnny Irving, Leslie also needed a backup plan and a way to get his burglary tools inside the bank without anyone noticing. A trip down to the Hartz Magic Repository on Broadway took care of one part of the problem. The second part would be far trickier.

Disguising Jimmy Hope with a fake mustache and curly black wig, he had Hope rent office space in the basement of the bank. The bank only occupied the first floor of the building. The entire basement was rented by William Kell. Posing as an insurance agent, Hope was able to rent a small office that opened out onto Fulton Street. Using forged documents, Hope showed Kell his credentials signed by the New York Insurance Department. Claiming to be Lewis Cole, president of the fictitious insurance company, Hope was able to rent the small office for $1,000, paid in advance. (Leslie chose the name Cole because of his admiration for outlaw Cole Younger, who rode with his hero, Jesse James.) Shortly afterward he had a desk, chair, and a huge cabinet moved into the office.

Having carefully surveyed the structure of the bank, Leslie knew that the small office in the basement that Jimmy Hope had successfully secured sat directly below the bank vault. *One man's ceiling, another man's floor.*

When the time came to enter the bank the second time around, during the weekend, Johnny Irving wouldn't be working at the bank so he wouldn't be able to let them sneak inside. Leslie decided he would simply drill a hole in the ceiling of the rented office, which would give them direct access to the bank vault and the safe. Of course, there was the question of all the saws and tools they would need, but Leslie had already thought of that. Everything they needed was stored in the huge cabinet that Hope had delivered to the rented office—pure genius on Leslie's part.

Over the course of a weekend in June 1869, George Leslie, Johnny Dobbs, and Red Leary were able to slip into the Ocean National Bank—twice. Billy Porter, the wheelman for the heist, was parked up the street in a getaway carriage. Gilbert Yost, Jimmy Hope, and Shang Draper all served as lookouts. Leslie made all of them wear theatrical disguises procured from the Opera House, different disguises each time. On the night of the second break-in of the bank, Leslie asked Draper to dress as a woman and keep watch in front of the bank. No one would ever suspect that a well-dressed woman, sporting a parasol and a hat, would be a lookout for a bank robbery. Draper balked at the idea, so Leslie went to Mandelbaum. Of all the members of the gang, Draper had the slightest build. He had small, round shoulders and small, delicate hands, and he was clean-shaven. It would not take very much to disguise him as a woman, Leslie thought. He knew Red Leary wouldn't do, not with his brawny build and flaming red beard.

The night of the robbery, Shang Draper, dressed in a powder-blue gown and wearing a long blond wig and carrying a parasol, stood watch in front of the Ocean National Bank while Leslie, Dobbs, and Leary broke in. The humiliation of it only fueled Draper's animosity toward Leslie.

On the night of the first break-in, Johnny Irving, working late sweeping up around the bank, let the three men in the back door. Using his renowned dexterity and nimble fingers, Johnny Dobbs removed the dial from the safe, following the instructions Leslie had given him. After becoming friends with the safe maker, Leslie had bought a smaller version of the same safe and had it delivered to the warehouse where he had built the replica of the bank. Using what he had learned, Leslie and Dobbs both had ample time to practice removing the safe dial without harming it. The three long months of planning that Leslie had put into the bank heist was paying off.

Dobbs removed the dial on the safe and inserted the little joker inside. Then he replaced the dial so that it appeared as though nothing was out of the ordinary. When bank officials opened the bank vault the next day, Leslie's joker would take care of the rest, recording the combination stops on the lock whenever someone opened the safe during normal business hours.

Leslie knew that there would be more money kept in the bank over the weekend than during the week, so they waited two days until Saturday night. Then they broke in again. This time they drilled a hole in the ceiling of the Lewis Cole & Co. office in the basement of the bank and gained access to the vault through the hole that came up directly opposite the vault. Leslie, Dobbs, and Leary climbed up through the hole to enter the bank for the second time.

Dobbs once again expertly took off the safe dial, removed the joker, and placed the dial back on the safe. Using the series of notches etched into the flat tin plate that had been inserted into the bank dial, Dobbs was able to record the tumbler stops. There were only so many different combinations, and Dobbs began the meticulous process of trying them out. It was only a matter of time before Dobbs established the right combination, and the door to the safe opened easily.

They were in.

Johnny Dobbs was one of the most successful safecrackers in New York City. Although there were plenty of deserving candidates to choose from, he was the best. His real name was Michael Kerrigan, and he had earned his reputation as one of New York City's finest criminals by working his way up the criminal ladder, starting as a fence for stolen merchandise and later graduating to bank robbery, safecracking, and ultimately murder. He was in on George Leslie's 1878 world-record bank robbery of the Manhattan Savings Institution, handpicked by Leslie. After the Manhattan bank robbery, Dobbs bought a small saloon where he tried his hand at going straight. Ironically, it was located almost across the street from the New York police headquarters on Mulberry Street. It was reported that when asked why he'd chosen a saloon so close to police headquarters, he replied, "The nearer to church, the closer to God." His attempt at leading a legitimate life didn't last long, and soon he was back plying his trade in the underworld. Johnny Dobbs enjoyed a near twenty-year criminal career. In 1898 Dobbs was found lying in a gutter, beaten to death. His body was taken to Bellevue Hospital. He died penniless. He was just fifty years old.

Leslie and his gang made off with close to $800,000 in cash, securities, and jewelry in the Ocean National Bank robbery, the largest bank heist in the city's history. They took only what they could carry and only what Leslie told them to steal—no secured certificates and no bags of heavy gold. Not a shot had been fired. Not a single person injured. Not a stick of dynamite used. Not one bit of property wrecked.

Nothing like it had ever been pulled off in the annals of New York City crime. Even the city newspapers gave credit to the culprits: "A masterful bank job pulled off by one very special bank robber," the *New York Herald* proclaimed after authorities were notified of the robbery the following Monday morning. Boss Tweed was reported to have commented, "I couldn't have done better myself."

Leslie had thought of everything, including the fact that if the bank job was performed on the weekend, then bank officials and authorities would not discover it until the following Monday morning, giving Leslie and his gang plenty of time to unload the stolen cash with Marm and make their individual getaways.

Newly appointed police detective Captain Thomas Byrnes was put in charge of the robbery investigation. Despite his expert criminal detection skills, Byrnes's investigation went nowhere fast. Neither Byrnes nor any of the other detectives assigned to the case were able to uncover a single lead in the case. The only puzzlement about the robbery was why the robbers had left behind close to $2 million in cash and securities lying on the vault floor.

Although Byrnes, a top-notch investigator who would go on to become the chief inspector for the city and an incorruptible force in law enforcement, had no leads in the Ocean National Bank robbery, his instincts told him that he was dealing with a whole new breed of bank robber—someone whose intellect was far superior than the usual run-of-the-mill criminal. The only incident noted by Byrnes during his short-lived investigation was the complete withdrawal of funds from the Ocean National Bank by one George L. Leslie. Byrnes was concerned with even the tiniest detail. Through his various sources, Byrnes learned that Leslie was an architect by vocation and a well-to-do gentleman of solid upbringing and education. He wasn't, in Byrnes's estimation, the criminal type. When he learned that Leslie was a frequent guest of Marm Mandelbaum's many dinner parties, Byrnes reportedly remarked, "This can't lead to anything good." How very right he was.

EIGHT

The Northfield Bank Job

J. H. Hanson

BETWEEN THE 23RD OF AUGUST AND THE 5TH OF SEPTEMBER, A COM-
pany of strangers made their appearance at different localities in the State
of Minnesota, attracting attention by their peculiar bearing, remarkable
physique, and decidedly southern phraseology. They would appear sometimes in pairs, and at other times there would be as many as four or five in
company. At one time they would be cattle dealers from Texas, and again
they were gentlemen in search of unimproved lands for speculative pur-
poses, and then again they were a party of engineers and surveyors pros-
pecting for a new railroad when they would make enquires about roads,
swamps, lakes, and timber lands, carefully consulting maps they had with
them, and when opportunity offered Andreas' State Atlas of Minnesota.

These men visited St. Paul, Minneapolis, St. Peter, Red Wing, St.
James, Madelia, Garden City, Lake Crystal, Mankato, Janesville, Cordova, Millersburg, Waterville, and Northfield, putting up at the best
hotels, spending their money freely, and creating a general impression
of free handed liberality. But there was a certain air of audacity blended
with their *sangfroid* and easy manners which led men to think they were
no ordinary persons and aroused speculations as to their true character
and vocation. The registers of the hotels honored by these guests bear the
names of King, Ward, Huddleston, &c., generally written in one line, but
subsequent developments prove these to be merely *nommes de guerre*.

They are next seen on the streets on Monday morning when a young
man, Chas. Robinson who was acquainted with the notorious Jesse James,

went up to one of them and remarked, "How do you do, Jesse, what brings you up this way." When the man addressed, eyeing the speaker keenly from head to foot, replied, "I guess you have mistaken your man," and vaulting into the saddle, galloped away. With this incident, the five men who had attracted so much notice, excited so much admiration, and aroused many vague suspicions, disappeared from Mankato. The same day five similarly dressed, similarly mounted, and similarly appearing strangers arrived in Janesville, a village on the Winona & St. Peter railroad, in Waseca County, about eighteen miles from Mankato.

As at Mankato they stopped at different hotels, two staying at the Johnson house, and two at the Farmers' Home. No one knew where the fifth slept, but on leaving the village on the Tuesday morning they halted some little distance out, and one, taking off his duster, rode back toward the village waving it over his head; he was followed in the maneuver by another when all four rode away. It is thought this was a signal for the fifth man, who, it is supposed, stopped at some house in the neighborhood.

Those who stopped at the Johnson house never made their appearance at the public table until all of the rest of the boarders had finished their meals, and during their stay in the town declined to admit a chambermaid to their room to arrange it. After their departure several packs of playing cards were found in their room torn up and thrown on the floor, and several handful of buttons of various sizes were scattered about, showing that the inmates had been indulging in a protracted game of "poker." The girls who waited on them at table say they were quiet and polite, and never made any trouble.

Cordova is the next place these "gay cavaliers" turn up, all five of them staying at the same hotel, three occupying one room, and two another with a commercial traveler, W. W. Barlow, of Delavan, Wisconsin, who describes them as polite, jocose fellows. They talked considerably of cattle, and from their language and peculiar dialect, Mr. Barlow thought them to be cattle dealers from the south. They left the hotel at 7 o'clock in the morning, politely raising their hats as they rode off. Cordova is about eighteen miles almost directly north from Janesville.

The next night, Wednesday, saw these five men housed at Millersburg, about twenty-four miles west and north of Cordova, in Rice County. They left here at an early hour on Tuesday morning, and at about 10 o'clock appeared in the streets of Northfield, which lies about eleven miles northwest of the latter village.

On the same Wednesday evening, four men stopped at a hotel in Cannon City. The landlord thinks they were Bob Younger, Bill Chadwell, and the two men who finally escaped. He says that the next morning, the 7th, while three of the men were at breakfast, one retired to his room and remained a long time with the door locked. After all had departed, the chambermaid discovered a bloody shirt and a portion of a pair of drawers, one leg of the latter being torn off and carried away. The drawers were soiled with blood and matter, such as would come from an old inflamed gun wound, and it was evident that the wearer had such a wound on one of his legs. This is considered evidence that the man arrested in Missouri, in October, and supposed to have been one of the James brothers, was really him, but the alibi proved by that party appears to be sufficient to prove that it was not.

It will be seen by the foregoing that there were originally nine men engaged in the plot, which gives plausibility to the opinion held by many that the terrible tragedy which followed was the result of a plan conceived by some Minnesota desperadoes, who engaged these desperate southern cut-throats to assist in it.

Northfield is a thriving, pretty little village, situated pleasantly upon both banks of the Cannon River just thirty-nine miles from St. Paul, in Rice County, on the St. Paul and Milwaukee railroad. A neat iron bridge unites the northwest and the southeast sides of the town, and just above the bridge is one of the finest mill races in the state, the water in its incessant flow roaring like the ocean and appearing like a miniature Niagara. There is a large flouring mill on either side of the river belonging to Messrs. Ames & Co. The public buildings are not surpassed in the state for their beauty of design and adaptability of construction, and the Carlton college is another institution of which the town may well be proud. Placed as it is in the center of a rich farming district, the citizens are considered well-to-do, and the bank transacts a large business.

The five strangers appeared on the streets at an early hour of the morning of September 7th, and attracted a great deal of notice from the citizens, some of them recognizing two of the men as a party who visited the village about a week before, stopping at the Dampier House.

At about 11 o'clock two of these horsemen drew up at Jeft's restaurant on the northeast side of the river and asked for dinner. Jeft told them he had nothing ready, but could cook them some eggs and ham. The men told him to do so, ordering four eggs each. Their horses were left standing untied at the back of the premises. After ordering their dinner the two men went out into the street and after some time returned, when they were joined by three others and all sat down to their meal. They entered into familiar discourse with the proprietor of the house, and asked him what was the prospect of the forthcoming presidential election. Jeft's reply was that he took no interest in politics, when one of the men offered to bet him $1,000 that the state would go Democratic. They still chatted on and seemed to be waiting for someone. At length they left and mounted their horses which were a sorrel, a cream color with silver tail and mane, a black, a bay, and a brown, all fine animals, sleek and clean limbed, and showing indications of blood.

After leaving the restaurant, the five horsemen crossed over the bridge, two remaining in bridge square and the other three, riding up to Division Street dismounted, and tied their horses to the posts at the side of the Scriver block. They then sauntered up toward bridge square, and after talking for some few moments leaning against a dry goods box in front of Lee & Hitchcock's store (Scriver block), they walked back toward the bank which they entered. Three other horsemen then came upon the scene and commenced at once to ride up and down the street in dashing style, and calling upon the citizens who from their doors were watching the eccentric proceeding, to get back into their houses, commenced firing pistols in the air with immense rapidity.

Greater confusion could not be imagined than now ensued. Wherever persons were seen upon the street, a horseman would dash up to them in full speed, and pointing a long-barreled glittering pistol at their heads order them to "get in you G—d—s—of a b." The streets were cleared in a few moments and stores were closed in quicker time than it takes to tell it.

But though taken at a disadvantage, when many of the men were out at work or away chicken hunting, the scare of the Northfield boys was but momentary. Collecting their perturbed thoughts men rushed about in search of firearms, but this most necessary desideratum for a successful encounter with a body of desperadoes or madmen, armed to the teeth, was found to be very scarce on this eventful day.

Mr. J. B. Hide, however, succeeded in getting a shot gun with which he blazed away at the marauding scoundrels, or escaped lunatics, for it was not at first exactly understood what the fellows were. Mr. Manning, armed with a breech-loading rifle, came coolly upon the field of action, backed by Mr. L. Stacey and Mr. Phillips, while Dr. Wheeler armed himself with an old breech-loading carbine and, placing himself in a room (No. 8) in the third story of the Dampier House, delivered two very effective shots.

The battle was now at its height, and firing was raging in downright earnest. Manning, from the front of the Scriver block, Bates from the clothing store of Mr. Hanauer, and Wheeler from the window directly over the clothing store, and unobserved by the daring scoundrels, made it lively for the desperate gang, and kept them from passing into Mill Square.

One of the gang was about mounting his horse, and while stooping over the pommel of his saddle with his back toward Wheeler, that gentleman took deliberate aim and fired.

The fellow pitched right over his horse, falling on his head to the earth where he lay gasping for a few moments and soon was everlastingly still.

Manning in the meantime was not idle, and while Wheeler was searching for another cartridge, he advanced from his retreat and seeing a horseman riding towards him up Division Street, he took a steady deliberate aim and fired. The man immediately turned his horse and started off a few paces rapidly, but the horse steadied his pace, the man rocked to and fro, and suddenly the horse stopped and the man fell over to the ground, when another horseman galloped up, sprang from his horse, turned the fallen man over and took from him his pistols and belt, then springing again to his saddle, he rode up the street.

Another scoundrel alighted from his horse and getting behind it commenced a rapid fire down the street, seeing which the intrepid and cool Manning, with all the nonchalance in the world, raised his unerring rifle and stretched the living barricade lifeless at the bandit's feet. The enraged brigand then ran towards Manning, fearless of the formidable weapon of Bates, and sheltering himself behind some packing cases under the open stairway of Scriver block, he commenced a rapid fusilade, evidently with the intention of keeping Manning from firing up the street at others of the gang.

But Wheeler had succeeded in finding another cartridge and returning to the room from which he delivered his first shot, a young lady, who had remained at the window coolly watching the fight throughout, pointed out to Wheeler the man who was keeping Manning from effectual work.

"Only aim as true as you did before," said the brave girl, "and there will be one the less to fight," and Wheeler fired. Instantly the villain dropped his hand upon his thigh, and the girl cried out, "Oh, you aimed too low," thinking the shot had taken effect in the middle third of the right thigh. Wheeler at once left the room in search of another cartridge which unluckily he was unable to find. The wounded man who had changed his pistol to the left hand and discharged several shots at Manning, now turned about, and seeing Bates inside his store with a pistol in his hand and thinking it was from this source he had received his wound, as quick as a lightning flash sent a deadly missive at the unsuspecting Bates.

The ball crashed through the intervening glass of the store front, and burnt a scorching track across the victims face from ear to nose.

But during this time a bloody and terrible tragedy was being enacted in the bank.

Just a few moments before the raiders commenced their wild career on the streets, three men rushed into the bank, holding in their hands large pistols, the glittering barrels of which they directed toward the three gentlemen, Messrs. Heywood, Bunker, and Wilcox, who occupied the desks behind the counter. Springing over the counter these desperadoes shouted out, "Throw up your hands, we intend to rob the bank."

"Which is the Cashier?" one demanded, and instantly approaching Heywood, commanded him to open the safe. "I am not the cashier," was the reply.

The man then turned to Bunker, and made the same demand, but he also denied that he held that important post. The fellow next addressed the bewildered and fear-stricken Wilcox, whose terror prevented him from answering.

The baffled man again turned to Heywood, and with oaths and threats endeavored to make him open the safe. Heywood replied that he could not, when the scoundrel fired a pistol close to his ear, and said "if he did not at once open the safe he would scatter his brains."

The brave Heywood still insisted upon his inability to comply.

The ruffian then seized him by the collar and dragging him toward the safe drew out a long, keen-edged knife, and poising it over Heywood's throat, threatened to cut it from ear to ear if he did not at once open the safe.

But the brave man, faithful to his trust, stolidly refused, when the robber released his hold of his collar and went into the safe vault.

Now was the opportunity for the faithful Heywood.

"If I can but get that ponderous door closed," thought he, "and spring the bolts upon the scoundrel, the villains will be baffled, and my integrity saved from suspicion."

It was a supreme moment of dreadful anxiety to him, and such the intense excitement of his feelings, that when he rushed upon the door to close it, his strength was unequal to the task, and before he could recover himself to renew the effort, a powerful hand seized him by the throat, and threw him back from the vault, at the same time a ruthless arm struck him to the ground with the butt end of a pistol.

Taking advantage of this struggle between Heywood and the robbers, Bunker sprang to his feet and bounded toward the back entrance of the premises.

But before he reached the door a sharp report and the crashing of a ball showed him that he had only miraculously escaped from having his brains scattered by one of the bandits. Bounding out of the bank he ran madly down Water Street, not however till another shot from the murderous revolver crashed through his shoulder.

At this point another of the band of ruffians hastily entered the bank and exclaimed, "Clear boys, the game is up."

The three men instantly jumped upon the counter and made tracks for the door.

But one man paused in his headlong retreat, and seeing Heywood reaching for his desk, turned round and, leveling his revolver at the devoted head of the faithful teller, fired, and without a groan, the brave man fell to the floor, his life blood staining the desk and seat with its crimson stream.

In the street the baffled and retreating murderers sought their horses, and vaulting into their saddles they were soon rushing with frantic haste out of town westward.

It was some few moments before the citizens could sufficiently recover themselves to take in thoroughly the entire situation.

There lay in the open street a few paces from the bank entrance a bandit in all the hideous ghastliness of a bloody death. A few feet from him was stretched the lifeless body of a noble horse, while further down the street on the opposite side another grim corpse lay in a pool of seething gore.

Windows in all directions were shattered, and door posts showed scars of imbedded bullets.

Reluctantly the assembled citizens approached the bank, and the sight which there met their horror-stricken gaze caused a thrill of indignation to seize upon every nerve; and strong men turned pale as they clinched their fists and set their teeth, registering an inward oath to wreak vengeance upon the miscreant perpetrators of the dastardly outrage.

There lay poor Heywood! the man who dared death and defied three of the most notorious scoundrels who ever "cracked a crib" or broke a skull, who resisted torture, and finally gave his life blood in defense of his trust. Who was the man to carry the appalling news to the young wife and tell her that he, upon whom hung her very life, had left her for all time—that he had been torn from her and hurled into dread eternity by the ruthless hand of the bloody assassin!

Who was stout enough to bear the gore-covered mangled corpse to the new desolate and grief-stricken home!

But there were those who were willing to pursue the red-handed murderers.

Some, overcome with indignation, impetuously prepared for the chase, but others, perhaps more determined men, who were willing to follow on to the very death, were not so hasty in their departure, but as time proved were prepared to pertinaciously follow up the trail with the tenacity of the bloodhound.

Two of the former, Davis and Hayes, immediately sought for horses, and none being so ready as those of the two dead robbers, seized them, sprang into the saddles, and were soon in hot pursuit.

Both men were well armed with rifles—one an eighteen-shot Winchester with globe sight. At every point they heard of the retreating villains upon whom they were gaining rapidly. Dashing through Dundas, Hayes and Davis kept up the pursuit till at last they saw a group of horsemen surrounding a wagon from which they were apparently taking the horses. As the pursuers advanced one of the horsemen turned from the wagon, and advancing a few steps up the road ordered the pursuing men to halt.

Davis and Hayes instinctively obeyed, and strange to relate, these two men who had been so impatient to commence the pursuit, now that they were confronted by the audacious scoundrels found their courage waning, and they halted.

Nor did they again find their courage return, but they sat there and saw the marauders after securing one of the farmer's horses again boldly dash away.

After the robbers had gone, Davis and Hayes leisurely wended their way to Millersburg where they awaited the coming of the other pursuers, two men standing but little chance against six such desperadoes.

It is true that Davis and Hayes had the advantage of the bandits in arms, but it is doubtful after all, if there are many men to be found who would have done differently, confronted as they were by six stalwart fierce knights of the road well armed and unscrupulous in shedding human blood, as they had shown at Northfield.

After the departure of Davis and Hayes, about thirty citizens organized into a pursuing party, some mounted on horses, others were carried in wagons and buggies, and all set out in full speed along the road the robbers had taken.

Meantime the telegraph was set at work, and messages were sent to all points. Unfortunately the operator at Dundas was not in his office, and although the call was repeated for an hour no response was made. Had this gentleman been at his post, the people of Dundas would have been prepared to receive the bandits on their arrival.

It has been expressed as a wonder by many that the gang, before making the raid, did not cut the telegraph wires, but it appears from the confession of one of them, that their plan was a much better one. They intended to have destroyed the telegraph instruments before leaving, only the unexpectedly hot attack which was made upon them by the plucky boys of Northfield completely demoralized them.

The first indication received at St. Paul of the daring raid, was from the following telegram to Mayor Maxfield: "Eight armed men attacked the bank at two o'clock. Fight on street between robbers and citizens. Cashier killed and teller wounded. Send us arms and men to chase robbers." JOHN T. AMES.

This telegram reached St. Paul at about 3 p.m. The first train leaving the city for the scene of hostilities, at 4 p.m., was the Owatonna Accommodation, on the Milwaukee & St. Paul road. From St. Paul were dispatched Chief of Police King, detective Brissette, officers Brosseau and Clark, and Deputy Sheriff Harrison. At Mendota Junction, the party was joined by Mr. Brackett and a posse of police, consisting of Capt. Hoy, A. S. Munger, F. C. Shepherd, J. W. Hankinson, and J. West, of Minneapolis, all well armed with seven shooters and rifles. At Rosemount, Farmington, and Castle Rock, the excitement was immense, many persons at these points getting on the cars and proceeding to Northfield.

The train arrived at the scene of the most daring crime ever perpetrated in the state at 6:20, the whole platform being crowded with an excited populace.

The police were at once led by the sheriff to an empty store where were lying the inanimate and ghastly forms of the two bandits who had been shot down by the intrepid Northfield citizens. One was found to be six feet four and a half inches in height; his body exhibited a splendid physical development, with arms and limbs of sinewy muscles and skin as fair and soft as a lady's; his face was of rather an elongated oval with sharply cut features; high cheek bones, well-arched brow, and deep-set blue eyes. His hair was a very dark, reddish auburn, inclined to curl. He wore no hair on his face, but was closely shaved, and did not appear to be more than twenty-three or twenty-five years of age. He was clothed in a new suit of black clothes, worth about twenty-five or thirty dollars, a new colored shirt, and good boots.

The ball which brought him down entered about three inches, in a line with the left nipple and toward the center of the chest, and completely riddling the man, passed out on the same side beneath the shoulder blade. On his person was found the card of the Nicollet House livery stable, St. Peter, on which is printed the distances of the principal cities in this part of the state. He had also on him an advertisement of Hall's safes cut from a local paper. His pockets were well filled with cartridges, and he had round his waist, beneath his coat, a cartridge belt. There has been some dispute as to the identity of the man, but it is now pretty well settled that he is Bill Chadwell *alias* Bill Styles.

There were two men from Cannon Falls, who came to view the bodies before the interment, with the expectation of identifying one of the latter as a brother-in-law of one of the two. He said if it was his relative, a bullet scar would be found under the left arm. The scar was there, but the man would not say whether the fellow was his relation or not. The man whom the big fellow was thought to be, is a former resident of Minneapolis, who has a brother-in-law still living there. This Styles left for Texas some time ago. It is said he was a desperately bad man. It is told that his sister received a letter from him a short time before, saying that now he had lucrative employment, and if she wanted money he would send her some. He also wrote in his letter that he would shortly be up this way, and would call on her. This sister was adopted by a minister residing at Cannon Falls. A letter recently received from the father of Styles proves beyond doubt the identity of the man. Styles's father now lives at Grand Forks, D.T., and says that his son has for some time lived in Texas. The father expresses no surprise at the untimely end of his son, and says he was always a wild wayward boy with whom he could do nothing.

The other man was five feet eight inches in height, but much stouter built than the taller, with hair of the exact color, and like his inclined to curl. His face was rounder and covered with about two weeks' growth of beard; the eyes, like the other's, were blue.

The clothing was quite new, even to the shirt, which appeared to have been put on that day. He also wore a white linen collar (new) and a white linen handkerchief round his neck. On his feet were striped half hose and good boots, but of different make, one boot being finer and lighter than the other.

Gold sleeve buttons, gold pin and gold or filled case watch and chain, with linen ulster duster and new felt hat of fine quality, "John Hancock" make, completed his costume.

Beneath his clothing he wore a money belt of leather, but it was empty. About a dollar and fifty cents had been taken from the two men, but Chief King, in researching this fellow, found four dollars more. The wound was an ugly, jagged bullet hole, very large, and with the edges much torn, toward the center of the chest and about four inches below the heart. There were also several small shot wounds on the body of this one and three on the forehead; his hat was also riddled with shot, and it was evident that he had been hit twice from a shot gun, for several of the shot wounds were in the back. From photographs sent to the St. Louis police, the man was at once recognized as Clell Miller.

The empty store in which the two corpses lay is on Mill Square, which is immediately over on the south side of the handsome iron bridge which spans the Cannon River just below the mill race. On the north side of the square is the flouring mill of Ames & Co. On the west is Scriver's block and two or three small stores, among them that in which the bodies lay. On the east side is the office of the Rice County *Journal* and a wagon shop, and on the south is the Dampier House, under which are three stores, the last, eastward and just opposite the corner of the Scriver block, is the clothing store of Mr. Hanauer. The Scriver block has also a frontage of eighty feet on Division Street, twenty-two feet of which is occupied by the First National Bank of Northfield, in which one of the saddest and most daring tragedies was perpetrated—the heartless and deliberate murder of a faithful and brave man in the defense of the valuable property under his charge.

There are some four or five wooden buildings below the bank on Fourth Street, and it was in this narrow space, from Mill Square to Fourth Street, that the great fight which startled the whole country took place. Many indications of the fearful contest in bullet holes were found in every direction. Windows were pierced and shattered and balls must have been thrown around for a time as thick as hail, for the whole encounter took place within the short space of fifteen minutes. The conflict was a sharp and bloody one, and speaks volumes for the coolness and intrepidity of the citizens of the little provincial town.

From Mr. Bates, who took a prominent part in the encounter, the following was learned:

He said at about 11 o'clock his attention was called to four men who came from over the river. They came over the bridge and were mounted on four splendid horses. The men were well dressed, and Mr. Bates says, four nobler looking fellows he never saw; but there was a *reckless, bold swagger* about them that seemed to indicate that they would be rough and dangerous fellows to handle. Altogether he did not like the looks of them.

Again, at about 2 o'clock in the afternoon, as he was standing at the entrance of the store, talking to Mr. C. C. Waldo, commercial traveler from Council Bluffs, he saw the same men ride past—three came up the street from Mill Square and one down the street, meeting within thirty feet of the bank. They dismounted and tied their horses to the hitching posts and two, he thought, went into the bank and two came down to the staircase leading up into the upper stories of Lee & Hitchcock's buildings, and here they stood leaning against the banisters talking. Commenting upon their fine physique, and upon their unusually good mounts, Mr. Bates and Mr. Waldo withdrew to the far end of the store to look over some sample trusses.

They had not long been so occupied when they heard several shots fired in rapid succession, and the thought flashed upon the mind of Bates at once, that the bank was in danger—Mr. Waldo stating that he cried out: "Those men are going for the town, they mean to rob the bank." Mr. Bates, however, does not recollect saying anything, he became so excited. He remembers, though, rushing to the door, and seeing some men riding up from the bank—they came riding towards him with long pistols in their hands and called out, "Get in there you son of a b——."

Mr. Bates at once seized a shotgun and ran back to the door, but the gun would not go off. He then put down the gun and seized a fine seven shooter which was *not* loaded, and as the men came down again (they were riding to and fro, evidently intent upon keeping people from going towards the bank), he, standing behind the door jambs, called out, "Now, I've got you." And pointed the empty pistol as if drawing a bead on them.

They turned their horses suddenly and fired at Mr. Bates, the ball crashing through the plate glass. There were other men at the bank firing down the street. The next he saw was Mr. J. S. Allen running down the street from the bank, and two shots were fired at him.

Mr. Manning, of Mill Square, whose store is adjoining the block in which the bank is, next came upon the scene. He ran out of his store with a breech-loading repeating rifle, and took a deliberate aim and fired from the corner, Mr. Bates calling out: "Jump back now, or they'll get you."

Next Mr. J. B. Hide came up with a double-barreled shot gun and discharged the two barrels, and retired to re-load. Mr. Phillips also took a turn at the scoundrels, and L. Stacy delivered a cool, deliberate aim. Mr. Bates next heard a report over his head and saw one of the desperadoes fall from his horse. The horse made a faltering plunge forward and then suddenly stopped and the man pitched over with his face to the ground and in a few moments was dead. This shot was fired by Henry Wheeler from an old carbine from out one of the windows of the Dampier House.

Mr. Manning was still firing, and as he crept to the corner Mr. Waldo called out, "Take good aim before you fire."

Immediately after this shot one of the horses started up the street and the rider began to reel and swing to and fro and suddenly fell to the ground just opposite Eldridge's store. Another horseman immediately rode up, dismounted, and spoke to the prostrate man, who was stretched out at full length, supporting himself on his outstretched arms, when he rolled over on his back. Then the other man took from him his cartridge belt and two pistols, and, remounting his horse, rode off.

Another horseman, finding Mr. Manning's fire too hot, dismounted from his horse and got on the opposite side of it for protection, when an unerring ball from the breech loader brought the horse down, the man running behind some boxes which were piled beneath the staircase before mentioned, and now ensued a lively fusilade between this fellow and Manning, the scoundrel keeping himself well under cover, but a ball from Wheeler's musket struck the fellow in the leg, halfway above the knee.

He at once changed his pistol to the left hand and grasped the wounded limb with the right, still trying to get at Manning. Finding himself getting weak, he turned and limped off up the street, but, seeing Bates with a pistol in his hand, he sent a ball whizzing toward that gentleman, grazing the side of his cheek and the bridge of his nose, and burying itself in a collar-box in the store.

Mr. Bates says he feels the ring of that ball in his ear still, and the ball, he says, he will ever keep as a souvenir of the hottest day Northfield ever saw.

The man limped away, and when he got opposite to Mr. Morris's store, he cried out to his retreating companions, "My God, boys, you are not going to leave—I am shot!"

One of the party, riding a sorrel horse with a light tail and mane, turned and took the wounded man up behind him.

Mr. Wilcox, the teller of the bank, stated that he, in company with Mr. Heywood and A. E. Bunker, were in the bank at about 2 o'clock, when three well-dressed, powerful looking men entered by the door, which was open. They held large revolvers in their hands, and one of them cried out, "Throw up your hands, for we intend to rob the bank, and if you halloo, we will blow your brains out."

They then asked which was the cashier, to which Mr. Heywood replied, "He is not in." They then sprang over the counter and demanded the safe to be opened. Addressing each in turn they said, "You are the cashier," which each denied.

Seeing Heywood seated at the cashier's desk, one of the ruffians went up to him with his long, narrow-barreled pistol and said, "You are the cashier; now open the safe, you —— —— son of a ——."

Mr. Heywood said, "It is a time-lock and cannot be opened now." One of the men then went into the vault, the door being open. Heywood at once sprang forward and closed the door of the vault, shutting the robber in, when another of the men seized Heywood by the collar and dragged him away from the door and released the incarcerated robber.

The man who came out of the vault—a slim, dark complexioned man, with a black moustache, then called to the others to seize the silver which was lying loose (about fifteen dollars) and put it in the sack. They did not do this, but seized about twelve dollars in scrip and put it into a two-bushel flour sack which they had with them. The dark complexioned man, who appeared to be the leader, then again attacked Heywood, insisting upon his opening the safe, threatening to cut his throat if he did not, and actually drawing a big knife across his throat.

The heroic and faithful teller, however, was not to be deterred from his duty, and would rather sacrifice his life than betray his trust. Some few moments—it seemed ages to the bewildered and terror-stricken lookers-on—were spent in Heywood's struggling to break from the murderous villain and gain his liberty.

At length he broke away, and regaining his feet, ran toward the door crying, "Murder!"

The man at once struck him with a pistol and knocked him down, and, dragging him to the safe door, commanded him to open it. But the intrepid clerk stolidly refused, when the villain shot at him, but did not hit him.

Evidently the shot was intended rather to intimidate him than injure, but the scoundrel had reckoned without his host, for the effect was lost upon Heywood.

But upon the discharge of the pistol Bunker made a start for the back door and ran for dear life, one of the robbers pursuing and firing, the shot taking effect in the shoulder. Bunker, however, reached the street (Water Street) and ran to Dr. Coombs's office.

During the whole of this time four or five men were riding up and down the street, shooting in every direction, and keeping up an incessant fusilade.

One of the men outside came riding up furiously and called for the men to leave the bank. "The game's up," he said, "and we are beaten."

The three men in the bank then sprang over the counter and rushed to the door, and Heywood staggered to the chair, but, as the last one was getting over the counter, with one hand on the cashier's desk, he turned round and deliberately fired. Heywood fell senseless to the floor! The man then sprang on the rail and out at the front door, and he (Wilcox) cleared out of the back door into Manning's hardware store.

Wilcox was not sure whether the ruffian struck Heywood when the latter staggered to the cashier's chair, and he did not stop to see if he was dead when he fell. He said the reason he did not try to get out or help Heywood was that one of the men stood over him with a pistol in his hand.

Mr. Allen said he saw three men cross the bridge and go toward the bank. They were all big, powerful men, well dressed. One had sandy side-whiskers, shaved chin, and blue eyes. Another wore a black mustache, and was a slight but tall man, and better dressed than the others. The third man was heavy set, with curly brown hair, and beard of about one week's growth. They had tied their horses and talked a while, when another came up, and he went into the bank. Mr. Allen then waited half a minute, and then walked up to the bank to see what was up.

"As I got to the back door," he says, "one man came out and grabbed me by the collar, and said 'you son of a——, don't holler,' drawing a revolver. I got out and made tracks as fast as I could, two shots being fired after me."

Mr. Ben Henry says that he was first attracted to the strangers by seeing the horses tied, and he went up to one and was examining the saddle, when one of the men came up and said, "What are you doing here?"

"Looking at this saddle," was the reply. "I want an article like that, and thought perhaps I could strike a bargain with the owner."

Drawing a pistol, the fellow cried out, "Now you git" And he *did* "git," but as he walked away a bullet came hissing by his head and struck a wall close by. Henry deliberately picked up the ball and put it in his pocket, but made long strides for home.

It appeared that the object of the men on the street was at first only to keep people back from the bank, and not a desire to murder indiscriminately, but when they found that the Northfield people would not scare worth a cent, and that real work was before them, they showed all the savage bloodthirsty propensity of their nature, and wherever a face showed itself, whether it was man, woman, or child, the robbers fired murderously at it, crashing in windows in a lively style.

Early Friday morning it was reported in Northfield that Brissette and Hoy had joined their forces at Morristown and had a hot encounter with the gang, which had been reinforced by three others. The police succeeded in killing one man and capturing the wounded man carried from Northfield. The robbers then took to the woods and the police held them there. This report was proved at a later date to be a complete fabrication, but so excited were the people that every rumor received credence and grew in dimensions as it was handed round by the busy throng of news seekers.

The bank is in a small apartment, about twenty by fifty feet, situated in the Scriver block, folding doors in the center of the front opening into Division Street. It has a counter three feet high, running across to within three feet of the west wall, and going back the whole length of the building. This counter is mounted by a thirty-inch glazed rail, leaving a space of two feet in front, where the men jumped over, scratching the counter with their boots. Inside of the center is the safe vault fitted with the Detroit Safe Company's doors, and to the left is the cashier's chair where poor Heywood fell a victim to the assassin's hand. A blotting pad lay upon the desk stained with the life blood of the murdered man.

Poor Heywood was shot through the head, the ball entering at the right temple and passing downward and inward, scattering his brains all about, and doubtless depriving him instantaneously of consciousness, and putting him completely beyond all suffering, although he breathed for about twenty minutes, but did not speak. In addition to the bullet wound, there was a slight scratch in the right side of the neck as from a knife.

Mr. E. E. Bunker was not considered dangerously wounded, the ball passing in at the back of the right shoulder, below the point of the shoulder, passing downward and forward and upward, coming out just above the clavicle, making only a severe flesh wound. This wound, however, was very nearly being a fatal one, as the ball passed close to a principal artery, which no doubt, had it been severed by the deadly missive, would have produced death by hemorrhage.

Since the capture at Madelia of the Younger boys, Mr. Bunker has given his recollections of the bank raid, and as it differs in several points from others already given; we embody it in this narrative. It will be seen that the narrative recognizes two of the men who entered the bank as Charley Pitts and Bob Younger.

Mr. Bunker said that himself, Mr. Heywood, and Mr. Wilcox were sitting at their respective desks, when they heard a heavy rush from the bank door to the counter. They turned round and saw three men climbing over the counter and with their knees on it and revolvers pointed directly at the three bank officers. A man presumed to be Jesse James, and who acted as leader, called out, "Throw up your hands, we are going to rob the bank." James then ran across the room and passed Heywood into the vault, which was open, but seeing the safe door closed, turned back from the entrance, and seizing Heywood by the collar who, from being older than the others and from the position of his desk, was naturally supposed to be the cashier, ordered him to open the safe. Mr. Heywood said it was a time-lock, and it could not be opened. The other said that was a d—d lie.

Charley Pitts then came up on the other side of Heywood and threatened to kill him if he did not immediately open the safe. One of the others called out, "Let's cut his throat and be done with it." Heywood commenced shouting murder, and repeated the cry three or four times. They then hustled him about, and James struck him on the head with the butt end of his pistol, knocking him down. He was then dragged towards the vault, where he lay with his head partially in the vault. James then drew the knife across Heywood's neck, who did not say anything, appearing to be partially insensible, when another of them stooped down and fired close to the prostrate man's head, the ball penetrating a tin box containing papers in the vault.

All this time I was on my knees on the floor, with Bob Younger standing guard over me. I had a revolver under the counter, where I stand, and which was in full view, and I endeavored gradually to edge over and obtain possession of it, but Bob saw the attempt, and seeing the weapon, put it into his pocket, saying, at the same time, that I could do nothing with this, and it was of no use. He then commenced searching me, but did not take anything from me. The pistol was a Smith & Wesson, and we always regarded it as an excellent weapon. Bob having turned his head partially around to see what was going on in the other part of the room, I raised my head with the view of giving the alarm to anyone I saw in the street, but my movements were quickly observed by Bob who pulled me down, saying at the same time, that I had better keep quiet, for if I attempted to rise again he would kill me. He then inquired where was the cashier's till, and I pointed to a box containing some nickels and scrip, the former done up in cartridges. He seemed to know very well there was more loose money than that, and he told me he would kill me if I did not show him the till. I did not answer him, and he pulled out a drawer containing stationery, but the drawer having some $2,000 he did not open, supposing, probably, that its contents were the same.

Meantime, while the two men were engaged with Heywood, James told Bob Younger to bring out the sack. Bob took out a green bag and thrust a handful of scrip into it, but did not take any of the nickels.

The distance from where I was to the rear of the bank is about twenty-five feet, and the rear door of the two hardware stores adjoin the rear door of the bank. I thought if I could make my way out in this direction, I would have a chance of giving the alarm, so that the citizens would come to the rescue. In making this movement, I should have to pass where Mr. Wilcox was sitting, and I made a slight motion for him to move so that I could get past. He saw my motion and shifted his position. The man who stood over me having his attention directed to the proceedings of the others, I started, but was immediately followed by Charley Pitts, who fired at me, the ball going through the blinds of the door and lodging in a brick chimney, but not striking me. There was a stairway leading down, and Pitts standing on top of that, fired down on me, I having reached the bottom at the time, fired again, the ball just striking me below the scapula, passing through the thin portion of it, and down, passing out about half an inch below the collar bone, the course traversed being about seven inches, and narrowly missing the sub-claviel artery, where the wound would have been fatal.

I think it was James that said, while keeping us down, "Don't one of you move; we have fifty men on the street, and you will be killed if you move." The safe was not locked at all, but there was only about $15,000 in it, which they might easily have secured.

Mr. Bunker said he recognized the body killed at Madelia as that of Charley Pitts, and also identified Bob Younger, by the likeness published herein.

Several citizens of Northfield narrowly escaped with their lives during the encounter. A Norwegian, Nicholas Gustavson by name, was struck with a bullet at the right side of the head, just at the ear, the ball running under the scalp and out at the top of his head. He says when he was struck, and for several minutes after, his whole left side was paralyzed. But after a few minutes of unconsciousness, he was able to reach his boarding house, but the next day he was unable to rise from his bed. It was evident that the skull was fractured, and depressing upon the right lobe of the brain, and if the patient was not opportunely relieved by trepanning the skull, the man must succumb. Subsequent events proved the correctness of this view, for the operation was not performed, and the poor fellow expired on the eleventh—four days after the dreadful tragedy, thus adding another victim to rekindle the fire of indignation in men's minds.

Illustrative of the dangerous nature of the weapons that the lawless ruffians carried, it should have been stated that balls fired from one side of Mill Square struck and completely riddled buildings on the other side of the square, a distance of one hundred and fifty yards.

Friday afternoon the coroner, Dr. Waugh, from Faribault, held an inquest upon the bodies of the two scoundrels who met with such a richly deserved end, and the following gentlemen were sworn as a jury: A. H. Rawson, S. L. Bushnell, R. Silk, J. L. McFee, R. Plummer and C. W. Gross. The jury were not long in arriving at the following verdict: "That the two unknown men came to their deaths by the discharge of firearms in the hands of our citizens in self-defense and in protecting the property of the First National Bank of Northfield."

The same jury, with the coroner, held an inquest over the remains of the lamented victim of the raid. The witnesses who gave evidence were E. Hobbs, ex-policeman J. S. Allen, F. Wilcox, and E. L. Fuller, whose statements were similar to those the same gentlemen made to the writer, and recorded elsewhere in these pages. The verdict found was: "That J. H. Heywood came to his death by a pistol shot fired by an unknown man attempting to rob the First National Bank of Northfield."

The grand jury that had been summoned included twenty-two of the best men in the county, but the prisoner's counsel reduced it to seventeen, by challenging a number who had too freely expressed their ideas in regard to the affair. There is no doubt but that by continuing the same line of questioning the grand jury could have all been found wanting, but it was not the intention of the defense to delay the trial by reducing the number below the legal minimum, but simply to refer the bills to as few men as possible, feeling that the chance of their finding all of the indictments could be materially lessened.

It took the jury but a very short time after they commenced their work to find four true bills against the prisoners, and the evidence given by the witnesses that testified before them was but a recapitulation of what they were entirely familiar with. In the case of the Swede, whom Cole Younger was charged with killing, evidence was given by a man and a woman, both of whom testified that they saw Cole shoot him coolly and deliberately.

On the day after the court convened, the sister and an aunt of the Younger boys arrived in Faribault. The sister, Miss Henrietta Younger, is a very pretty, prepossessing young lady of about seventeen years, and she conducted herself so as to win the esteem of all who met her. Mrs. Fanny Twyman, their aunt, is the wife of a highly respectable physician practicing in Missouri, and appears to be a lady of the highest moral character. These ladies passed the greater portion of their time sitting with their relatives, behind the iron bars, reading, talking, and sewing. On Thursday, the 9th of November, the grand jury signified that they had completed their labors as far as the cases of the Younger boys were concerned, and the sheriff was instructed to bring the prisoners to hear the indictments read.

This summons had been expected, and the boys were ready, dressed neatly, and looking wonderfully well after their unaccustomed confinement that had continued for more than a month. They quietly stood up in a row ready to be shackled together. Cole in the middle, Bob at the right, and Jim at the left. The shackles were placed on their feet; Bob being secured by one foot to Cole, and Jim by the other. When the handcuffs were placed on Cole, he remarked that it was the first time he had ever worn them. The prisoners showed signs of nervousness, evidently fearing that the crowd outside would think it best to dispose of them without due process of law. However, nothing occurred except some almost inaudible mutterings among the spectators, but which were quickly quieted by right-minded citizens. Slowly the procession passed to the temple of justice, the prisoners seeing the sun and breathing the pure air for the first time in thirty days. In advance of them was an armed guard, led by the captain of the minute men, then came the sheriff by the side of his prisoners, the chief of police of Faribault, and his lieutenant, and finally another squad of minute men with their needle guns. On reaching the court house, the guards broke to the right and left, and allowed none to enter except those known to their captain.

The cortege passed to the court room by a rear stairway, and when the prisoners arrived in front of the Judge, the court room was thoroughly filled with people, all gazing with the greatest curiosity on the three bloody brothers.

The shackles having been removed from the arms and legs of the prisoners, they were ordered to stand up while the indictment charging them with killing Heywood was read to them by the county attorney. As their names were read, the Judge asked them if they were indicted by their true names, to which all responded in the affirmative. During the reading, Cole Younger never moved his sharp eye from the face of the attorney; in fact, his gaze was so intense, that Mr. Baxter appeared to feel it, and to be made somewhat nervous thereby. Bob did not appear to take great interest in the matter, and he gazed coolly about on the crowd.

The sister and aunt of the boys were by their sides during this scene, and they walked with them as they returned to the jail under the same guard that escorted them forth. Until the following Saturday had been taken by the prisoners' counsel to plead to the indictment, and during the interval of three days the subject of how to plead was discussed for many hours. Bob was as independent as ever, declared he would not plead guilty, but the persuasions of sister and aunt finally prevailed, and when taken into court on Saturday in the same manner as before, each responded "guilty" when the question was asked by the clerk. Judge Lord then, without preface or remark, sentenced each to be confined in the state prison, at Stillwater, at hard labor, for the term of his natural Life. After the dread words had been uttered, the sister broke down and fell sobbing and moaning on the breast of her brother Cole.

Thus these bloody bandits escaped the gallows where their many crimes should have been expiated, and in a few days from the time they were sentenced, they were on their way to Stillwater, under a strong guard, but no attempt was made to molest them, although large crowds were collected at each station on the railroads by which they traveled. Sheriff Barton knew well the citizens of his state, and he had no fear that he would be interfered with while discharging his duty. The bandits were accompanied to their final home in this world by their faithful relatives, who left them within the prison walls, taking away as mementoes the clothes which the wicked men had worn. The robbers were immediately set at work painting pails, a labor which called for no dangerous tools to prosecute, and a special guard was set upon the renowned villains, as it is not intended that they shall escape to again terrify the world by their wicked deeds.

NINE

Hijack!

Geoffrey Gray

THE JET IS CLIMBING. TEN THOUSAND FEET, FIFTEEN THOUSAND FEET. In the cockpit, Scotty and copilot Bill Rataczak aren't sure how to respond. A bomb? Is it real? Does it matter?

In total, there are thirty-six passengers in the cabin, six crew members. As captain, Scotty is in charge. What to do?

Scotty radios Northwest Orient flight operations in Minnesota.

A man in the back says he has a bomb, Scotty says. He doesn't know who the man is or what he wants. Not yet.

—⁓—

"Take this down."

Flo Schaffner reaches into her purse and retrieves her pen. She can no longer see the man's eyes. He's put on sunglasses. The frames are dark. The lenses are brown.

"I want two hundred grand by five p.m., in cash," he says.

She writes down the words on the envelope he gave her. "Put it in a knapsack," he says.

The pen scratches paper and the words she writes appear in a messy swirl of cursive.

Anything else?

"I want two back parachutes and two front parachutes. . . . When we land, I want a fuel truck ready to refuel."

Anything else?

He wants meals for the flight crew, in case anyone gets hungry.

"No funny stuff, or I'll do the job."

She writes down those words, too.

"No fuss. After this we'll take a little trip."

"No fuss," she writes and her mind reels and her chest heaves. No, Flo, no, don't do this. Do not panic. The images of the airplane in the sky are easy to conjure. KABOOM! Smoldering debris bobbing in the water. Charred bodies. She is a corpse. Her pa is getting calls in Fordyce . . . from the newspapermen . . . from the morgue. This isn't happening, Flo, this isn't happening. Focus on the details. No, no. Details are worse. Parachutes? What did he want parachutes for? Is he taking a hostage? Is that hostage her? A fuel truck? Where are they going? What is this "little trip"?

The word flashes in her mind. Rape.

How would she know how to pull the parachute cord? Would he pull the cord for her? They could parachute into a dark forest. He could steal her uniform and leave her there—with cougars, bears. She would have to run through the woods in bare feet and find a road. A pair of headlights would flash against her naked body, and she would have to scream out into the headlights, Stop, stop. Please stop.

"I have to go to the cockpit," she tells him.

He does not want her to leave. That is his rule. *Sit by me.* His rule does not make sense, she says. If he wants his demands met, she has to take the note to the captain, no?

Kneeling in the aisle, stewardess Tina Mucklow is eavesdropping on the conversation.

"Do you want me to take the note?" Tina says.

"No," he says.

Flo is pushy.

"I have to go to the cockpit," Flo tells him. He thinks it over.

"All right. Go ahead."

"Do you want me to stay here?" Tina says. He looks her over.

"Yes," he says.

Flo steps out of the seat and into the aisle and strains to walk toward the cockpit. The jet is still climbing. The gravitational pull forces her back toward the lavatory. She pushes off the armrests and propels herself forward. In first class she passes Alice. The first-class stew can see the fear on Flo's face. Alice looks back into the tourist cabin to see the hijacker. Tina, she can see, is sitting next to him. He is wearing sunglasses. Tina was right. This is no joke.

As the oldest stew, Alice has to do something. She wants Tina away from this man. She walks to her.

"Tina, can you help me find a deck of playing cards?" Tina is not listening. Alice walks away. Is Tina in shock?

Inside the cockpit, the Northwest pilots hear the door open. Flo slips in. The envelope with the hijacker's instructions is in her hand.

"Did you get a good look at the bomb?"

"What was in the briefcase?"

"Red sticks," she says.

"Dynamite?"

"They looked like dynamite."

"What else?"

"Lots of wires, a battery."

Copilot Rataczak reads the hijacker's note. He notices the fine lettering, the felt-tip pen. The hijacker could be a master criminal, he thinks. The pilots better play his game. No funny stuff.

Scotty reaches for his radio. He calls Northwest Flight Operations back in Minnesota. His words are recorded via Teletype.

PASSENGER HAS ADVISED THIS IS A HIJACKING. EN ROUTE TO SEATTLE. THE STEW HAS BEEN HANDED A NOTE. HE REQUESTS $200,000 IN A KNAPSACK BY 5:00 PM. HE WANTS TWO BACK PARACHUTES, TWO FRONT PARACHUTES. HE WANTS THE MONEY IN NEGOTIABLE AMERICAN CURRENCY. DENOMINATION OF THE BILLS IS NOT IMPORTANT. HAS BOMB IN BRIEFCASE AND WILL USE IT IF ANYTHING IS DONE TO BLOCK HIS REQUEST.

Dispatch is calling. "PD 32, PD 32."

PD 32 is the number of Special Agent Ralph Himmelsbach's unmarked '68 Plymouth. He's driving back to the field office from Yaw's Top Notch, a drive-in burger joint on the outskirts of Portland. He had a light lunch—grilled cheese, chased down with a glass of milk—because his wife is cooking a pre-Thanksgiving dinner and he needs to be home with a healthy appetite. There is tension in the marriage. Himmelsbach is never around, either working cases or flying his airplane. He suspects she is having an affair with her boss.

"164 in progress, Portland International."

In the Bureau, each crime has a code number. 164 is an airplane hijacking. Is it real or a prank?

"Verified," the dispatcher says. "Report to Northwest Airlines Operations Office."

Himmelsbach reaches for the radio.

"PD 32," he says. "Ten four."

He slams the brakes, banks into a U-turn, cuts off traffic, and heads toward the Portland airport. He places the sirens on the car roof. He wants to drive faster. Can't move. Traffic.

"Damn, this is a long light," he says.

Himmelsbach hates what Portland has become. His city has been sacked! From the East, the liberals have come from New York and Boston, purchasing property and running for office. From the South, the hippies come from Northern California. He can see them in bus stations begging for money or rides. The spoiled kids don't have the decency to cut their hair. The women don't shave under their arms. They do drugs and sell drugs. They don't believe in relationships. Only a short drive from Portland, a group of girls has built the first lesbian commune. The girls have rules. Monogamy is forbidden. Imagine that!

Ralph Himmelsbach can't. In the rearview mirror of his Bureau squad car, the agent's reflection is all straight lines. His jawline is sharp and angular. His Wyatt Earp mustache is full and trimmed. His eyebrows are hawklike, fitting for the hunter he is.

It is elk season and he could be hunting elk on a day like today. Elk can be invisible creatures. One of the best places to hunt them is in the eastern part of Washington, up in the Blue and Wallowa Mountains. Himmelsbach and his brother, a district attorney there, set up camp in waist-high snow, crouch near the trees, look for tracks, and wait. But in ten years hunting them, Himmelsbach has never taken an elk.

"PD 32, PD 32."

Dispatch again.

"On the 164 . . . we've learned the suspect has an explosive device."

Himmelsbach leans on the horn. Bastards, let's move. The guy has a bomb!

Another one? Was this a copycat? Ten days ago, a Canadian man slipped on a mask, brandished a shotgun, and threatened to blow up an Air Canada flight with forty pounds of plastic explosives. The man, Paul Cini, told the flight crew he was a member of the Irish Republican Army (he wasn't) and wanted the plane rerouted to Ireland. He also demanded $1.5 million in cash. He couldn't make up his mind though. He wanted the pilots to refuel in Saskatchewan and then changed the location to Great Falls, Montana, where the governor negotiated a lower ransom of $50,000. On the ground in Great Falls, the hijacker listened to the news of his hijacking on the radio in real time, and in glee, passengers later reported, as if he had achieved his fifteen minutes of fame.

Cini then demanded the pilots fly him to New York. In the air, Cini then shocked the crew and passengers by stepping into the harness of a parachute. The plane was a DC-8, which like the Boeing 727 had aft stairs that could be opened during flight.

Cini nearly made it. As he was planning to jump, according to news reports, the Air Canada purser on the flight "let him have it with a fire ax."

The story of Cini, who was rushed to the emergency room after the plane landed, was national news. Images of the bloodied hijacker, who was too foolish and deranged to execute his daring escape with $50,000, also ran on the national news.

Agent Himmelsbach cursed the media outlets for publishing them. Like bank robbers, Cini could inspire others to board planes with bombs and crazy demands, hold the passengers hostage, and attempt to make a getaway via parachute.

In Seattle, the Bureau field office is located in an old bank downtown, a few blocks from the piers off Alaskan Way. The boss, J. Earl Milnes, steps out of his office.

The first agent he sees is Bob Fuhrman, a recent transfer. Fuhrman is trained as an accountant. Hoover wants only lawyers and accountants to be G-men.

Milnes points a finger at Fuhrman. "You," he says. "Drive me to the airport."

Fuhrman follows Milnes out to an ummarked car and turns over the keys. The radio is on. Voices are on the frequency. What is the procedure for hijackings? Should the feds cooperate with the hijacker and give him $200,000 and parachutes? Should they storm the plane, take him out? Is it even their responsibility to make the decision?

The airlines and agencies are feuding over how to handle skyjackings. Who is in control? At the FAA, officials argue that it is the pilot who is responsible for the plane and its passengers. At the FBI, Hoover argues that once a plane lands, the hijacker has violated federal air piracy laws; therefore, he is within the Bureau's jurisdiction and should be apprehended immediately. It's too dangerous to think otherwise. What if the hijacker had a manic episode, killed the pilot, and crashed the plane into downtown Cleveland? Hundreds of bystanders would die in the explosion. Or worse. What if hijackers demanded that pilots fly airplanes into skyscrapers?

In New York, tenants have already moved into the North Tower of the World Trade Center. Construction on the South Tower is almost finished. With a hijacker at the controls, a domestic airplane becomes its own bomb. Thousands could die.

The jockeying over who controls a hijacked plane unfolded only weeks before on the front pages. A charter jet to the Bahamas was taken over by a man with a gun and a bomb.

Onboard, the flight crew could see the man was delusional. The captain begged Bureau agents to let them refuel. He felt that if the plane was back in the air, the armed hijacker would relax and nobody would get injured. After landing in Florida to refuel, the request was denied. Agents fired gunshots at the plane's tires. The skyjacker panicked. He fatally shot the captain, his wife, then himself.

Hoover's lawyers raced into court, to keep the transcriptions between the pilots and Bureau agents sealed. A federal judge tossed out the request. The transcript made national news.

> Pilot: *This is fifty-eight November. Uh, this gentleman has about 12.5 pounds of plastic explosives back here and, uh, I got no yen to join it right now so I would please . . . appreciate it if you would stay away from the airplane.*
>
> Tower: *This is the FBI. There will be no fuel. Repeat. There will be no fuel.*
>
> Pilot: *Uh, (gasp) look, I don't think this fellow's kiddin'—I wish you'd get that fuel truck out here.*
>
> Tower: *Fifty-eight November. There will be no fuel. I repeat. There will be no fuel.*
>
> Pilot: *This is fifty-eight November. You are endangering lives by doing this, and for the sake of some lives we request some fuel out here, please.*

Skyjacking had a twisted history. Early on, passengers who hijacked planes wanted to flee Communist countries and come to America. The skyjack was a means of escape, and the United States welcomed political dissidents from Eastern Europe and later Cuba. By the late 1960s, the direction had turned.

Since the United States cut off ties with Fidel Castro and banished travel to Cuba in 1961, eighty airplanes had been successfully hijacked to Cuba. The frequency of hijackings to the island was so high, airline pilots began to carry approach maps for the Havana airport. "Take me to Cuba" became a catchphrase. One government plan was to build a replica of the Havana airport near Miami as a decoy to hijackers.

Around the world, an airplane was taken over once every week. In newspapers and on television, passengers reported live from the new war zone: airplane cabins. "We had no control," one passenger said after a grenade went off on an Ethiopian Air flight. "We were weaving all over. When that bomb took off I thought, *This is it*." On a flight out of Sacramento: "I counted twenty-two shots. There was a pause and a man shouted, 'I'm shot.' The bullet went through the back of his seat and out his chest. The wound—it was as big as a fist. He said good-bye to his wife. She embraced him and said, 'God have mercy on him.'"

Struggling to keep their companies afloat during the recession, airline presidents don't want to spend millions to install magnetometers, or metal detectors, in airport terminals. Won't the devices be an inconvenience to their customers, most of whom are businessmen? Executives would cringe at having to walk through the detectors and have each bag checked for weapons and explosives. President Nixon, who counts several airline presidents among his supporters and contributors, does not want to force the airlines to comply with costly security mandates. Nixon prefers a voluntary approach, and has introduced the sky marshals, a new breed of armed undercover agents who travel on airplanes to deter hijackers. At the Federal Aviation Administration, officials have also developed a secret psychological profile of hijackers, and brief airport officials on what types of passengers to look for. As effective as the program is, it is left up to airline officials to screen passengers. Security is now a judgment call, and somewhere along the flight path of Northwest 305, a hijacker was allowed to board.

At Northwest Orient, the decisions on how to handle the hijacker—comply with his requests, or turn him down—go to the airline's president, Don Nyrop. Nyrop. A bit to the left of Genghis Khan, one executive calls him. Nyrop is stubborn, abrasive, unpredictable, cheap, a brilliant administrator.

According to company legend, Nyrop popped into a hangar one afternoon to check on Northwest's mechanics. After inspecting the work, Nyrop used the hangar bathroom and heard the rustling of paper in the stall next to him. Reading a newspaper on company time! All men's bathroom doors in Northwest buildings were removed henceforth.

In turn, the thousands of Northwest stewardesses, pursers, mechanics, pilots, and ground crewmembers rob his planes blind. After flights, they steal toilet paper, booze, pillows, blankets, silverware. They went on strike last year over pay and working conditions. Picket lines formed. Nyrop wouldn't budge. President Nixon had to help negotiate a settlement. Nyrop's stinginess made him a hero to Northwest management and the company's stockholders. During the recession, other airlines tanked. Northwest Orient posted profits.

Nyrop's decision is swift. At the airport in Minnesota, Nyrop tells the feds he wants to comply with the hijacker. The airline has insurance. They will cover the $200,000 ransom. Now the feds in Seattle need to find parachutes.

Throughout Northwest's facilities, officials listen to the radio. In the hangar, mechanic John Rataczak, father of copilot Bill Rataczak, can hear his son's voice on the frequency. Who is the man in the back with a bomb? What if it detonates?

—◆—

In the cockpit, the phone is ringing. It is Tina.

The hijacker is getting nervous, she says.

About what?

About the radio currents on the plane. Why?

He thinks the radio currents might be too strong, she says. They could accidentally detonate the device he's packed in his briefcase.

Is he sure? No.

On the radio, Scotty and Rataczak hear new voices. It's the feds.

"Do you know where he wants to go?"

"Negative. Have asked him once and so we don't want to ask him again. . . . Would suggest we wait and see where he wants to go."

"Can bring out the manuals to Alaska if you think so."

Outside the cockpit window, it is getting dark. The weather is changing. The storm should hit any minute.

"Approach, NW305, ah . . . a little rain up over here. We'd like to hold it at about . . . ah . . . turn back on the radio now and go out to about, oh, thirty would be a little better."

On the ground in Seattle, officials are concerned about the radio communications. Can the hijacker hear the conversation between the pilots and the authorities on the frequency?

"I don't know. I think it's free to call us. Nobody's giving us any trouble up here. He's in the back."

In the back row of the jet, he fishes a pack of cigarettes from his pocket. "You smoke?"

"Quit," Tina says. The word is out. Smoking kills. This past summer, Congress banned smoking ads from television and radio.

She offers to light the cig for him. The matchbook he has is blue. The words *Sky Chef* are on the cover. He leans in close as she flicks the cardboard stick against the strike pad and watches the sulfur fizzle into flame.

"Want one?"

He holds out the pack.

Why not? Tina takes a butt and sticks it in her mouth. She lights it.

"Where are you from?" he asks.

She grew up in Trevose, a small city outside of Philadelphia. She now lives with roommates in an apartment near the Minneapolis-St. Paul airport. The stew zoo.

"Minneapolis is very nice country," says the hijacker.

Tina takes a drag of her smoke. She knows where they are going: Cuba, where all the other hijackers want to go. She jokes with him.

"You know Northwest Orient has strict policies against traveling to Cuba. Can't bring home rum or cigars. Customs confiscate them in the airport."

The hijacker laughs.

"No, we're not going to Cuba. But you'll like where we're going."

In the seat across from them, Bill Mitchell, a college sophomore, waits for his chance. What is the young stew doing talking to such an older guy? Mitchell notices that as the man talks to the stew, he spills his drink. What is that stewardess thinking wasting her time on him? When will she get up so he can make his move?

The jet banks into a turn around Seattle, circling the city twenty miles to the south. The hijacker wants to know the time. His deadline is 5:00 p.m. He peers out the window.

In Portland, Special Agent Ralph Himmelsbach sprints into the terminal. In the doorway, a lady is lugging hat boxes. Himmelsbach nearly knocks her over. He heads for the management office of Northwest Orient. His boss, Julius Mattson, special agent in charge of the Bureau's field office in Portland, is listening to a panel of radios cued in to the cockpit of the hijacked plane.

"There you are, Ralph," Mattson says. "Where you been? We got a hot one going here."

"Got here quick as I could. Damn traffic on Sandy was fierce. Dispatch said the guy has a bomb. What else do we know?"

"Not a lot more," says Mattson. "He wants money and a parachute. So far that's about all that we've been able to put together."

"How much cash?"

"Two hundred thousand," says Frank Faist, a Northwest official.

"Whew. That's a hell of a hit, Frank. Are you going to make it?"

"I imagine so. He's holding all the high cards."

"Any idents on the guy with the bomb?"

"We've asked the crew to pass on anything they can, but so far no info."

"Have your people found out anything more?"

We got the ticket lists and the flight manifest. We know there are twenty-nine men aboard that aircraft. He could be nine or ninety for all I know now."

Over the radio, there is a crackle of sound. It is the Northwest pilots on the frequency. Himmelsbach and Mattson strain their ears.

"Our future destination not yet advised. . . . Name of man unknown. . . . About six feet one inch, black hair, age about fifty, weight a hundred and seventy-five pounds. Boarded at Portland."

Portland! He was here, Himmelsbach thinks. But who was he? How did he get here? Taxi? Car? Did he stay overnight? Walk from a hotel? Take the bus?

Agents fan out across the terminal, searching for witnesses. The day before Thanksgiving is one of the busiest travel days of the year. Agents approach airport officials, security personnel, passengers, taxi drivers, bus drivers, parking lot attendees, rental car agents, gift shop employees, coffee shop employees, bartenders in the cocktail lounge, waiters and waitresses in the restaurants, and salesmen working in the insurance stands.

See anybody suspicious? About six foot one? Black hair?

"Yes, as a matter of fact, there was a gentleman that looked awfully suspicious," Hal Williams says.

Williams is a gate clerk for Northwest. He noticed the gentlemen. He was odd, not like the others. He boarded Flight 305. What was so odd about him? He was dressed in black, all black, Williams tells the feds.

Anything else?

The man was a lone wolf, Williams says. Before the flight, other passengers on the 305 gathered by the terminal window. With the storm coming, they joked about how they would all have to run across the tarmac. Everybody would get drenched in the rain. The man in black was not part of the group. His attitude was different.

How different? How would he describe the attitude?

"Blah," Williams says.

The agents have the passenger list for Flight 305. Recognize any names?

Williams looks at the list. "No," he says.

The feds hunt for more eyewitnesses. To get on the plane, the hijacker must have purchased a ticket. Who sold it to him?

Dennis Lysne was working the ticket desk that afternoon, agents learn. Where is Lysne? He's left for the day, Northwest officials tell the feds.

In Portland, agents race to Lysne's home. They find his wife. Where is Lysne?

The supermarket, she tells them. Doing some Thanksgiving shopping. In the supermarket parking lot, Lysne loads up his car with groceries. He gets in the driver's seat. His engine won't start. He walks to a pay phone and calls his wife.

"Better hurry home," she tells him. "The FBI wants to talk to you." At his house, Lysne is briefed. Flight 305 was hijacked. The man says he has a bomb. Does Lysne remember selling a ticket to anybody suspicious?

"Yes," Lysne says. There was one suspicious passenger. Does Lysne happen to remember the passenger's name? He does.

"Cooper. Dan Cooper."

Cooper was the last passenger to buy a ticket for Flight 305. What did Cooper look like?

He was wearing dark clothes. Had darkish skin. Olive in color. Anything else?

Lysne remembers snippets of their conversation.

"Can I get on your flight to Seattle?" he asked. "That's a 727, isn't it?"

Does Lysne remember anything else? The fare was $20. Cooper paid with cash.

Did Cooper display any nervous behavior or fidgeting? He did not.

Did Lysne notice what Cooper was keeping his money in? He did not.

Could he recognize Cooper again if he saw him? Lysne isn't sure.

⸺

In his unmarked car in Seattle, homicide detective Owen McKenna races to the Seattle First National Bank downtown. Two employees from the bank's security department are waiting for him. They have a leather satchel. Inside is a canvas bag that contains $200,000, all in twenty-dollar bills.

The money is not coated with powders or rigged with exploding packs of dye. But the bills are marked. To prepare for a robbery, Seattle First National has set aside a cache of bills, and each serial number of each bill has been recorded on microfiche. They count out a hundred stacks of twenty-dollar bills, each stack worth $2,000. The load must weigh twenty pounds, maybe more.

McKenna drives the bank officials and the satchel to SEA-TAC. He thinks about the man with the bomb on the hijacked plane circling above them.

As a detective, McKenna has little respect for the airlines. One cold case haunts him. He found her body on a houseboat near the University of Washington. She had been beaten, strangled, raped. She was a stewardess, and he suspects the killer was a passenger she met. The airlines are selling sex in their stewardesses, but what are they doing to protect them? So many of the stews tell the same story: small-town girls, left home to see the world before they got married. What about the creeps? The killers? And now parachuting hijackers?

On the police radio, there are more voices on the frequency. The feds want to know where the parachutes are.

With sirens flashing, state troopers descend on Issaquah Skyport, a parachute jump center twenty miles east of SEA-TAC airport. Inside, proprietor Linn Emrich hands the troopers two front or reserve chutes. These front chutes will clip onto the harness of the rear or main parachutes. A trooper puts them in the trunk of his car and speeds off to SEA-TAC.

The rear parachutes are already at the airport. Norman Hayden, a local pilot, sent them in a taxicab. Hayden recently purchased the chutes from Earl Cossey, a local parachute rigger.

Inside the airport, the bank officials from Seattle First National lug the ransom into the Northwest flight operations office. The bank officials cut open a seal of the leather satchel and hand FBI boss J. Earl Milnes the canvas bag inside. Its dimensions are roughly a foot by a foot, and eight or nine inches tall. Milnes looks at the money. He does not count it. He hands the bag to Al Lee, Northwest's director of flying. Lee lugs the sack of cash into the trunk of McKenna's unmarked car, along with the rear parachutes, eight meals for the crew, and instructions on how to use a parachute.

— ⁓ —

Thousands of feet above them, in the cockpit of the Northwest jet, Scotty worries about the passengers. Won't they get edgy when the plane doesn't land? Won't they start asking questions? Should he tell them the flight has been hijacked?

"You know, Scotty, I don't think it's a good idea," Rataczak says. "I know we picked up some good old Montana mountain boys and they're pretty good sized, and they're sitting up in first class and they're on their second and third martinis. We don't need them to look at each other and say, 'Hey, let's go back and get a hijacker.'"

The pilots have an idea. Why not ask *him* what he wants to do? They call back to Tina. She asks the hijacker if he wants the passengers alerted. "No," he says.

She relays the message back. Now the crew needs a ruse to explain the delay. Rataczak switches on the in-flight intercom system.

"Ladies and gentlemen," he says, "there's been a slight mechanical problem. We've been asked to circle Seattle, to burn off excess fuel."

A clap of thunder. The storm has hit. In the jet windows there are flashes of lightning against the dark sky. In the bulkhead row, prosecutor Larry Finegold can see them. He tries to make sense of what the pilot had just said. It doesn't make sense. How could any mechanical problem on a jet be *slight?*

He thinks, *This is the one, oh boy, here we go, get ready to crash.* He thinks about his wife. Sharon was in law school at Berkeley when they met. She had such long hair. He was a preppy in jeans and penny loafers. Once they started talking, he didn't want the conversation to end. He couldn't stand to be apart from her. After they met, he went with friends on a three-day fishing trip. After the first night, he made his friends dock. He hitchhiked to her dorm room and proposed. Now she's pregnant with their first child. A boy, they've learned. His son.

The jet is shaking. More lightning. The cabin drops in spasms. His stomach is rolling like a waterbed.

Across the aisle, passenger Barbara Simmons wakes up from a nap. She looks out the window and sees the lights of the Space Needle. The futuristic structure was the tallest west of the Mississippi when it was built for the 1962 World's Fair in Seattle. It is located several miles north of SEA-TAC.

"Oh my gosh," Simmons says to her husband. "Either we're on the wrong plane or we're being hijacked."

One passenger gets out of his seat and marches toward the back.

Tina gets up and intercepts him at row 14.

"I'm bored," he says. "You have any sports magazines to read back there?"

She escorts him to the rear. She looks for a sports magazine. She can't find any.

"How about *The New Yorker?*" she says.

In a nearby seat, a passenger gets up to use the lavatory.

When he comes out, another passenger is blocking the aisle. He's a cowboy type, wearing a Stetson. He's furious, demanding that Tina tell him more about this "mechanical difficulty." Why do they have to burn fuel? When will they be on the ground? Does Tina know *anything?*

The man headed to the lavatory notices the man in sunglasses sitting next to Tina. He seems amused by the cowboy's antics. Then he gets annoyed when the man won't stop. He tells Stetson Man to go back to his seat. The hijacker and Tina are alone again.

"If that's a sky marshal, I don't want any more of that," he says.

He remembers something: his note. Flo has it. He wants it back.

Tina picks up the phone and tells the captain. She eases back into her seat. She asks the hijacker if he wants anything to eat or drink.

"No."

She asks him about the passengers. When can they get off?

He goes over his instructions again. She needs to pay attention.

First, the fuel truck; he wants it out at SEA-TAC and ready to pump gas when the plane lands.

Second, the money; he wants the car carrying the ransom parked so he can see it from the windows at all times.

Third, her; he wants Tina to get out of the plane and fetch the bag of money.

She worries. The bag may be too heavy for her to carry.

"You'll manage," he says.

Once the money is on board, the passengers will be released. Then Tina will get the parachutes and meals. He also has Benzedrine pills in his pocket. He doesn't want the crew to get sleepy.

The jet banks another wide loop. Tina tries to chat him up.

"So, where you from?" she says.

He won't tell her. He's not that stupid.

She wants to know his motive. Why hijack this plane? "Do you have a grudge against Northwest?" she says.

He looks at the stewardess, the sunglasses shielding his eyes.

"I don't have a grudge against your airline, Miss," he says. "I just have a grudge."

—◆—

In the air, the jet banks another turn. In the bulkhead row, prosecutor Finegold looks out the portal window for the roof of his house. In the rain, in the dark, he can't find it. Behind him passengers shift uneasily in the powder blue fabric chairs and flip through Northwest Orient's inflight magazine.

Sitting in his seat over the wing of the plane, passenger Patrick Minsch, a heavy-equipment operator from Alaska, worries about his connection. In Seattle he is changing planes to go to his grandmother's house in the San Juan Islands. The plane has been circling for three hours. He'll miss his flight. He'll have to spend the night in SEA-TAC. He looks out the window and sees the lights on the wing illuminate the rain streaking by. He feels the plane move.

Another loop. The jet banks again, over Everett, where Boeing's 747 factory is located.

The 747 was a gamble that nearly bankrupted the company. In the recession, Boeing has been forced to lay off more than half the workforce. A company town, Seattle has the highest unemployment rate of any American city since the Great Depression. It's over 12 percent. Aeronautical engineers with advanced degrees are forced to mow lawns to feed their families. Foreclosure rates skyrocket. Homeless shelters are at full capacity. Across the board, local budgets are slashed. Police officers in Seattle are placed on unpaid leave. Dope is sold outside drive-in restaurants.

Down near the piers off Puget Sound, the homeless sleep in wet bundles under the freeway as smack junkies warm their hands by oil-drum fires. An exodus is under way. A new billboard is up: "Will the last person to leave Seattle please turn off the lights?"

Outside the city, in old logging towns, the government is collecting on back taxes. Auditors snake through the maze of country roads in rural Washington where many loggers and their families are living off the grid.

The tax bills are higher than what many homes are worth. Laborers are forced to move, forced to sell. Locals vow to get back at the government for stealing their homes.

The hijacker wants to know what time it is.

After five, Tina tells him.

Five was his deadline. What are the feds trying to do? Stall? For the first time, Tina sees panic on his face.

"They're not gonna take me alive," he says.

Tina calls the cockpit. The hijacker is starting to lose control. What's the delay?

The front chutes are not at the airport yet.

"Ask him if he wants to start our descent without the chutes present." She asks him.

"Yes," he says.

She relays the message. The phone rings again. It's Scotty.

"The front chutes are now at the airport," he says. "We're going down." At SEA-TAC, agents rush to the windows of the terminal to watch the jet come in. Along the wet runways and on the rooftops, Bureau snipers get into position. In Washington, D.C., officials at the FAA and the FAA's psychiatrist listen to the drama on the radio frequency.

In Minnesota, Don Nyrop and other Northwest officials pray the feds in Seattle will let Scotty handle this and not storm the plane. At his lakefront home outside Minneapolis, Scotty's wife is crying in the upstairs bathroom. Scotty's young daughter, Catherine, has gone to the sock hop at her high school. Her friends and the music area blur. Who is the man in the back of the jet? Why does he want to kill her father?

"Seattle Approach, we're ready to make our approach."

"Okay Northwest 305, would you have any objection to a right turn from your present position?"

"That should not present any problem and we understand we're landing at 1606. Is that correct?"

"Correct. . . . If you want some light we can turn the high-intensity runway lights up after you land, and they're pretty bright."

The airport is closed. Planes are told to circle. Air traffic controllers in the towers monitor the loops at different altitudes, careful not to cause a collision. Other jets are rerouted.

On the tarmac, on a domestic flight to Denver, pilots listen to the hijack unfold on the radio frequency. The conversation between the Northwest pilots and the FBI is so entertaining they play the radio over the cabin's intercom speakers so their passengers can follow what is happening in real time.

In his unmarked car, police detective McKenna and Northwest flight director Lee wait for Flight 305 to land. The high beams of the detective's car carve tunnels of light in the falling rain. McKenna and Lee look into the dark sky for the plane. First they see the lights on the wing, then the landing gear; now the jet is landing. Its wheels deflate on impact against the slick runway. From the car, McKenna and Lee can see the caps of the Northwest pilots in the cockpit. Through the cabin windows, they can see the heads of passengers.

Lee speaks into a hand radio. "305, this is Al. If you want to stay on the runway, that's fine with us."

"We might pull off to the right side just a little bit off the runway . . . until we make contact with our friend in the back."

Down on the tarmac, McKenna wants to storm the plane, take this guy out. He is carrying his service weapon.

"Okay, Al, can you hear me?"

"Yes sir."

"Okay, he at the present time is in the lavatory and apparently desires to stay there."

"I'll go back and get the fuel truck started."

"Okay, fine. Okay, be sure to get the fuel out here right now."

The jet rolls to a stop. The passengers are anxious to get off. In row 15, passenger Nancy House looks toward the back of the jet. She sees the man in sunglasses coming out of the lavatory. She sees that he is holding an attache case on its side with both arms, like a pizza box. On top of the attache case is a bag. The bag is about four inches tall and about the same size of the attache case. The bag is a light color, made from manila, or perhaps burlap. It is yellow, with a tinge of pink. What is in this bag?

Passengers scramble to collect their luggage. They want off. In the front row, prosecutor Finegold can see flashing beacons of a fuel truck out the window.

"They care more about the fucking gas than they do about the passengers!" he screams.

A pickup truck appears. A set of airstairs is attached to the rig. The stairs connect to the jet's front door. The pressure seal is cracked. It's time. The man in the back wants Tina to get the money. *Now.*

Tina moves up the crowded aisle, through the passengers, to the front exit door. On the tarmac, the SEA-TAC ground crew has set up klieg lights. The runway is illuminated like a movie set.

Al Lee scurries out of the detective's car and around to the trunk. He opens it. He grabs the canvas sack of money and waits for Tina in the rain. Tina peeks her head out of the airplane and slinks down the wet steps. In the rain, she is a smear of blond and red. She walks up to Lee. She is talking.

Lee can't understand a word. The stewardess must be in shock. He hands her the money bag. In the driver's seat of the unmarked car, McKenna watches.

Last chance to storm the plane. He can sneak under the pickup's stairs, slip into the cabin on his belly, slither under the seats, and take out this motherfucker.

Tina clutches the canvas bag in her arms, like a giant sack of mail. She clinks back to the jet in her heels and up the wet stairs into the maw of the cabin. She drops the money bag on the floor—it *is* heavy—and drags it down the aisle. The hijacker is waiting. The sack has no drawstring, no handle, no straps. The mouth is loose. This isn't right. He asked for a knapsack—with straps. What are the feds trying to do?

He peers inside. "Looks okay," he says.

He plunges his hands in the bag, and his fingers swim around the tightly wrapped twenties.

"There's a lot of cash in that bag," Tina says. "Can I have some?" She is joking.

The hijacker pulls out a stack of bills and hands it to her anyway. He wants her to have the money.

"Sorry, sir," she says. "No tips. Northwest Orient policy."

She asks about the passengers.

"Why not let them go now? You've still got the crew and the plane."

He agrees. The passengers can go.

Soon the announcement is made. The passengers flood the aisles, retrieve their bags, hats, coats. Flo Schaffner is out of the cockpit and stands near the front door with Alice Hancock. From the rear, Tina Mucklow joins them, helping the angry, hostile passengers off the jet and into the rain.

"Happy Thanksgiving!" she says.

The cabin is clear. The hijacker wants Tina to get the parachutes. She protests. She is not strong enough.

"They aren't that heavy. You shouldn't have any trouble."

She turns for the front exit door again. That's when she sees him. A passenger! He's snuck back on board. What is he doing? "Forgot my briefcase," he says.

Tina follows him back to his seat, stuffs the briefcase in his arms, and escorts him out the door. The Northwest pilots are flustered.

"Is this Al?"

"Yeah."

"Okay, please go stand by the bottom of the stairs and secure that area. We just had a passenger that came back up the steps because he forgot a bag. We just had to literally push him back off the steps."

Scotty checks the fuel gauge. It hasn't moved. What's going on?

"We want as rapidly as possible another fuel truck and a third fuel truck to stand by. We've got some difficulty in pumping at the present time and we're not able to take on fuel. Understand? Two fuel trucks, and get them out there as fast as you can."

In the Northwest Orient operations office at SEA-TAC, agents ask the Northwest pilots about the bomb.

"305, as long as you're free to talk, can you give me any more information and type of device or anything about it that you can talk now?"

"Ground, stand by."

"This is Al again."

"Yes, Al."

"Yeah, the fuel truck should be on the way."

"Okay, is this the other fuel truck now with the flashing headlights?"

"No, there's a school bus running around there with flashing amber lights."

"You better alert him and get those things off."

"305, this is Al. Are you going to let those girls out?"

"Well, that's what we're working on now. What we're trying to figure out is some way that we can get everybody up here and down those stairs, and we're kept still on the backend."

"Well, how many girls you got trained?"

"A good bunch."

"That one that came down here, she's pretty sharp; get her, and then make a mass exodus and leave this sonofabitch. *Go!*"

In the empty cabin, Alice Hancock inches toward the hijacker. She wants her purse.

"Sure," he says. "I'm not going to bite you."

Flo Schaffner wants her purse, too. As she walks down the aisle toward him, she notices the hijacker's mood has changed. He is giddy, almost boyish, clutching the money bag.

He asks Flo to hold it. Feel how heavy the money is? She puts her arms around the bag. She lifts.

"It is heavy."

She heaves the sack back to him.

He fishes around the pockets of his pants for the $19 he received from Flo nearly four hours ago, on the tarmac in Portland, for the bourbon and seven he ordered and spilled. He offers the change.

Flo and Alice shake their heads. "Sorry."

"No tips."

The stews turn and scurry off the plane.

Tina does not leave. She stands with him in the rear. He is angry. The fuel has not been pumped. What is taking the feds so long? "Close the shades," he says.

She shutters each window, closing them like heavy eyelids.

When she returns, he is grumbling about the knapsack he asked for. The canvas money bag is useless. What will he stuff the ransom in now?

Think.

The front reserve chutes. He grabs one. He pulls the ripcord. The pink canopy of the chute bursts open and covers the seats like popped bubblegum.

The hijacker reaches into his pocket and retrieves a pocket knife.

He cuts the knots that tie the canopy to the chute. Finally, the chute is free and the container is empty. Maybe he can stuff the ransom bills in here.

No. It won't work. The container is too small. What else? Think. The parachute canopy. The shroud lines.

He uses the knife to cut a cord. Then one more. Tina watches him.

He takes the shroud lines and wraps them around the canvas money bag to secure it. Next he wraps the shroud lines around the mouth of the bag and ties a noose-like knot into a makeshift handle.

———

"305, this is Al."

"Go ahead, Al."

"I just talked to the stews here [Flo and Alice] and if you'll call back there and tell him everything is under control then he'll let this other one [Tina] off."

"Whose word is that? Whose idea is that?"

"This is the two stews that got off. They were saying the guy don't really care if she stays on or not, but they suggested to call back and tell him everything is under control and that he'll let that third stew off."

"That's contrary to what's going on up here, Al. He's not going to let her come off right now and we're trying to work out a way that we can get her up here somehow before we go. Right now he wants her to sit back there with him during takeoff."

"Okay, I was just wondering, you know. About the fuel, how much do you want on board or how much more can you take?"

"Well, we got a long way to go and he's getting antsy and that's our problem right now."

"Have you been able to get in the back end of that cockpit or won't he come out?"

"He doesn't want any of us in the aisle. The only one he negotiates with is the stewardess and he doesn't want anybody beyond that first curtain. We've never left the cockpit."

"Did you get the maps I sent out there?"

"Yeah, we got all that stuff."

"And you got that deal from Boeing on how to get out of there?"

Inside the cockpit is a rope ladder. To exit the plane and escape, the pilots and flight engineer can open the cockpit windshield and shimmy down the rope onto the tarmac.

"Yeah, we got that. If we could get the gal out, well, we could make tracks ourselves."

"Is it possible to communicate with her to have her come forward to get food?"

"No, we tried that. . . . We don't want to try that kind of stuff."

"Seattle-Tacoma Tower now for one—stand by. Fuel truck just crossed in front of Northwest hangar."

"Alpha Two, go on."

"Stand by."

"What did he say now?"

"He was giving instructions there."

<hr>

"We're going to Mexico City," the hijacker tells Tina.

"Or anyplace in Mexico. Gear down, flaps down. You can trim the flaps to fifteen. You can stop anywhere in Mexico to refuel, but not here in the United States. Cabin lights out—no one behind the first-class curtain."

The pilots must also keep an altitude of 10,000 feet. No higher. There is more.

"The aft door must be open and the stairs must be down."

Tina picks up the interphone and relays the instructions to the Northwest pilots: Mexico City, gear down, flaps at fifteen degrees, altitude of 10,000 feet, no higher.

In the cockpit, the pilots are talking to the feds. There's an update.

"305, is the individual in the back? He can't hear?"

"You can have all the conversations you want."

"Okay, 305, did you hear the message from Washington, D.C., from the FAA's chief psychiatrist? He believes the second parachute is for the stewardess to use with him to go out, and after he leaves the airplane will be blown up."

On the tarmac, a bus approaches. The name on the bus is Western Tours. The passengers file in. The bus drives the passengers across the airfield to the SEA-TAC terminal. Here, two federal agents board. One says he's going to take a roll call and if you hear your name on the list, say something or raise your hand.

Menendez. Minsch. Pollart.

The hands go up. Larry Finegold raises his hand. George Kurata raises his hand. Cliff McDonald, a real estate salesman, raises his hand. George Labissoniere raises his hand.

Cooper?

Dan Cooper?

The bus is dark. The agents look for a hand, a face. They wait for a sound.

"Dan Cooper?"

In Portland, reporters hear the news of the hijacking over police scanners. Clyde Jabin, a stringer for United Press International wire service, asks a Bureau agent in Portland if they have any suspects. As a matter of fact, they do.

"D. Cooper," the agent says.

Jabin does not hear what the agent says. "'D' as in dog, 'B' as in boy?" Jabin says. "Right," the agent says.

Jabin scribbles down the "D" and "B" and the name "Cooper."

He calls in the story. The name of the hijacker—D.B. Cooper—hits the wires.

Mexico City?

In Portland, Special Agent Ralph Himmelsbach goes over the flight path in his mind. As a pilot, he knows the most sensible route south at the low altitude of 10,000 feet is Vector 23. The flight path would follow the Interstate 5 freeway and take the hijacked plane back to Portland.

"What do you think?" his boss, Mattson, asks. "Do you think he's corning back to us?"

"I sure hope so," Himmelsbach says. "I'd like to take him here."

Himmelsbach calls around. He learns there is a Huey helicopter at the National Guard hangar at Portland International. His idea is to chase the hijacked plane in the helicopter. He races over to the hangar, where the on-duty Guard pilots are waiting.

Himmelsbach also considers another detail. The request to have the plane flown at the altitude of 10,000 feet was telling. At 10,000 feet, the cabin would not be pressurized. If Cooper cracked the rear door of the jet, he would not get sucked out. Clearly, the man the agents were after knew airplanes.

꧁ — ꧂

The rain is light. The wind speed is ten knots, from the southeast. Clouds are scattered at 2,500 feet. Visibility is seven miles. The night is black. From the cockpit, the pilots can see the high beams of the detective's unmarked car.

"Yeah, say, this is Al again. I'm down here in a car."

"Yeah, Al. We're all set. We're going to crank the engines. You've probably heard me say he's indicated that he wants the show on the road, so we're going to get her cranked up here and pick our clearance in the air."

"Or maybe you can get him downtown toward Portland. He might get homesick and want to land there again, I don't know."

"Well, we'll hope for something to happen here, that's all. You go ahead and pull out. We're going to get cranked up here now. So we'll see you later."

"Yes sir."

"Ground, no force on 305. Be advised that I will be trying to take her up to altitude any way we can. Any other restrictions that may be imposed upon us?"

"No restrictions at all. You fly in the best way you can do her."

"And, 305, there'll be people with you all the way down."

The company is a pair of F-106s, interceptor turbojets designed to shoot down bombers with air-to-air missiles. If the Northwest pilots lose control of the jet and Flight 305 is headed into a populated or residential area, the F-106 pilots could be ordered to unlock their weapons systems and take the jet out.

At SEA-TAC, agents are busy debriefing passengers and Flo and Alice about the hijacker. What color was his hair? Did he speak with an accent? Was he wearing a wedding ring? On the runway, Flight 305 picks up speed. Soon the nose is up and the wheels are off the ground.

<hr />

In Portland, outside the Guard hangar, the giant blades of the Huey are spinning. Himmelsbach and a partner hop in the cockpit. As they rise, winds from the storm bully the chopper around the airfield. Himmelsbach can see the lights of the Portland suburbs. He thinks he sees his house. His wife and daughters are probably inside preparing a turkey. He was supposed to have been home hours ago. Happy Thanksgiving, he thinks.

The chopper picks up speed. They try the radio, but the frequencies are different. There is no way to communicate with the Northwest pilots. Himmelsbach looks out into the night. He can see nothing. They are moving 120 knots into the storm. They are moving too slowly to catch Flight 305. Above the chopper, somewhere, the F-106 fighter jets are moving too fast. To maintain any radar reading on the passenger jet, the fighter pilots are forced to carve wide turns, snaking through the night sky. As they make these S-turns, Northwest 305 comes in and out of their radar screens. They are losing him.

Other jets join the aerial posse. In Boise, Idaho, a pair of F-102 interceptor jets is dispatched. The F-102s cannot make contact with Flight 305, either. To the west, Norman Battaglia, a National Guard flight instructor, is on a night training mission in a T-33 reconnaissance fighter plane. The training mission is canceled.

"We want you to tail an aircraft," an air traffic controller says.

"The one that's hijacked?"

"That's the one."

In the sky, Battaglia positions the T-33 about three quarters of a mile behind Flight 305. It's hard to keep up. The Northwest jet is moving so slowly. And, every forty-five seconds or so, the plane changes courses. Battaglia tries his radio to contact the Northwest pilots. It doesn't work. The frequencies are also different.

In the cockpit of Northwest 305, the phone is ringing. It's him again. He needs help with the aftstairs. The pilots relay the message over the radio.

"Fourteen miles on Vector 23 out of Seattle. He is trying to get the door down. The stew is with us. He cannot get the stairs down."

"After a while, someone will have to take a look back there and see if he is out of the aircraft."

"Miss Mucklow said he apparently has the knapsack around him and thinks he will attempt a jump."

The pilots notice a change in their instruments.

"We now have an aftstair light on."

Copilot Rataczak picks up the receiver to use the jet's intercom. The air swirling around the cabin must be fierce, a tornado of wind twisting up and down the aisles. Rataczak calls back into the cabin as if trying to reach a man trapped in the belly of a mine.

"Can you hear me? Is there anything we can do for you?"

The hijacker picks up the cabin phone.

"No," he says.

With the aftstairs released, the temperature in the cabin must be far below freezing. In the cockpit window, pilots look at their thermometer. The reading in the sky is minus seven. It's also loud. The jet's engines are blasting away.

"Everything okay back there?"

"Everything is okay."

The jet is moving south. The flight crew notices another change in reading.

"We're getting some oscillations in the cabin. He must be doing something with the air stairs."

Harold Anderson, flight engineer, checks his instrument panel. The cabin pressure gauge is spiraling out of control. Rataczak calls back again on the interphone.

"Sir?"

There is no response. Tina picks up the plastic receiver.

"Sir?"

Underneath the jet, the lights of the cities in Oregon pass: Portland, Salem, Eugene. The configurations of the plane keep the jet moving slow and strain the engines. In Northern California, an HC-130 rescue plane is dispatched from Hamilton Air Force Base, as well as another pair of F-106 interceptor jets. At Red Bluff, California, the pilots and the jets following them turn east, approaching Reno on the Nevada border. Time to descend. Time to refuel. Tina calls back into the cabin.

"Sir, we are going to land now. Please put up the stairs. We are going to land anyway, but the aircraft may be structurally damaged. We may not be able to take off after we've landed."

Northwest officials in Minneapolis and air-traffic controllers in Reno want to know if the hijacker has jumped from the plane.

Tina uses the intercom phone again.

"Sir?"

The screech of the dangling aftstairs against the runway in Reno sounds like a car crash. Police cars trail the jet to ensure the hijacker does not roll out onto the tarmac. The Northwest pilots are talking with Reno.

"See any sparks coming off the tail at any time on touchdown?"

"Negative. None at all. The only thing that's visible on the tail is lights on your ramp."

"Roger."

"I do see some sparks now, just a few, trailing you as you're taxiing in."

The plane rolls to a stop.

Scotty turns and unlocks the cockpit door. He calls out into the cabin.

"Sir?"

Tina is behind him. She calls out over his shoulder.

"Sir?" she says. "Do you want us to refuel?"

Scotty inches into first class. The seats are empty. He creeps forward into the cabin. He is facing the first-class curtain. He unhinges the clasp. He pulls the curtain back.

"*Sir?*"